The Complete Stereo Cookbook

The Complete Rice Cookbook

The Complete Rice Cookbook

Carlson Wade

South Brunswick and New York: A. S. Barnes and Company
London: Thomas Yoseloff Ltd

© 1972 by A. S. Barnes and Co., Inc.

A. S. Barnes and Co., Inc.
Cranbury, New Jersey 08512

Thomas Yoseloff Ltd
108 New Bond Street
London W1Y OQX, England

Library of Congress Cataloging in Publication Data

Wade, Carlson.
The Complete Rice Cookbook.

1. Cookery (Rice)   I. Title.
TX809.R5W33   641.6′31′8   72-146775
ISBN 0-498-07844-2

Printed in the United States of America

To my mother,

who made a bowl of rice into a joy of culinary art.

Contents

Contents

Measures

	American	English
1 cup of breadcrumbs (fresh)	1½ oz.	3 oz.
1 cup of flour or other powdered grains	4 oz.	5 oz.
1 cup of sugar	7 oz.	8 oz.
1 cup of icing sugar	4½ oz.	5 oz.
1 cup of butter or other fats	8 oz.	8 oz.
1 cup of raisins, etc.	5 oz.	6 oz.
1 cup of grated cheese	4 oz.	4 oz.
1 cup of syrup, etc.	12 oz.	14 oz.

1 English pint	20 fluid ounces
1 American pint	16 fluid ounces
1 American cup	8 fluid ounces
8 American tablespoons	4 fluid ounces
1 American tablespoon	½ fluid ounce
3 American teaspoons	½ fluid ounce
1 English tablespoon	⅔ to 1 fluid ounce (approx.)
1 English tablespoon	4 teaspoons

The American measuring tablespoon holds ¼ oz. flour.

The Complete Rice Cookbook

1.
What This Rice Cookbook Can Do for You

Rice is the world's number one food grain, and one of the most convenient and versatile foods we have. It's easy to cook, combines well with innumerable foods, keeps well, is easy to store, and is economical. This cookbook will show you how to use rice for just about every occasion: holiday festivities, parties, eating alone, or dining with those who are "fussy" by choice or circumstance. You will learn how to prepare rice to satisfy not only the budget and time clock but the tummy as well.

Rice Is Easy to Prepare. There is no waste—every bit is edible. What's more, there is no peeling, scraping, or washing, for modern rice is machine-milled and comes to you ready to cook.

Rice Is Low Cost and Saves You Money. Just one cup of cooked rice costs about five cents! This tasty food is unique because it provides so much nourishment for so little cost.

Rice Is a Treat for Those Meatless Days. Looking for a satisfying food to take the place of meat? Rice is the answer. When eaten alone, it imparts a tummy-satisfying delight that makes a meatless day a joy. When combined with fruit, vegetables, fish, or eggs, rice can make the dish taste better than meat!

Rice Is a Traveler's Companion. When you go on an outdoor camping adventure, take along several packages of instant or precooked rice. Follow package directions for cooking and enjoy a mini-feast at an outdoor grill or campfire. Instant rice is especially welcome on such occasions because it is ready to serve as soon as it's cooked and it will not stick to pots and pans. No rinsing or draining is necessary.

Rice Can Be Eaten "On the Run." There are occasions when you are in a rush to eat. Rice is one food that can be eaten quickly because it is soft, requires less chewing than more solid foods, and is also more speedily digested.

Health Treats of Rice

Rice is a treasure of nutrients that work together to give you energy, growth, and vitality. Let's take a look at some of the unique nutritive qualities that make rice so admirably suited for special requirements, as well as being a healthful food for all purposes.

Superior Protein. The protein in rice, which makes up to eight percent of the grain, is considerably superior to protein in other grains. According to reports, rice protein is more beneficial than those in corn and oats. Rice protein has eight of the essential amino acids (out of about 11) in proper proportions. When rice protein is digested and transformed into amino acids, a complete internal revitalization takes place. Amino acids create strong muscles, healthy skin and hair, proper eye nourishment. They enter into the blood and lymph, nourishing the heart and lungs, tendons and ligaments, brain and nerves, and hormones. Just about all that you can see (and cannot see) depends upon amino acids for sustenance. Rice is regarded an especially abundant source of such nutrients that are needed by your body.

Vital Vitamins. Rice contains three vitamins of the B-complex family—thiamine (B-1), riboflavin (B-2), and niacin. These vitamins give living energy and help nourish the skin and blood vessels.

Nourishing Minerals. Rice is a good source of the essential minerals needed to nourish the hormonal system, heal wounds, create a healthy heartbeat, stabilize blood pressure, and keep you well nourished from within. Rice has calcium, needed for strong bones, sound teeth, and nerve stability; iron, needed to feed your bloodstream; phosphorus and potassium, needed to metabolize other nutrients and maintain internal water balance. Rice minerals may be regarded the "sparkplugs" of health.

Youthful Energy. Rice will provide you with the energy for that ball game, party, or hike, and is not fattening. Any food— if eaten in large amounts—will put pounds on you. Rice is able to *satisfy* your craving for food so that you can actually eat while you reduce!

For Those with Special Eating Problems

Rice fits in deliciously well for those who have special eating problems. By using it in different culinary creations (this book will show you how to transform simple rice into a royal banquet-in-a-dish fit for a king) , you can enjoy a meal along with the rest of the family. No longer need you feel "different" or be "left out" of the joys of family mealtime. Rice cookery is the answer. It will benefit those who have digestive upsets, allergic disorders, restrictions on intake of fat, fiber, cholesterol, gluten, or salt. You can feel reasonably free to use rice with such health problems. Let's see some of the benefits of rice for those on such restricted diets.

Easy to Digest. Rice is one of the most easily and quickly digested foods, being fully digested in one hour, while most other foods require two to four hours. It is 98% digestible. Rice starch is 100% amlyopectin—the most rapidly and completely digested grain starch. This ease and quickness of digestion makes rice particularly desirable as a food for babies and those with digestive disturbances.

Non-Allergenic. Rice is non-allergenic. For this reason, it is usually the first cereal allowed babies. It is used in diets for children and grownups who are allergic to other foods. Persons who are allergic to wheat and rye flour turn to rice flour for relief.

Low Fiber Content. The very low fiber content renders rice easy on the digestive system, as well as making it more digestible. This makes rice favored for soft diets and diets for the elderly, and for those who have colitis, ulcers, or other internal sensitivities.

Low Fat, Low Cholesterol. Rice contains only a tiny trace of fat and is virtually free of saturated fats. It is very low in cholesterol.

Gluten Free. Rice is absolutely gluten free. Gluten is an elastic substance that gives adhesiveness to dough. It is formed when protein in flour absorbs water. Gluten helps create a shape in cooked products because it coagulates when heated. Some people are allergic to gluten and may turn to rice or rice-based products. Also, rice is beneficial to infants suffering from celiac disease (an inability to properly assimilate foods from the intestinal tract) and adults with non-tropical sprue (a form of diarrhea). Gluten in wheat products often creates such distress to cause these health problems.

Salt Free. Rice is virtually free of sodium or salt, making it well suited for special restrictive diets and particularly diets for the elderly.

Added Benefits of Rice. Many researchers have long observed that in countries where there is a low incidence of high blood pressure, rice is the main food consumed. Dr. Walter Kempner of Duke University made a 20-year study of rice and reported that a special diet, followed in conjunction with advice from your family physician, is helpful in the treatment of high blood pressure and related cardiac and kidney disorders. The nutrients in rice are most beneficial to the health and maintenance of these functions.

Rice Puts Taste Back into Foods. By combining rice with normally low-taste foods, a unique flavor emerges. Rice actually helps put taste back into foods! Babies love it, children and teen-agers thrive on it, adults like it for everyday meals as well as gourmet specials, senior citizens rank it high among their diet-preferred foods.

2.
How to Buy and Cook Rice

Ordinary rice (*Oryza sativa*) is not quite as ordinary as that. Farming and milling processes have transformed rice into a wonderful array of varieties. Actually, there are about 7,000 varieties of rice but we usually divide them into the following three main groups. Note that each of these groups favors a special type of recipe for maximum eating joy.

Long-Grain Rice. This rice, favored by connoisseurs, is about four times as long as the grain is wide. When cooked, the grains tend to separate and are light and fluffy. It cooks tender. It is especially good for salads, curries, stews, chicken, or meat dishes, and as a side dish with a sauce or gravy, too. It is excellent for casseroles and combination dishes.

Short and *Medium-Grain Rice.* These varieties, less costly, have short, plump grains that cook tender and moist, with the particles tending to cling together. They are favored by many and are especially good for croquettes, puddings, or rice rings, which require a tender rice that is easily molded.

Rice Varieties to Suit Your Mood and Need

For a variety of texture and flavor, there are several different kinds of rice to try. Food stores offer rice milled for convenience or traditional use. You will be able to enjoy rice to fit your mood and need with these different varieties.

Regular Milled White Rice. This is probably the most familiar and popular variety of rice. It is often called "regular rice." The hull, germ, outer bran layers, and most of the inner bran have

17

been removed. It may be either short, medium, or long grain. Regular milled white rice is cleansed and graded in the milling process, and comes to you ready-to-cook without washing. It is easily prepared (directions follow in this chapter), and one cup of uncooked regular milled white rice will yield three cups of cooked rice.

Parboiled Rice. Also known as converted rice, it is white rice that has been partly cooked before milling. This treatment aids in the retention of much of the natural vitamin and mineral content. After cooking, the grains will be fluffy, separate, and plump. This parboiling process gelatinizes the starch in the grain, retaining much of the nutrient content, since this method seals the vitamins and minerals into the body of the rice. One cup of parboiled rice will yield four cups of cooked rice.

Pre-Cooked Rice. Known to many as instant rice because it needs so little preparation. This is milled rice that has been completely cooked and then had the water extracted. This popular "instant" rice is ideal for hurry-up meals or speedy desserts. Follow preparation instructions on the package. One cup of pre-cooked rice will yield approximately two to three cups of cooked rice.

Brown Rice. This is the whole unpolished grain of rice, with only the outer hull and a small amount of bran removed. It has a delightful nut-like flavor and a slightly chewy texture. It also has a firmer texture but a shorter shelf life. One cup of uncooked brown rice will yield three cups of cooked rice.

Wild Rice. Also known as Indian rice (*Zizanie aquatica*), this is not a true rice but the seed of a reed-like water grass native to Minnesota and other Northern states. Wild rice is an annual grass, growing partly submerged along the margins of lakes. It was once an important food of the Indian tribes of the region of the Great Lakes and the upper Mississippi Valley. The amount of labor involved in finding the rice and harvesting it make the price very high. No more than a half million pounds are for sale every year. Indians harvest it from their canoes, knocking the ripe grains into a box. Law requires it to be harvested by these primitive Indian methods since machines would clean the stalks so thoroughly no grain would be left for reseeding the crop and the reed-like water plant might be extinguished. The methods of the Chippewa Indians are still being used. In a canoe, one man bends the stalks of the plant over the boat with one stick, knocking the ripe kernels into the bottom of the boat with another stick. The other man pushes the craft through the heavy growth by use of a long forked pole. You can readily appreciate the high cost of wild rice when you consider this necessary hand method of harvesting. Wild rice has a unique flavor and texture; its kernels vary considerably in size and consistency. One cup of uncooked wild rice will yield three cups of cooked rice.

Seasoned Converted Rice. Available in package form with prepared sauces, this offers you convenience, speed, and interesting variety in flavor. Follow the cooking directions on the package.

It's Easy to Buy Rice the Right Way

There are many packaged brands available to suit your needs. Good marketing is as important as good cooking. Here's how to buy rice the right way:

1. Decide upon the best type of rice for the dish you are cooking. For example, many prefer the medium-grain type for gumbo, the long-grain type for soups because the grains do not split. Know your needs in advance.

2. Consider the time you have for cooking. Pre-cooked rice is great for speed. White rice is perfect for leisurely cooking. Plan ahead to get the most from rice and the most from your budget.

3. Determine in advance the yield per serving. While rice can be stored (directions follow), your circumstances may be such that you will want to avoid leftovers. Here is an at-a-glance chart to show you the yield of the different kinds of rice:

1 Cup Uncooked	*Measure After Cooking*
Regular Milled White Rice	3 cups
Parboiled Rice	4 cups
Pre-Cooked Rice	2 to 3 cups
Brown Rice	3 cups
Wild Rice	3 cups

4. You may want to benefit from enriched rice, which is rice to which extra food value (vitamins, minerals) has been added. In particular, enriched rice has Vitamin B-1 (thiamine), riboflavin, niacin, and iron added to it. These nutrients give you the pep and energy that you want. Use enriched rice in some of the dishes you prepare for your family and friends. The package label will state it is "enriched." This is the easiest way to give vitamins and minerals to your family—in the rice!

More Rice Products to Suit Your Taste

There are many valuable by-products of rice that add versatility to this wonderful food. You will discover a world of eating ecstasy when you use some of these products made from rice.

RICE BRAN. This is the outer cuticle layer and the germ of the rice grain that is removed in the milling process. It is high in nourishing niacin. There are many breakfast cereals made from rice bran, available at all markets.

RICE OIL. This is extracted from rice bran. It is a very fine cooking oil and extremely low in cholesterol. Use this when you need an oil for cooking or for a salad.

RICE POLISH. This consists of the inner grain layer plus small quantities of the outer layer of the kernel. It is produced during the final stages of the milling process. It is highly digestible and has a very high vitamin content. Medical science has discovered that rice polish is effective in the prevention and treatment of certain diseases such as arthritis, neuritis, and certain nervous disorders.

RICE FLOUR. Milled rice is ground into flour. This rice flour can be used in place of wheat for baking. Rice is non-allergenic and this flour is particularly valuable to those who are allergic to wheat flour products. Ask for rice flour at your local food outlet. Use it in any recipe calling for wheat flour. You'll discover a gourmet taste treat that will win you praise from your family and friends.

How to Cook Rice

There are different ways to cook rice which only adds to its appeal. Here are some of the most popular methods.

The Fluffy Rice Method: Measure 1 cup uncooked regular rice into a 3-quart saucepan with a tightly fitted lid. Add 2 cups water and 1 teaspoon salt. Heat to boiling, stirring once or twice. Reduce heat to simmer. Cover and cook 14 minutes *without removing lid or stirring.* All water should be absorbed. Test the rice by tasting it to see that it is tender. Simmer a little longer if needed. Remove from heat. Turn rice into serving dish. Fluff with fork or slotted spoon.

The Oven-Bake Method: Heat oven to 350°F. Combine 1 cup uncooked regular rice, 2 cups water, and 1 teaspoon salt into a

3-quart baking dish. Cover. Bake 25 or 30 minutes or until rice is tender.

The Feathered Rice Method: Heat oven to 375°F. Spread 1 cup rice in shallow baking pan. Bake, stirring occasionally, until rice grains are golden brown. Remove pan from the oven. Now turn oven heat to 400°F. Put toasted rice into 1½-quart casserole with a tight-fitting cover. Stir in 1½ teaspoons salt and 2½ cups boiling water. Cover. Bake 20 minutes. (*Note:* you can toast a quantity of rice at one time and then store it in a tightly covered jar for future use.)

Double Boiler Method: When rice is cooked in milk, it is most frequently cooked over boiling water; that is, in the top of a double boiler. Place 1 cup regular white rice in the top of a double boiler with 3½ cups milk and 1 teaspoon salt. Heat to boiling, then place over boiling water, and cook, covered, for 40 minutes, or until milk is absorbed. *For Extra Flavor* add a bouillon cube to the water in which you steam rice, or use a can of consommé in place of part of the water. IN BRIEF: You will have rice success if you follow this simple rule: *Use 2 cups of water and 1 teaspoon of salt with each 1 cup of rice.*

How to Make the Most of Cooked Rice

While rice is at its best when served as soon as it is cooked, there are times when you have to put it aside for a late arrival. It is good to remember this tip: if cooked rice is left in the cooking pan for longer than 5 or 10 minutes, it packs together. When necessary to hold rice for a longer time, transfer it to a shallow baking dish, cover with aluminum foil, and place in a warm oven.

Two Ways to Keep Cooked Rice Hot: Begin by running boiling water through the rice to separate the kernels, then: 1. Cover cooked rice with cloth and place over a pan of hot water. 2. Place in a square or oblong baking pan; cover with aluminum foil and place in a slow oven. (If rice is wet, do not cover. Let dry in oven 5 to 10 minutes; fluff with fork.)

Two Ways to Reheat Cooked Rice: Use either of these two simple methods: 1. Heat cooked rice in double boiler over hot water about 10 minutes or until rice is hot and fluffy. 2. Place rice in a heavy pan with a tightly fitted cover. Sprinkle water over rice, using about 2 tablespoons of water to 1 cup of rice. Cover. Heat over low heat 4 to 5 minutes or until hot and fluffy.

How to Refrigerate Leftover Rice. Cooked rice is one of the few foods that may be covered and refrigerated for about a week. Put the rice in a glass bowl. Be sure to cover so the grains will not dry out or absorb the flavors of other foods.

How to Freeze Leftover Rice. Rice has excellent freezing qualities, plain or with any combination of foods that can be safely frozen. To freeze rice, first let the dish cool. Remove dividers from an ice cube tray; place cooled rice in the tray. Quick freeze. When frozen, remove from the tray and wrap in foil or freezer paper. Place in freezer where it may be kept for 6 to 8 months. To serve, reheat as indicated above.

How to Store Uncooked Rice. For good keeping, store rice at room temperature. Rice will absorb some moisture so it is suggested that you pour the uncooked grains from the package into a glass container with a tight fitting lid.

Put Color in Your Rice

Serving rice in various colors is a popular method of providing a festive air to meals. Rice may be tinted by mixing a few drops of food coloring in liquid in which the rice is to be cooked. Blend to the preferred shade. Add rice and follow the usual cooking directions. The rice will absorb the color and cook a shade lighter.

Another method of coloring rice is by preparing it with liquids that will lend their own color to it.

Maraschino Cherry Juice. Use 1 cup rice, 1½ cups water, ½ cup cherry juice, 1 teaspoon salt; cook 15 minutes.

Orange or Tangerine Juice. Use 1 cup rice, 2 cups juice, and 1 teaspoon salt; cook 15–20 minutes.

Tomato Juice. Use 1 cup rice, 1 cup water, 1 cup tomato juice, and 1 teaspoon salt; cook 15 minutes.

Carrot Juice. Use 1 cup rice, 1½ cups water, ½ cup carrot juice, and 1 teaspoon salt; cook 20 minutes.

(If using brown or parboiled rice, increase total liquid specified by ½ cup water; adjust cooking times.)

For Flavor-Plus, Try These Tips

Try different flavors when cooking rice for salads, main dishes, casseroles, etc. Cook rice in chicken broth, beef broth, or consommé. Flavored bouillon cubes are excellent when added to the water in which rice will be cooked. Small amounts of dehydrated soup and salad mixes may also be added to the water when cooking rice for new and exciting flavors.

How to Become a Gourmet Rice Chef

Here is a set of tips about rice to bring out the best in flavor and taste:

1. Don't wash or rinse rice since this causes loss of vitamins and minerals.

2. Don't peep into the pot when boiling rice. Lifting the lid beforehand only lets out steam and lowers the temperature.

3. Never stir rice after it comes to a boil. This will mash the grains and make the rice too gummy.

4. Never let rice remain in the cooking pot for more than 5 or 10 minutes after it has cooked or it will pack.

5. Don't add cold water to boiling rice. If you must add water, boil some in a separate pot before adding it to the rice. It must be bubbly-boiling when you pour it into the already boiling rice.

6. *Never* stir rice. Lift it gently with your fork.

7. Make sure that the water is at a brisk boil before you add the rice.

8. To prevent sogginess, keep the liquid above the boiling point until the rice is done.

9. To maintain a snowy whiteness, add a bit of lemon juice before putting the lid on the cooking pot.

10. Keep rice hot until served to retain its fluffy appeal.

20 Quick and Easy Ways to Serve Rice in Minutes

First: Cook according to package directions . . . then:

1. Top a serving with gravy.
2. Top a serving with a pat of butter.
3. Top with paprika.
4. Toss cooked rice with chopped chives.
5. Toss with crumbled bacon and sour cream.
6. Toss with shredded Cheddar cheese.
7. Toss with sautéed mushrooms and sliced water chestnuts.
8. Toss with chopped ripe olives.
9. Toss with toasted slivered almonds.
10. Toss with grated Parmesan cheese.
11. Toss with drained chopped pimiento.

12. Toss with chopped parsley.
13. Toss with chopped peanuts.
14. Toss with chopped green pepper.
15. Toss with sliced pimiento stuffed olives.
16. Toss with cooked chopped onion and mushrooms.
17. Toss with curry powder blended with melted butter.
18. Toss with cooked green peas.
19. Toss with chopped ripe tomatoes.
20. Pack into buttered ring mold, then unmold on platter.

3.

The Mystery, the History, and the Romance of Rice

The growing and use of rice began long before the time of written records. Its very earliest mention dates back to 2800 B.C., when a Chinese emperor established a ceremonial ordinance for the planting of rice. It is believed that this Oriental potentate named the grain "rice," which is the Chinese word for culture and agriculture. From fragments that have come down throughout the centuries, it appears that rice was being grown back in 3000 B.C., when it appeared as a plant called "Newaree" in ancient India.

Rice is also referred to in the Jewish Talmud (the body of Jewish civil and canonical law). It was cultivated in the Euphrates Valley, near the Persian Gulf, in 400 B.C. The ancients revered the value of rice because it served as their main means of sustenance. Rice helped many races and nationalities survive in times of distress or famine.

The nourishing importance of rice spread throughout the East and then throughout the West. The Greeks learned of rice from the Persians. The classical Greek poet Sophocles (495–406 B.C.) talks about the "god-bestowed" values of rice in his famous *Tragedies*.

During Medieval times, the Saracens (Moslem invaders of Europe) brought rice to southern Europe where it became established as an important crop. Entire armies subsisted almost exclusively on rice in time of food shortages. Starvation was many times averted because of the nourishing value of this basic food.

25

Gradually, by this time, the entire Orient came to look upon rice as their most important food. Some of the earliest manuscripts of India contain descriptions of particular varieties of rice that were used in religious offerings. Similar evidence as to the antiquity and importance of the crop has been found in the early literature of Thailand, Burma, Malaya, and French Indo-China.

The Chinese have always held rice in veneration. When two Orientals greet one another and ask, "Have you eaten your rice?" it would be the same as if we would ask, "How are you?" This reverence for rice is seen throughout the whole of the East. Rice is so close to these people that some refer to it as "mother" during ordinary conversations.

The custom of throwing rice at newly married couples is a survival of the ancient religious practices of the Chinese and Hindus. In the Orient, rice is the symbol of fertility. To throw rice on a just-married couple is symbolic of bestowing fertility upon them. The custom still retains some of its original significance in India. There, the bridegroom throws three handfuls of rice over his bride and the bride does the same over her groom.

The divine power of rice is regarded so strongly by these people that they throw rice at a wedding in order to placate the evil spirits said to be hovering about. The belief is that throwing rice at the evil spirits would keep them busy eating and away from the groom of whom they were jealous.

In India, rice throwing can be traced from its earliest literature down to the present day. The poet Kalidasa (author of the classical *Sakuntala*, said to have lived around 525 A.D.) describes how Prince Aja and his bride, sitting on a golden chair, were strewn with wet grains of rice. First to do so were the young Brahmans, then the King and all his relatives, and finally the noble women. All this was said to feed evil spirits and also assure the young royal couple of a fruitful marriage.

The people of Celebes, a Dutch isle of the Malay Archipelago, believe that the soul of the bridegroom, unless bribed with rice, may fly away at marriage and never return. Therefore, rice is scattered over him to prevent the flight of his fickle soul.

Among other primitives, when two people eat rice together out of a common bowl, it is as binding as a marriage ceremony. Some regard mutual rice eating as symbolic of friendship. (This is much healthier than smoking a peace pipe!) No other food will serve this purpose except rice.

The Indonesians believe that rice possesses a soul like that of man. They treat rice with the same respect as they would a soul.

Among some Asiatics, rice in bloom is respected as a pregnant woman. Farmers in rice fields will refrain from firing guns or making loud noises lest they frighten the soul of the rice, which would miscarry and bear no grain. They prohibit any unkind words to be spoken in the blooming rice field.

These same Asiatics feed the blooming rice with different types of foods, just as they would nourish a pregnant woman. Rice-ears, just beginning to form, are looked upon as infants. Women pass through the fields, feeding them with rice-pap as if they were human babies.

Among the Burmese, if a rice field does not flourish, they assume that the soul (known as *kelah*) has become detached from the grain. Local priests are called upon to chant a special ceremony to join the soul with the rice.

In the interior of Sumatra (another Dutch isle in the Malay Archipelago) rice is sown by women who, during their labors, let their hair hang down loosely. This is believed to help the rice grow more luxuriantly and have long stalks.

Among the Khonds (aboriginal hill people of India, of Dravidian stock), a birth is celebrated on the seventh day after the event by a feast. The local priest drops rice grains into a cup of water, naming each grain a deceased ancestor of the child. From the movements of the seed in the water, and from observations made on the reactions of the infant, the priest pronounces which of his progenitors has reappeared in him. This is how the child is named.

In the East Indian island of Buru, the close of the rice harvest calls for the gathering of the tribes at a common sacramental meal. Each member of the tribes contributes a little of the new rice that he helped harvest. This meal is called "eating the soul of the rice," a name that clearly indicates the sacramental character of the special feast. Some of the rice is also set apart to be offered to the spirits hovering about.

Among the Hindus of southern India, the eating of the new rice is the occasion of a family festival called Pongol. The new rice is boiled in a new pot on a fire that is kindled at noon, on the day when, according to Hindu astrologers, the sun enters the Tropic of Capricorn. (This is the tenth sign of the zodiac, entered by the sun at the winter solstice.) The boiling of the pot is watched with great anxiety by the whole family, for as the milk boils, so will the coming year be fulfilled. If the milk boils rapidly, the year will be prosperous; but it will be the reverse if the milk boils slowly. Some of the new boiled rice is offered to the image of Ganesa, a local diety. Then everyone partakes of the rest of the boiled rice.

Legend has it that Harmenszoon van Rijn (better known to the world as the great painter Rembrandt, 1606–1669) would eat a steaming bowl of rice before starting on any new work of art in his home town of Leiden in the Netherlands. He thoroughly enjoyed the creative-stimulation of *rijst*.

For a long time, early Americans remained unaware of rice— that is until the year 1694. In that year, a ship sailed from the island of Madagascar, off the east coast of South Africa. The ship was bound for England. While enroute, a storm of such ferocity arose, the ship was forced off its course. It had to land for repairs at Charleston, South Carolina. When the ship was finally ready to continue on its voyage, its captain was so grateful for the hospitality, that he presented the governor of the colony with a small package of rough rice. It was his token of appreciation for the needy assistance and shelter. The rough rice seeds were planted and from this humble beginning, rice production was born in the United States of America—before our Nation itself was born! Thus, rice production is older than the U.S.A.

Before long, enough rice was growing to supply South Carolina and neighboring colonies. The quality of Carolina rice was excellent. Soon a thriving export trade with England was under way. Slowly other states planted the rough rice grains as seed, and production as well as demand began to spread.

However, the War Between the States (1861–1865), ravaging hurricanes, competition from Western areas better suited for rice culture brought about destruction of the South Carolina rice industry. To this day, only a small amount of rice comes from this region.

Rice production moved to Louisiana and other states. In 1889, rice became an important food crop in Texas. In 1905 rice was heralded in Arkansas as being a valuable enterprise. In 1912 California caught the "rice fever." In 1949 latecomer Mississippi entered the picture.

Currently, the major rice producing states are Arkansas, Louisiana, Mississippi, Texas, and California. A whopping seven billion pounds of rough rice was produced in just one year. Other states grow rice, too, and the consumer demand continues to increase.

Around the world, there is probably no other food more universally known and eaten than rice. It is to be found everywhere and is known in hundreds of languages and dialects. Rice is a giving food. That is, it will grow where wheat and other grains hesitate. Rice also yields far more for each planted acre than other grains. In overpopulated countries of the world, rice is the poor man's friend and his basic source of life-giving nourishment.

Half of the world's population live chiefly on rice. It can be eaten in its simplest boiled form. Small wonder that an anonymous bard once wrote hopefully:

All the wrong in the world would be right in a trice
If everybody fed upon nothing but Rice.

This may be something of an exaggeration but it does point up the value and importance of rice. Here in our own nation the rice industry is a rapidly growing empire. Rice production has expanded dramatically during the 20th century, increasing 16-fold from 1900 to the present day. Production is on a steady increase. That sure adds up to a lot of rice—whether for religious ceremonies, a snack, a meal, or life-giving nourishment!

4.
Breakfast Dishes

APPLE RICE GRIDDLE CAKES

1 cup sifted flour
1 tablespoon sugar
1 tablespoon baking powder
½ teaspoon salt
½ teaspoon cinnamon
¼ teaspoon nutmeg
2 eggs
¾ cup milk
1 cup finely grated apple
1 cup cooked rice
2 tablespoons melted shortening

Sift together dry ingredients. Beat eggs. Blend in milk, apple, rice, and shortening. Add dry ingredients and mix well. For each cake, spoon about 3 tablespoons of batter on very lightly greased hot griddle. Spread batter slightly. Bake slowly until bubbles form and edges dry. Turn and brown other side. *Makes about 14.*

RICE BUTTERMILK PANCAKES

2 cups sifted flour
2 teaspoons baking powder
1 teaspoon salt
1 teaspoon baking soda

2 tablespoons sugar
3 eggs, separated
2½ cups buttermilk
5 tablespoons shortening or butter
1 cup cold cooked rice

Sift dry ingredients together in a mixing bowl. Beat egg whites and yolks separately. Combine egg yolks, buttermilk, and shortening and add to dry ingredients, mixing well. Stir in rice. Fold in stiffly beaten egg whites. Bake on hot griddle. *Makes 16 4-inch pancakes.*

ORANGE HONEY BUTTER

¼ pound butter or margarine
⅓ cup honey
1 tablespoon orange juice
1 teaspoon lemon juice
1½ tablespoons grated orange rind (fresh or bottled)

Melt butter; beat in honey, orange juice, lemon juice, and orange rind. Serve warm over Rice Buttermilk Pancakes.

BREAKFAST CALAS

1½ cups cooked rice, very soft
½ package yeast, active dry or compressed
½ cup warm, not hot, water
3 eggs, beaten
1¼ cups sifted flour
¼ cup sugar
½ teaspoon salt
¼ teaspoon nutmeg

Mash rice grains and cool to lukewarm. Soften yeast in warm water and stir in lukewarm rice. Mix well. Cover and let rise overnight. The next morning, add eggs, flour, sugar, salt, and nutmeg. Beat until smooth. Let stand in a warm place for 30 minutes. Drop by tablespoons into deep hot fat (360°F.) and fry until golden brown, about 3 minutes. Serve sprinkled with powdered sugar or sugar mixed with cinnamon. *Makes 2 dozen.*

SUGGESTION: Flavorful if served with fruit or maple syrup.

EASY BUFFET
(*Or* Sausage Scramble)

1 package beef-flavored rice mix
1 pound link sausage
⅓ cup chopped onion
¼ teaspoon basil
¼ cup barbecue sauce

Cook beef rice according to package directions. Fry sausage in large skillet. Remove sausage to paper towel, also remove one-half drippings from pan. Sauté onion until done in remaining drippings. Add basil and barbecue sauce. Combine with rice and top with sausage. Cover and simmer for 5 minutes. *Serves 4–6.*

SUGGESTION: Delicious with poached eggs or breakfast waffles.

SOMETHING DIFFERENT

1 package chicken-flavored rice mix
8 strips bacon

Cook rice according to package directions. Fry or broil bacon until crisp. Crumble bacon into rice and lightly mix. *Serves 6.*

RICE PANCAKES OR WAFFLES

⅔ cup enriched pre-cooked rice
⅔ cup water
¾ cup milk
2 egg yolks, slightly beaten
1 tablespoon liquid shortening
1 cup pancake mix
2 egg whites, stiffly beaten
butter and maple syrup

Combine rice and water; set aside. Mix milk, egg yolks, and shortening in a bowl. Add pancake mix and stir lightly until moistened. Stir in rice mixture. Fold in egg whites. Bake on a hot griddle, turning only once, or bake in a hot waffle iron. Serve hot with butter and syrup. *Makes 12 pancakes or 8 waffles.*

BREAKFAST RICE

1⅓ cups enriched pre-cooked rice
2½ to 2¾ cups milk
½ teaspoon salt
¼ cup chopped dates or raisins
light cream, maple syrup, *or* brown sugar

Combine rice, milk, salt, and dates in a saucepan. Bring to a boil; cook and stir over medium heat for 5 minutes, or until mixture is creamy. Serve with cream, maple syrup, or brown sugar. *Serves 4.*

FARMER'S OMELET

2 tablespoons butter or margarine
2 cups cooked, hot parboiled rice
2 tablespoons chopped chives
4 eggs
2 tablespoons cream
salt, white pepper

Melt butter in a skillet. Add rice, chives. Beat the eggs and cream together lightly. Season with salt and pepper; pour over rice. Cook over low heat, stirring and turning, until the eggs are set. *Serves 4.*

SUGGESTION: To make a meal, such as brunch, serve this omelet with chilled orange juice, grilled Canadian bacon, hot biscuits or popovers (made from scratch or from a mix) with lime marmalade, and lots of your favorite hot beverage.

RICE PREPARED WITH MILK

**(This slightly creamy, extra-fluffy rice is
superb with highly seasoned dishes)**

1½ cups milk
1 tablespoon butter
½ teaspoon salt
1⅓ cups enriched pre-cooked rice

Bring milk, butter, and salt to a boil in a saucepan. Stir in rice.
Cover, remove from heat, and let stand 10 minutes. Fluff with a
fork before serving. Serve as a vegetable, or sprinkle with sugar
and cinnamon or top with sweetened fruit and serve as a cereal.
Serves 4.

RICE GRIDDLE CAKES

2 cups rice flour
1½ tablespoons baking powder
1 teaspoon salt
1 tablespoon sugar
2½ cups milk
1 egg, beaten
1 tablespoon melted shortening

Mix and sift dry ingredients twice. Add milk gradually, beating
well. Add beaten egg and shortening. Batter should be smooth.
Bake on a medium hot iron skillet or grill, lightly greased.
Makes 12.

RICE FLOUR WAFFLES

1 cup rice flour
2 teaspoons baking powder
½ teaspoon soda
½ teaspoon salt
1¼ cups buttermilk
2 eggs, well beaten
¼ cup melted butter

Sift together dry ingredients. Combine buttermilk and eggs; add to flour mixture and beat until smooth. Stir in melted butter. Bake in hot, greased waffle iron. Waffles come out light and tasty. *Makes 4.*

SUGGESTION: To make *Raisin-Pecan Waffles,* add ½ cup stewed raisins and ½ cup chopped pecans to batter. (To stew raisins, cover with water and cook until water is absorbed.)

BREAKFAST WITH RICE

Hot cooked rice—an excellent source of energy to begin the day. Add butter or margarine, cream, and sugar. For an added touch of flavor, sprinkle a small amount of cinnamon on top.

Rice with fruit—makes a delightful change for breakfast or a mid-morning snack. Top hot cooked rice with cream, sugar, and slices of fresh, canned, or frozen fruit.

Rice Pancakes—add 1¼ cups cold cooked rice to every 3 cups of pancake batter. There is a secret: add 1 teaspoon walnut or almond extract to the water when cooking rice.

LATE BREAKFAST HONEY RICE PEACHES

8 large canned peach halves
1 cup cooked rice
3 tablespoons honey
⅛ teaspoon ginger
2 tablespoons slivered almonds
1 tablespoon butter or margarine

Drain peach halves. Place rounded side down on baking sheet. Combine rice, honey, and ginger. Spoon into peach halves. Insert slivered almonds into rice. Dot with butter. Broil about 5 minutes. *Serves 4.*

5.

Soups

RISOTTO à la MILANESE

2 tablespoons butter or margarine
1 cup rice
¼ cup chopped green onion
1 teaspoon salt
dash of black pepper
2 cups water
2 chicken bouillon cubes
2 tablespoons dehydrated parsley
¼ cup Parmesan cheese

In heavy saucepan, sauté rice and onion in butter until onion is tender. Stir in salt, pepper, water, bouillon, and parsley. Bring to a boil, then lower heat and simmer 20 minutes. Stir in Parmesan cheese and serve. *Serves 6.*

PLANTATION CHOWDER

3 medium onions, sliced
2 green peppers, cut into small pieces
3 large carrots, cubed
½ cup olive oil
2 packages deveined frozen shrimp
1 pound package frozen fish fillets
water to cover (about 5 cups)

36

1 cup cooked tomatoes
1½ tablespoons salt
¼ teaspoon pepper
3 cups cooked rice
saffron (optional)

Sauté vegetables in oil in a large kettle. Add shrimp, then fish fillets. Add water, tomatoes, and seasonings. Cover and cook to boiling. Reduce heat and simmer 20 minutes. *Meanwhile,* following directions on the package, cook enough rice to make 3 cups. Add saffron for color and flavor, if desired. In individual bowls, serve fish and soup topped with scoops of freshly cooked rice. *Serves 6.*

QUICK TOMATO RICE SOUP

1 package spanish-flavored rice mix
1 large can tomato juice

In large saucepan, combine rice and tomato juice; bring to a boil for 5 minutes. Turn low and simmer for 35 minutes. *Serves 6–8.*

ANY TIME ENTRÉE

1 package curry-flavored rice mix
1 can Cheddar cheese soup
½ cup water
2 cups cubed cooked or canned meat
4 hard-cooked eggs

Cook curry rice according to package directions. Combine all other ingredients in a large skillet or electric skillet, bring to a boil, then simmer for 5 minutes. Serve soup mixture over rice. *Serves 6.*

BEEF AND RICE CHOWDER

1 pound ground beef
½ cup chopped onion
1 tablespoon butter

1 can (4 ounces) sliced mushrooms
1 package (10 ounces) frozen succotash or mixed vegetables
1 can (1 pound, 12 ounces) tomatoes
3 cups water
1 to 2 teaspoons salt
¼ teaspoon oregano
⅛ teaspoon pepper
1 cup enriched pre-cooked rice

Brown meat and onion in butter. Add remaining ingredients except rice; bring to a boil, separating frozen vegetables with fork if necessary. Add rice, cover, and simmer 8 to 10 minutes, or until vegetables are tender. Serve in soup bowls. *Serves 10.*

PEASE PORRIDGE HOT

4 slices bacon
¾ cup chopped onions
2 cans (11 ounces each) condensed green pea soup
3 cans (4 cups) water
¾ teaspoon salt
1⅓ cups enriched pre-cooked rice

Fry bacon in medium saucepan until crisp; drain on absorbent paper and crumble. Pour off all drippings except 2 tablespoons. Sauté onions in reserved drippings until soft and golden. Add pea soup; then gradually stir in water. Add crumbled bacon and salt. Bring to a boil; then add rice, cover loosely, and simmer about 10 minutes. *Makes 7½ cups or about 7 servings.*

SUGGESTION: To make Easy Pease Porridge Hot, omit bacon and onions and substitute 1 can (10½ ounces) condensed vegetable beef soup for 1 can of the pea soup, and decrease water to 2 cans (2⅔ cups) and enriched pre-cooked rice to ⅔ cup. *Serves 5.*

CHICKEN-RICE CHOWDER

¼ cup chopped onion
2 tablespoons butter
3⅓ cups (two 14½-ounce cans) evaporated milk

1⅔ cups water
2½ teaspoons salt
1 teaspoon sugar
½ teaspoon baking soda
¼ teaspoon pepper
1 can (1 pound) tomatoes
1 can (8¾ ounces) whole kernel corn, drained
1 cup diced cooked chicken
1⅓ cups enriched pre-cooked rice
1 tablespoon chopped parsley

In a large heavy saucepan, sauté onion in butter until transparent. Add evaporated milk, water, salt, sugar, soda, pepper, tomatoes, and corn. Bring to a boil, breaking up the tomatoes with a spoon. Stir in chicken and rice. Cover and simmer 10 minutes. Stir in parsley. *Serves 8.*

COCKALEEKIE SOUP

4 cans (12½ ounces each) chicken broth
1 cup water
6 leeks, split and cut in 1-inch pieces (or 2 bunches
    scallions, cut in ½-inch pieces)
½ teaspoon salt
⅛ teaspoon pepper
1 cup enriched pre-cooked rice
2 tablespoons minced parsley

Combine broth, water, leeks, salt, and pepper in a large saucepan. Bring to a boil. Cook over medium heat 15 minutes, or until leeks are just tender. Add rice and simmer 5 minutes. Place chicken in soup tureen. Ladle in soup and sprinkle with parsley. *Serves 6–7.*

SOUP KETTLE SUPPER

½ pound bacon, diced
1 cup diced cooked ham or beef
1 can (10½ ounces) condensed beef broth
2 cups water
1⅓ cups enriched pre-cooked rice

1 can (1 pound, 1 ounce) whole kernel corn
1 can (15½ ounces) French-style green beans, drained
1 can (1 pound) tomatoes
1 to 2 teaspoons salt
⅛ teaspoon pepper
1 tablespoon finely chopped parsley

Fry bacon in large heavy saucepan until crisp; drain on absorbent paper. Pour off all but 2 tablespoons of the drippings. Sauté ham in reserved drippings until lightly browned. Add bacon and remaining ingredients except parsley. Bring to a boil. Cover, remove from heat, and let stand 5 minutes. Add parsley just before serving. (If soup becomes too thick, add a little water.) *Serves 8.*

SAVORY TOMATO-RICE SOUP

1 tablespoon finely chopped onion
1 tablespoon butter
1 can (1 pint, 2 ounces) tomato juice
1 can (10½ ounces) condensed beef consommé
⅓ cup water
½ teaspoon celery salt
¼ teaspoon salt
1 bay leaf
dash of pepper
⅓ cup enriched pre-cooked rice

Sauté onion in butter in medium saucepan until soft. Add remaining ingredients except rice. Bring to a boil; then add rice, cover loosely, and simmer 5 minutes. If desired, garnish each serving with a slice of lemon. *Serves 4.*

BLACK BEAN-RICE POTAGE

1 can (10½ ounces) condensed black bean soup
1 can (13 ounces) tomato consommé
⅔ cup water
1 tablespoon butter
1 tablespoon dry sherry

2 teaspoons lemon juice
½ teaspoon salt
⅔ cup enriched pre-cooked rice

Blend soup and consommé with water in a 2-quart saucepan. Add butter, sherry, lemon juice, and salt. Bring to a boil. Stir in rice. Reduce heat, cover loosely, and cook gently 10 minutes, stirring occasionally. Garnish with finely chopped hard-cooked egg and lemon slices, if desired. *Serves 4.*

POTAGE MONGOLE WITH RICE

1 can (10½ ounces) condensed tomato soup
1 can (11 ounces) condensed green pea soup
2½ cups water
1 tablespoon butter
1 teaspoon salt
⅔ cup enriched pre-cooked rice

Blend soups with water in a 2-quart saucepan. Add butter and salt. Bring to a boil. Stir in rice. Reduce heat, cover loosely, and cook slowly 10 minutes, stirring occasionally. Garnish with chopped parsley, if desired. *Serves 6.*

BEEF BROTH WITH RICE

⅔ cup enriched pre-cooked rice
2 cans (10½ ounces each) condensed beef broth
1 can (1⅓ cups) water

Combine all ingredients in a saucepan. Bring to a boil; then simmer 5 minutes. Serve with a sprinkling of chopped parsley, if desired. *Serves 4.*

RICE RANCHERO

2 cans (10½ ounces each) chili-beef soup
1½ soup cans water
¾ cup finely chopped onion

3 cups cooked rice
1½ cup corn chips, slightly crushed
1 cup grated cheese

Mix soup, water, and onion. Heat and stir until boiling. Add rice. Pour into a greased 2-quart casserole. Top with corn chips and cheese. Bake at 375°F. for 25 to 35 minutes. *Serves 6.*

6.
Salads

RICE PICNIC SALAD

1 tablespoon cider or tarragon vinegar
2 tablespoons salad oil
1 tablespoon prepared mustard
¾ teaspoon salt
dash pepper
2½ cups hot cooked long-grain rice
½ cups sliced stuffed green olives
1 hard-cooked egg, chopped
¾ cup sliced celery
2 tablespoons chopped dill pickle
2 tablespoons chopped pimiento
1 small onion, minced
¼ cup mayonnaise

Blend salad oil with vinegar, mustard, salt, and pepper. Then blend with hot rice and allow to cool. Add remaining ingredients and toss lightly. Chill overnight. *Serves 4.*

HOT CURRIED CHICKEN SALAD

3 cups diced, cooked chicken
2 cups chopped celery
1 teaspoon curry powder
½ teaspoon salt

43

⅛ teaspoon pepper
½ cup slivered almonds, toasted
1¼ cups salad dressing
1 cup oven-toasted rice cereal
1 tablespoon regular margarine or butter, melted

Combine chicken, celery, curry powder, salt, pepper, almonds, and salad dressing. Mix thoroughly. Spoon chicken mixture into 6 individual ramekins. Toss oven-toasted rice cereal with melted margarine until well-coated; sprinkle over chicken mixture. Bake in slow oven (325°F.) about 30 minutes or until thoroughly heated. Garnish with parsley. *Serves 6.*

GOLDEN RICE SALAD

3 cups cooked rice
¼ cup minced green onion
6 hard-cooked eggs, diced
1 cup diced celery
¼ cup diced dill pickles
¾ cup mayonnaise
¾ teaspoon salt

Chill rice thoroughly and toss it lightly with other ingredients. Serve on lettuce and garnish the bowl or platter with salad greens, tomato wedges, and radish roses. Stuffed olives may be used in place of pickles. *Serves 8.*

CHINESE FRIED RICE

½ cup diced green onion
1 cup diced celery
3 tablespoons butter
1 jar (2½ ounces) sliced mushrooms, drained
3 cups cooked rice
2 tablespoons soy sauce
1 egg, slightly beaten

In skillet, sauté the green onion and celery in butter until almost tender. Stir in mushrooms, rice, and soy sauce. Cook 10 minutes over low heat, stirring occasionally. Stir in beaten egg and cook only until egg is done. If desired, serve with extra soy sauce. *Serves 6.*

CRABMEAT RICE SALAD

1 can (6½ ounces) crabmeat
1½ cups cold cooked rice
2 tablespoons French dressing
¼ cup mayonnaise
2 tablespoons finely minced onion
2 teaspoons anchovy paste
½ teaspoon dry mustard
¾ cup sliced celery
2 tablespoons minced parsley
crisp greens
2 hard-cooked eggs, sliced
1 tomato, sliced

Combine crabmeat with rice and French dressing. Marinate in the refrigerator for about one-half hour. Combine mayonnaise with onion, anchovy paste, and mustard. Add with celery and parsley to rice mixture. Toss very lightly. Serve in crisp greens garnished with egg and tomato slices. *Serves 4.*

BOMBAY RICE

¾ cup French dressing
1½ teaspoons curry powder
1 teaspoon paprika
3 cups hot cooked rice
1 tablespoon grated onion
½ cup chopped pimiento
1½ cups diced celery
1½ cups cooked green peas

Blend French dressing, curry powder, and paprika and add to warm rice, tossing gently. Stir in onion and pimiento and cool. Add celery and peas to cooled rice mixture. Chill. To serve, mound mixture on platter and surround with slices of cold turkey, roast lamb, ham, beef, or other sandwich meat. *Serves 6.*

RICE AMANDINE

1 cup uncooked rice
2 tablespoons butter or margarine, melted
1 cup chopped green onions and tops
2 cups chicken broth
1 teaspoon salt
½ cup slivered almonds

Cook rice and onions in butter or margarine until golden but not brown. Add broth and salt. Heat to boiling, stir, cover. Lower heat and simmer for 14 minutes or until rice is tender. Remove from heat and toss lightly with slivered almonds. *Serves 6.*

SOUTHERN RICE DRESSING

1 tablespoon shortening
1 tablespoon flour
2 cups chicken or beef broth
1 clove garlic
1 cup chopped giblets or ground meat
1 chopped onion
1 cup diced celery
½ cup raisins
2 tablespoons chopped parsley
4 cups cooked rice
⅔ cup chopped nutmeats
salt and pepper to taste

Cook flour in shortening over low heat until brown. Add broth, garlic, and giblets. Cook for 20 minutes. Add onions, celery, raisins, and parsley. Simmer for 10 minutes. Mix with cooked rice, nuts, and seasonings; simmer for about 10 minutes. *Serves 6.*

RICE PICNIC SALAD

3 cups hot rice
¼ cup French dressing
¼ cup minced onions
1 teaspoon salt

¼ teaspoon pepper
½ cup minced celery
⅓ cup minced green pepper
¼ cup minced sour pickles
⅓ cup sweet relish
2 tablespoons minced pimiento
2 hard-cooked eggs, chopped
⅔ cup mayonnaise

Combine rice, French dressing, onions, salt, and pepper. Let stand while preparing remaining ingredients. Add celery, green pepper, sour pickles, sweet relish, pimiento, eggs, and mayonnaise; toss lightly with a fork. Chill thoroughly. *Serves 6*

GREEN AND GOLD RELISH

1 cup shredded raw carrots
½ cup chopped green pepper
1 cup crushed pineapple, drained
2 teaspoons lemon peel
2 tablespoons lemon juice
¼ cup sugar
1½ cups cooked rice

Combine all ingredients and mix well. Cover and chill about 2 hours before serving. *Serves 8.*

FRENCH SPINACH AND RICE SALAD BOWL

¼ to ½ pound fresh spinach
1 small onion, thinly sliced
½ cup thinly sliced celery
¼ cup sliced radishes
3 hard-cooked eggs, sliced
1½ cups cold cooked rice
¾ teaspoon salt
¼ teaspoon pepper
1 cup Lemon Dressing

Wash spinach thoroughly. Break off stems and measure 1 quart.

If leaves are large, tear into bite-sized pieces. Shake spinach in a towel to dry well. In a salad bowl arrange attractively with other vegetables the eggs and rice. Season with salt and pepper. Chill. When ready to serve, add Lemon Dressing and toss lightly. *Serves 5–6.*

LEMON DRESSING

1 tablespoon flour
⅓ cup salad oil
½ cup water
1 egg yolk, slightly beaten
½ teaspoon salt
½ teaspoon dry mustard
3 tablespoons lemon juice

Blend flour and 1 tablespoon of the oil in a small saucepan. Stir in water. Cook until thickened, stirring constantly. Gradually stir hot mixture into egg yolk. Blend in salt, mustard, remaining oil, and lemon juice. Beat until smooth. Chill. *Makes 1 cup.*

HOT RICE SALAD WITH CRISP BACON

1½ cups hot cooked rice
2 tablespoons French dressing
2 tablespoons minced onion
½ teaspoon salt
dash of pepper
¼ cup minced celery
3 tablespoons minced green pepper
⅓ cup sweet relish
2 tablespoons pimiento, chopped
2 hard-cooked eggs, chopped
⅓ cup mayonnaise
8 slices crisp bacon

Combine rice, French dressing, onion, and seasoning. Let stand while preparing remaining ingredients. *Next:* add together celery, green pepper, relish, pimiento, eggs, and mayonnaise. Toss lightly. Turn into a casserole and bake covered 15 minutes in a 450°F. oven. Serve with 8 slices of crisp bacon. *Serves 2.*

GOLDEN RICE SALAD

¼ cup salad oil
2 tablespoons vinegar
2 tablespoons prepared mustard
1½ teaspoons salt
⅛ teaspoon pepper
4½ cups hot cooked rice (1½ cups rice cooked in 3 cups
                                        chicken broth)
1 cup ripe olives, cut in large pieces
2 hard-cooked eggs, diced
1½ cups celery, sliced
¼ cup dill pickles, chopped
¼ cup pimiento
1 small onion, minced
½ cup mayonnaise

Blend together salad oil, vinegar, mustard, salt, and pepper; pour over hot rice; toss and set aside to cool. Add remaining ingredients and toss. Chill thoroughly. Serve on lettuce leaf and garnish with extra sliced eggs. *Makes 8 one-cup servings.*

TROPICAL RICE SALAD

1 cup uncooked rice
2 cups orange juice
¼ teaspoon salt
1 teaspoon grated lemon rind
1 tablespoon lemon juice
1 cup coarsely chopped dates (about 20 whole)
½ cup toasted slivered almonds
6 thin cantaloupe slices, peeled
6 thin honeydew melon slices, peeled

Combine rice, orange juice, and salt in a 3-quart saucepan. Bring to a boil and stir gently with a fork. Cover tightly, reduce heat to simmer, and cook about 20 minutes, or until rice is tender. Chill. Mix in lemon rind and juice, dates, and nuts. Serve in ring of alternating slices of cantaloupe and honeydew melon topped with Minted Sour Cream Dressing. *Serves 4–6.*

MINTED SOUR CREAM DRESSING

Combine 1 cup sour cream with 1 tablespoon finely chopped mint, 2 teaspoons sugar, 1 teaspoon lemon juice, and a pinch of salt. Chill.

RICE SALAD U.S.A.

5 cups cooked rice (cooked in chicken broth)
1 cup diced green pepper
1 cup chopped celery
3 tablespoons minced onion
¼ cup chopped pimiento
salt and pepper to taste
½ cup prepared vinegar and oil dressing
4 tomatoes, peeled and quartered

Combine rice, green pepper, celery, onion, pimiento, salt, and pepper; mix well. Chill. When ready to serve, pour dressing over rice-vegetable mixture. Toss lightly. Spoon onto salad plate and surround with quartered tomatoes. *Serves 10–12.*

COUNTRY INN SALAD

1 package herb-flavored rice mix
½ cup mayonnaise
1 can (4 ounces) chopped mushrooms, drained
¼ cup chopped pimiento
2 tablespoons chopped celery
2 cups cooked seafood or chicken
2 tablespoons mayonnaise
2 teaspoons lemon juice

Cook herb rice mix according to package directions and cool. Combine mayonnaise, pimiento, and celery. Add to rice and mix. Combine seafood, mayonnaise, and lemon juice. Add to rice mixture. Serve on greens and garnish with tomato wedges and hard-cooked eggs or cucumber slices. *Serves 6.*

COME-TO-LUNCH SALAD

1½ cups cooked parboiled rice
2 hard-cooked eggs (chopped)
¼ cup ground pickles (sour or dill)
½ cup diced cold chicken
¼ cup sweet pickles
¼ cup diced celery
¼ cup diced onions
2 pimientos, diced
⅛ teaspoon paprika
½ teaspoon salt
1 tablespoon prepared mustard
⅓ cup mayonnaise

Combine all ingredients; chill. Garnish with tomato wedges and endive. *Serves 4.*

SUGGESTION: To make a meal: serve to luncheon guests with cups of jellied madrilène with lemon wedges; heated, buttered rusks; orange ice with crème de menthe topping. If you prefer, use flaked tuna in the salad in place of chicken.

EASY RICE-FRUIT SALAD

2 cups enriched pre-cooked rice
¼ cup pecans, broken
1 banana, cut into ½-inch pieces
½ cup pineapple cubes
1 orange, peeled and sectioned
1 apple, cut into ½-inch pieces
maraschino cherries (with stems) for garnish

Cook rice according to package directions. Set pan of rice in cold tap water to cool quickly. Combine with pecans and fruit (except cherries). Mound individual servings on crisp lettuce leaves. Garnish just before serving with maraschino cherries. Top each serving with Orange Cream Dressing. *Serves 6.*

ORANGE CREAM DRESSING

⅓ cup orange juice
2 teaspoons lemon juice
¼ cup sugar
½ teaspoon salt
2 egg yolks
½ cup whipping cream

Combine first four ingredients in a saucepan. Bring to a boil on high heat. Cool slightly; add egg yolks, one at a time, beating well after each addition. Cook over low heat until mixture thickens, stirring occasionally. Cool. Fold in whipped cream.

DANISH RICE SALAD

2 packages sour cream sauce mix
milk
2 hard-cooked eggs
3 cups cooked parboiled rice
½ cup minced green pepper
½ cup minced celery
½ teaspoon salt
lettuce leaves
1 cup diced pickled beets
parsley

Blend sour cream sauce mix with milk to a smooth sauce according to package directions. Chop egg whites; reserve yolks. Stir rice, egg whites, green pepper, celery, and salt into sauce; chill. Spoon onto lettuce leaves. Circle with pickled beets and top with reserved egg yolks sprinkled with parsley. *Serves 4.*

CURRIED SHRIMP SALAD

¾ cup mayonnaise
2 teaspoons curry powder, or enough to taste
1½ cups cooked cleaned shrimp, quartered
1½ cups cold cooked parboiled rice
¾ cup sliced celery

2 tablespoons grated onion
½ cup halved seedless green grapes
½ cup slivered blanched almonds

Mix curry powder to taste with mayonnaise. Combine remaining ingredients. Toss well with the curried mayonnaise. *Serves 6.*

SUGGESTION: To make a meal: serve pickled beets with a dab of sour cream, parsley-butter finger sandwiches, lime sherbet and ginger cookies for dessert.

EGG-AND-RICE SALAD

1½ cups cooked rice
4 hard-cooked eggs, chopped
¼ cup chopped or ground pickles (sour or dill)
¼ cup chopped sweet pickles
¼ cup chopped celery
¼ cup chopped onion (optional)
2 chopped pimientos
salt, pepper, paprika to taste
mayonnaise
prepared mustard

Toss with small amount of mayonnaise combined with a little prepared mustard. *Serves 4–6.*

ITALIAN RICE SALAD

3 cups enriched pre-cooked rice
2¼ cups chicken broth
1 cup diced green pepper
1 cup chopped celery
3 tablespoons minced onion
¼ cup chopped pimiento
½ cup bottled Italian dressing
4 tomatoes, peeled and cut into wedges

Cook rice in chicken broth according to package directions. Combine rice, green pepper, celery, onion, and pimiento. Mix well;

chill. When ready to serve, pour dressing over rice-vegetable mixture. Toss lightly. Spoon onto salad plate and surround with tomato wedges. *Serves 6–8.*

HE-MAN'S RICE SALAD

    2 cups cooked parboiled rice
    6 hard-cooked eggs, chopped
    6 slices crisp bacon, crumbled
    3 tablespoons finely chopped green pepper
    1 tablespoon minced onion
    1 teaspoon salt
    ½ teaspoon prepared mustard
    ⅛ teaspoon pepper
    ½ cup mayonnaise
    ½ cup Cheddar cheese, diced
    8 bologna slices

Combine rice, eggs, bacon, green pepper, onion, and seasonings. Add mayonnaise and mix well. Toss lightly with diced cheese. Roll some of the mixture in bologna slices and arrange around edge of bowl. Fill center with remaining salad mixture; chill. Serve with crisp greens and tomato wedges. *Serves 4.*

HERBAL RICE TREAT

    1 cup uncooked rice
    1 teaspoon instant minced onion
    2 cups water
    1 tablespoon butter or margarine
    1 teaspoon salt
    2 tablespoons minced parsley

To prepare, place rice and onion in a buttered casserole. Heat water, butter, and salt to boiling. Pour over rice; stir well. Cover tightly and bake at 325°F. for 35 minutes. Remove from oven. Add parsley and toss lightly. *Serves 4.*

SUGGESTION: For a main dish, add 2 cups chopped ham or diced chicken.

SKY-HIGH RICE SALAD

3 cups cooked rice
1 cup whole kernel corn
1 cup thinly sliced celery
¼ cup chopped green pepper
¼ cup pimiento stuffed olives, sliced
3 tablespoons minced onion
¼ cup chopped dill pickle
¾ teaspoon salt
freshly ground black pepper to taste
⅓ cup bottled French dressing
¼ teaspoon curry powder
2 tablespoons finely chopped chutney
crisp salad greens
hard-cooked egg slices

Combine rice, corn, celery, green pepper, olives, onion, and pickle. Season with salt and pepper. Blend French dressing with curry powder and chutney; pour over rice mixture and toss lightly. Chill at least 30 minutes before serving. To serve, mound on salad greens and garnish with egg slices. *Serves 6.*

FRESH SPINACH AND RICE SALAD BOWL

¼ to ½ pound fresh spinach
1 small onion, thinly sliced
½ cup thinly sliced celery
¼ cup sliced radishes
3 hard-cooked eggs, sliced
1½ cups cold cooked rice
¾ teaspoon salt
¼ teaspoon pepper
bottled French Dressing

Wash spinach thoroughly. Break off stems and measure 1 quart. If leaves are large, tear into bite-sized pieces. Shake spinach in a towel to dry well. Arrange attractively with other vegetables, eggs, and rice in a salad bowl. Chill. When ready to serve, season, add dressing, and toss lightly. *Serves 5–6.*

7.
Casseroles

INDIVIDUAL CHICKEN RICE CASSEROLE

3 cups hot, cooked rice
2 tablespoons butter or margarine, softened
2 cups grated processed cheese
1 cup cream
½ teaspoon salt
dash of white pepper
1 teaspoon Worcestershire sauce
1½ cups cooked chicken, sliced
1 4-ounce can mushrooms, drained
1 cup cooked peas, drained
½ cup bread crumbs

Add butter to hot, cooked rice and mix well. In top of a double boiler, mix cheese, cream, salt, pepper, and Worcestershire sauce. Cook, stirring constantly, until cheese is melted. Layer rice, chicken, mushrooms, and peas into individual casseroles. Make the top and bottom layers of rice. Pour cheese sauce over each casserole and sprinkle with bread crumbs. Bake at 350°F. about 20 minutes or until bubbly hot. *Serves 6.*

COUNTRY CASSEROLE

3 cups cooked rice
1 pound pork links, browned and drained of all fat

1 medium onion, finely chopped
1 10½-ounce can condensed cream of tomato soup, undiluted
2 tablespoons grated American cheese

In a buttered casserole, arrange rice and sausages in alternate layers, sprinkling each layer with chopped onion. Top with soup and grated cheese. Cover. Bake in moderately hot oven (350°F.) for 30 minutes. *Serves 6.*

SUGGESTION: Ingredients may be prepared beforehand and kept refrigerated until time to bake. Bulk sausage may be used instead of links.

CASSEROLE MEXICANA

1 pound ground beef
½ cup chopped onion
¼ cup chopped green pepper
1 15-ounce can kidney beans
1 cup cooked rice
1 8-ounce can tomato sauce
1 teaspoon salt
⅔ cup grated cheese

In skillet, brown meat, onion, and green pepper. Drain excess fat. Layer meat mixture and next four ingredients in a one-quart casserole. Sprinkle with cheese. Bake at 325°F. for 20 minutes. *Serves 4–6.*

MUSHROOM RICE AS A VEGETABLE DISH

Coarsely grind 1 pound fresh mushrooms. Sauté with 2 tablespoons chopped green pepper and 2 tablespoons chopped green onions in 2 tablespoons butter or margarine until tender. Combine with 2½ cups cooked rice and ½ teaspoon salt in an earthenware casserole. Bake at 350°F. about 15 minutes. (For more flavor, cook rice in chicken stock instead of water.) *Serves 2.*

HAM AND RICE CASSEROLE

2 cans (10½ ounces each) cream of celery soup

1 cup light cream
1 cup grated sharp Cheddar cheese
½ cup grated Parmesan cheese
1½ tablespoons minced onion
1 tablespoon prepared mustard
1 teaspoon grated lemon rind
¼ teaspoon rosemary
⅛ teaspoon pepper
4 cups cooked rice
4 cups cubed cooked ham
1 can (1 lb. 4 ounces) cut green beans
1 can (3½ ounces) French fried onion rings

Combine celery soup and cream; stir until smooth. Heat slowly until hot, being careful not to boil. Stir in cheese. Then blend in onion, mustard, lemon rind, rosemary, and pepper. Remove from heat. Combine sauce with rice and ham. Alternate layers of ham and rice mixture with green beans in 3-quart casserole, ending with ham and rice mixture. Sprinkle with French-fried onion rings. Bake, uncovered, at 350°F. for 15 to 20 minutes or until bubbly. *Serves 10.*

SUGGESTION: If your family is small, freeze half of this casserole for later serving.

OVEN-BAKED RICE

½ cup uncooked rice
1¼ cups canned tomatoes
½ cup water
½ teaspoon salt
⅓ cup sliced stuffed olives
2 tablespoons salad dressing
¼ cup minced onions
½ cup grated Cheddar cheese

Combine all ingredients in a one-quart casserole. Cover. Bake in a 350°F. oven about 40 minutes or until rice is tender. Uncover and toss lightly with a fork. Cook another 15 minutes or until all liquid is absorbed. *Serves 2.*

LAMB RISOTTO CASSEROLE

½ lemon
4 thick lamb chops
¾ cup brown rice, uncooked
1 can consommé (10½ ounces)
2 carrots, cut in julienne strips
10 small onions
1 cup Sauterne
¼ teaspoon marjoram
⅛ teaspoon oregano
½ teaspoon salt
dash of pepper

Squeeze lemon over chops. While this is standing, put in the casserole brown rice, consommé, carrots, onions, and Sauterne. Add lamb chops. Bake covered 1 hour in 350°F. oven. At the end of ½ hour, take out and stir, and add seasoning. Return to oven and finish cooking. *Serves 4.*

RICE SOUFFLÉ

1 cup heavy white sauce
4 eggs, separated
1 cup cooked rice

Combine white sauce with slightly beaten egg yolks and rice. Beat egg whites until stiff but not dry. Fold into rice mixture. Pour into an ungreased 2-quart casserole and bake for 1 hour in a 325°F. oven. *Serves 4–6.*

WHITE SAUCE

Melt ¼ cup butter in a saucepan. Stir in ¼ cup flour. Then blend in 1 cup milk and ½ teaspoon salt. Cook, stirring constantly, until thickened.

VARIATIONS:
1. Swiss cheese or sharp cheese—Blend 1 cup of grated cheese into the hot white sauce.

2. Apricot—Add 1 cup apricot pulp to the rice mixture before folding in the egg whites.

3. Fold in ¾ cup finely diced chicken, ¾ cup cooked rice, ¼ cup chopped nuts, and ¼ teaspoon nutmeg. Cook 50 minutes in a 325°F. oven.

4. Add to the white sauce, ¾ cup tuna fish, ¾ cup cooked rice, 1 teaspoon dillweed, and ¾ teaspoon paprika. Bake 50 minutes in a 325°F. oven.

5. Add to the white sauce, ¾ cup salmon, ½ teaspoon liquid smoke, which has been brushed over the salmon, ¾ cup cooked rice, salt and pepper to taste. Bake for 50 minutes in a 325°F. oven.

6. Combine with the white sauce, ¼ teaspoon nutmeg, ¼ teaspoon paprika, ½ teaspoon basil, 2 tablespoons minced parsley, ½ cup boiled onions (drained and minced), ¾ cup cooked rice. Bake 45 minutes in a 325°F. oven.

7. Add to the white sauce, ½ cup whole kernel corn, ¾ cup cooked rice, 1 tablespoon chopped pimiento, and 2 tablespoons minced green pepper. Bake 45 minutes in a 325°F. oven.

SCALLOPED OYSTERS AND RICE

4 tablespoons butter or margarine
¾ cup onions, chopped
1 cup celery, diced
3 cups cooked rice
1 pint oysters
2 teaspoons salt
¼ teaspoon pepper
1 cup milk
1 cup grated sharp cheese
1 cup rice concentrate cereal, buttered

Melt butter in skillet. Add onions and celery; sauté until tender, but not brown. Remove from stove and stir in cooked rice and mix well. Butter a casserole and add a layer of oysters that have been salted and peppered, then a layer of rice mixture. Proceed in this manner until all the oysters and rice have been added. Pour the milk over all. Spread grated cheese over the rice mixture and top with buttered rice cereal. Bake in a covered casserole at 400°F. for 30 minutes. Serve piping hot. *Serves 8.*

HOPPING JOHN
(Rice and Peas)

1 cup dried black-eyed peas and water to cover
¼ pound smoked bacon or salt pork, diced
1 red pepper pod, diced
3 cups cooked rice
salt and pepper to taste

Soak peas overnight. Cook with the bacon and pepper pod until peas are very tender. Add rice and salt and pepper to taste. Pour into casserole. Cover. Bake in moderate oven (350°F.) until liquid is absorbed and dish is thoroughly heated. *Serves 8.*

ARKANSAS GREEN RICE

1 cup uncooked rice
¼ cup minced onion
2 cups water
1 tablespoon butter or margarine
1 teaspoon salt
2 tablespoons minced parsley

To prepare, place rice and onion in a buttered casserole. Heat water, butter, and salt to boiling. Pour over rice; stir well. Cover tightly and bake at 325°F. for 35 minutes. Remove from oven. Add parsley and toss lightly. *Serves 4.*

MISSISSIPPI RICE MEDLEY

2 tablespoons butter or margarine
½ cup diced celery
3 cups cooked rice
1 can (4½ ounces) deviled ham
1 egg, beaten
¼ teaspoon salt
dash of pepper
½ cup cheese, grated

Melt butter in skillet; sauté celery until tender but not brown.

Add rice, ham, egg, salt, and pepper. Heat thoroughly, stirring constantly. Pour into buttered casserole. Top with cheese. Place under broiler only until cheese is melted. *Serves 6.*

BAKED RICE ITALIANO CASSEROLE

1 tablespoon butter or margarine
¾ cup chopped onion
½ pound Italian sausage (or any highly seasoned type), skinned and finely chopped
3 cups cooked parboiled rice
1 cup fresh or frozen peas
1 can (2 ounces) sliced mushrooms (or stems and pieces) drained
1 can (8 ounces) tomato sauce
¼ cup grated Parmesan cheese

Brown onion and sausage lightly in melted butter or margarine. Add peas and mushrooms and stir for several minutes. Add tomato sauce; cover and simmer for 10 minutes. Combine with cooked rice and place in buttered 1-quart casserole. Sprinkle with cheese and bake in 375°F. oven for about 15–20 minutes. *Serves 4.*

SUGGESTION: To make a meal, serve a salad-antipasto of carrot curls, cucumber fingers, crisp scallions, cubes of mild cheese, green and ripe olives, tomato wedges—all on a bed of shredded lettuce. Pass oil and vinegar. Use long and thin bread sticks called *grissini*. Finish the meal with *spumoni* or Italian ice cream.

BACON CHEESE BAKE CASSEROLE

8 slices bacon
1 cup minced onion
1 cup diced celery
3 cups cooked parboiled rice
1 cup sliced stuffed olives
½ teaspoon pepper
1 can (10½ ounces) condensed cream of chicken soup
2 cups shredded Cheddar cheese

Fry bacon in a large skillet until crisp. Remove from pan. Drain well on absorbent paper; crumble into small pieces. Drain all but 3 tablespoons drippings from pan. Add onion and celery and cook until tender but not brown. Remove from heat and stir in rice, sliced olives, and pepper. In a saucepan, heat chicken soup and 1 cup cheese until cheese has melted. Add sauce and bacon to the rice mixture. Turn into a greased 1½-quart casserole; top with remaining cheese. Then bake in 375°F. oven for 15 minutes. *Serves 6.*

RICE-BROCCOLI CASSEROLE

1 box (6 ounces) long-grain rice
1 package (10 ounces) frozen chopped broccoli, partially
                                                  defrosted
1 can (10½ ounces) cream of mushroom soup
1 can (6½ ounces) chunk-style tuna, drained
2 eggs, separated

Cook rice as directed on package, but only 15 minutes. Break broccoli apart and spread on top of rice. Continue cooking until rice and broccoli are tender and liquid is absorbed. Remove from heat. Add soup, salt, tuna, and slightly beaten egg yolks. Beat egg whites until stiff. Fold in rice mixture. Bake in 2-quart casserole 20 to 30 minutes in 350°F. oven. *Serves 6–8.*

SUGGESTION: Cut off tops of 8 large green peppers and remove seeds. Parboil in salted water for 5 minutes; drain. Stuff with the rice mixture. Bake in a greased casserole in a 350°F. oven for 25 to 35 minutes.

RICE BENITO CASSEROLE

1 large onion, thinly sliced
6 tablespoons butter or margarine
1 cup parboiled rice
2 cups chicken broth, hot
1 cup cooked green peas
1 cup cooked diced ham
2 tablespoons chopped pimiento

Sauté onion in 4 tablespoons butter or margarine until soft. Stir in rice and sauté until lightly browned. Pour in hot broth. Bake, covered, 30 to 35 minutes in 350°F. oven or until the rice is tender and the liquid is absorbed. Stir in peas, ham, 2 tablespoons butter, and pimiento. Garnish with ham cut in julienne strips. *Serves 5–6.*

TUNA-WILD RICE BAKE CASSEROLE

1 box (6 ounces) long-grain rice
¼ cup melted butter or margarine
3 tablespoons finely chopped onion
⅓ cup flour
1 teaspoon salt
black pepper to taste
2 cups milk
2 cans (6½ ounces each) tuna fish
¼ cup chopped ripe olives
1 tablespoon lemon juice
⅓ cup mayonnaise
⅓ cup crushed potato chips
2 diced hard-cooked eggs

Cook rice as directed on package. Sauté onions in butter or margarine. Blend in flour, salt, and pepper. Gradually stir in milk. Cook until thickened. Mix in rice, tuna fish, olives, lemon juice, mayonnaise, and 3 tablespoons potato chips. Fold in eggs. Pour into 2-quart casserole. Cover with remaining potato chips. Bake in 425°F. oven 20–30 minutes. *Serves 6–8.*

CONTINENTAL RICE CASSEROLE

¼ cup minced onion
¼ cup slivered almonds
¼ cup butter or margarine
1 cup parboiled rice
2¼ cups chicken stock or bouillon
½ teaspoon salt
¼ teaspoon white pepper
1 cup cubed cooked chicken

1 cup cubed cooked beef
1 cup cubed cooked ham
1 medium apple, peeled, sliced
1 cup (4 ounces) grated Cheddar cheese
¼ cup Sauterne
1 tablespoon chopped green celery tops (optional)

Sauté onion and almonds in butter or margarine until golden. Stir in rice and sauté until light brown. Add stock or bouillon, salt, and pepper. Bring to boil; cover. Simmer 15 minutes. Stir in chicken, beef, ham, and apples. Return to boil, cover. Simmer 10 minutes. Pour into 2½-quart casserole. Sprinkle with cheese and wine. Bake 10 to 15 minutes in 350°F. oven. Garnish with celery tops if desired. *Serves 5–6.*

WINTER CASSEROLE

1 tablespoon chopped onion
1 tablespoon butter or margarine
2 cups enriched pre-cooked rice
¼ cup chopped parsley
¾ plus ¼ cup shredded sharp Cheddar cheese
½ teaspoon salt
1 can (10½ ounces) cream of mushroom soup
¾ cup hot water
¼ cup sliced almonds (optional)

Sauté onions in butter or margarine. Add rice, parsley, ¾ cup cheese, salt, soup, and water. Mix well. Pour into 1½-quart greased casserole; cover. Bake in 375°F. oven until rice is tender and liquid is absorbed, about 30 minutes. Sprinkle top with remaining cheese and almonds. Broil until cheese is melted. *Serves 4–5.*

CHICKEN CASSEROLE

½ cup flour
1 teaspoon salt
½ cup melted butter or chicken fat
2½ cups chicken stock
2 cups enriched pre-cooked rice

2 cups cubed cooked chicken
1 cup fresh broiled mushrooms
½ cup chopped ripe olives
½ cup green peas
¾ cup slivered almonds

Stir flour and salt into butter or chicken fat in a saucepan. Stir in chicken stock. Cook until thickened, stirring constantly. Alternate layers of cooked rice, chicken sauce, and vegetables in greased 2-quart casserole. Top with slivered almonds. Bake in 350°F. oven for 30 minutes. *Serves 6–8.*

RICE 'N' SALMON CASSEROLE

2½ cups cooked parboiled rice
1 can (6 to 8 ounces) salmon
3 tablespoons butter or margarine
3 tablespoons flour
¾ cup milk (or part salmon liquid)
½ teaspoon onion juice
½ teaspoon paprika
¾ teaspoon salt
⅛ teaspoon each: pepper, marjoram
dash cayenne
½ cup grated Cheddar cheese

Flake salmon (remove bones or crush finely) and combine with rice. Melt butter or margarine; remove from heat, blend in flour. Stir in milk and seasonings and cook over low heat until sauce is thickened. Combine sauce with rice mixture and place in 1½-quart casserole or 4 individual casseroles. Top with cheese. Cover, bake in 350°F. oven 30 minutes. *Serves 4.*

CHEROKEE CASSEROLE

1 pound ground beef
1 tablespoon salad or olive oil
¾ cup finely chopped onions
1½ teaspoons salt
dash of pepper

⅛ teaspoon garlic powder
⅛ teaspoon thyme
⅛ teaspoon oregano
½ small bay leaf
2 cans (8 ounces each) tomato sauce (or 1 can of tomatoes)
1 can (10½ ounces) condensed cream of mushroom soup
1 cup enriched pre-cooked rice
3 stuffed olives, sliced
2 or 3 slices process American cheese, cut in ½-inch strips

Brown meat in oil over high heat. Add onions and cook over medium heat until tender. Stir in remaining ingredients in order given, *except cheese*. Bring to a boil, reduce heat, and simmer for 5 minutes, stirring occasionally. Discard bay leaf. Spoon into a shallow 1½-quart baking dish or casserole. Arrange a lattice of cheese over top. Broil just until cheese melts. Garnish with additional sliced stuffed olives, if desired. *Serves 4–6.*

NOTE: Legend says the Indians called this "Dohm Minna Bou," meaning, "everything in the pot."

SAUCY RICE CASSEROLE

¼ cup chopped onion
1 tablespoon salad oil
½ clove garlic, crushed
1 pound ground beef
2 cans (6 ounces) tomato paste
1¼ cups water
2 teaspoons brown sugar
1 bouillon cube
¾ teaspoon salt
¼ teaspoon pepper
⅛ teaspoon oregano
1⅓ cups boiling water
1⅔ cups enriched pre-cooked rice

Lightly brown onion in oil. Stir in garlic; then add meat and sauté until browned, stirring occasionally. Pour off excess fat. Add remaining ingredients except boiling water and rice. Cook over low heat 10 minutes, stirring occasionally. Pour boiling water into a 2-quart casserole. Sprinkle in rice. Gently ladle the bubbling sauce over rice. Do not stir. Cover. Bake at 400°F. for 10 minutes. Sprinkle with grated Parmesan cheese before serving, if desired. Makes 4½ cups sauce plus rice. *Serves 5–6.*

MEXICAN CASSEROLE

1 can (10½ ounces) condensed tomato soup
1 can (1⅓ cups) water
1 egg
1 tablespoon coarsely chopped parsley
1¼ teaspoons salt
⅛ teaspoon pepper
1 cup soft bread crumbs
1 pound ground beef
1⅓ cups enriched pre-cooked rice
½ cup chopped ripe olives
¼ cup chopped onion
2 teaspoons chili powder
¾ teaspoon salt
1 cup grated Cheddar *or* process American cheese
1 tablespoon butter, melted

Mix soup and water. Blend ½ cup soup mixture into the egg in a mixing bowl; stir in parsley, 1¼ teaspoons salt, pepper, and bread crumbs. Add beef and mix lightly. Shape into 6 patties. Combine rice, olives, onion, chili powder, ¾ teaspoon salt, and remaining soup mixture in a greased, shallow, 2-quart casserole. Sprinkle with cheese. Place meat patties on top and brush with butter. Bake at 350°F. for 35 minutes, or until lightly browned. *Serves 4–6.*

UPSIDE-DOWN HAM CASSEROLE

3 tablespoons butter, melted
3 tablespoons brown sugar
1 can (8½ ounces) sliced pineapple, drained
4 servings sliced cooked ham, about ¼-inch thick
2½ tablespoons all-purpose flour
½ teaspoon salt
⅛ teaspoon pepper

1½ teaspoons minced onion
1⅓ cups enriched pre-cooked rice
1 cup milk
1 cup water

Blend butter and brown sugar in a 9-x-5-inch loaf pan or a shallow 1½-quart baking dish. Arrange pineapple and ham in mixture. Place in 400°F. oven while preparing rice mixture. Combine remaining ingredients in saucepan. Bring to a boil over medium heat. Then cover and simmer 5 minutes, stirring occasionally. Spread over ham and pineapple. Cover and bake at 400°F. for 10 minutes. Invert on serving platter and let stand about 1 minute before removing baking dish. Makes 4½ cups rice mixture. *Serves 4.*

CAREFREE CASSEROLE

1⅓ cups enriched pre-cooked rice
1 can (10½ ounces) condensed cream of mushroom soup
1¼ cups water
2 cups diced cooked or 1 can (12 ounces) boned chicken
1 cup cooked peas *or* peas and carrots
½ teaspoon salt
½ cup grated Cheddar cheese

Measure rice into a 1½-quart casserole. Blend soup and water in a saucepan. Stir in chicken, peas, and salt. Bring quickly to a boil, stirring occasionally. Stir into rice. Sprinkle with cheese. Cover and bake at 400°F. for 20 minutes. Stir. Garnish with potato chips or hot French fried onion rings, if desired. *Serves 4.*

SUGGESTION: In place of chicken, use 1 can (7 ounces) tuna, drained and flaked.

MARDI GRAS CASSEROLE

3 tablespoons butter
3 tablespoons all-purpose flour
dash of pepper
¼ teaspoon salt
1⅔ cups (14½-ounce can) evaporated milk
1 cup shredded Cheddar cheese

1⅓ cups enriched pre-cooked rice
1 tablespoon chopped parsley
½ teaspoon oregano
½ teaspoon salt
1⅓ cups water
1 can (1 pound) tomatoes, drained and sliced
½ medium onion, thinly sliced
2 cans (7 ounces each) tuna, drained and flaked

Melt butter in saucepan; blend in flour, pepper, and ¼ teaspoon salt. Gradually add milk, stirring constantly over medium heat. Continue to cook and stir until thickened. Add cheese. Cook and stir until melted. Combine rice, parsley, oregano, ½ teaspoon salt, and water in a shallow 11-x-7-inch baking dish. Place two-thirds of the tomato slices on rice. Then add onion and tuna. Spread cheese sauce over tuna and top with remaining tomato slices. Bake at 375°F. for 15 minutes. *Serves 6.*

QUICK SEAFOOD CASSEROLE

1 package (9 ounces) frozen cut green beans
1 can (1 pound) stewed tomatoes
1 can (7 or 7½ ounces) tuna or crabmeat, drained
¾ cup water
2 tablespoons butter
½ teaspoon celery salt
½ teaspoon sugar
½ teaspoon salt
⅛ teaspoon pepper
¾ cup enriched pre-cooked rice
1 cup grated Cheddar cheese

Combine all ingredients except rice and cheese in saucepan; bring to a boil. Scatter rice in a 2-quart casserole. Pour in the bean mixture. Cover and bake at 450°F. for 10 minutes; then uncover, sprinkle with cheese, and bake 5 minutes longer. *Serves 4.*

CAPTAIN'S CASSEROLE

1 can (10½ ounces) condensed cream of mushroom *or* cream of vegetable soup

½ cup milk
⅔ cup grated Cheddar cheese
1⅓ cups enriched pre-cooked rice
½ teaspoon oregano (optional)
dash of pepper
1 can (1 pound) tomatoes
1 cup water
½ onion, thinly sliced
2 cans (7 ounces each) tuna, drained and flaked
⅓ cup sliced stuffed olives
½ cup crushed potato chips (optional)

Combine soup, milk, and cheese; heat until cheese is melted, stirring occasionally. Meanwhile, combine rice, oregano, and pepper in a greased 1½-quart shallow baking dish. Drain tomatoes, measuring ½ cup of the juice. Stir juice and water into rice. Slice tomatoes and arrange about three-quarters of them on rice mixture. Add onion, tuna, and olives. Pour on soup mixture and sprinkle with potato chips. Arrange remaining tomato slices on top. Bake at 375°F. for 20–25 minutes. *Serves 5–6.*

SEVEN SEAS CASSEROLE

1 can (10½ ounces) condensed cream of celery soup
1⅓ cups water
¼ cup finely chopped onion (optional)
1 teaspoon lemon juice (optional)
¼ teaspoon salt
dash of pepper
1⅓ cups enriched pre-cooked rice
1½ cups drained cooked peas
1 can (7 ounces) tuna, drained and flaked
½ cup grated Cheddar cheese
paprika

Combine soup, water, onion, lemon juice, salt, and pepper in a saucepan. Bring to a boil over medium heat, stirring occasionally. Pour about half of the soup mixture into a greased 1½-quart casserole. Then, in layers, add rice, peas, and tuna. Pour on remaining soup mixture. Sprinkle with cheese and paprika. Cover and bake at 375°F. for 10 minutes; then cut through mixture, cover and bake about 10 minutes longer. *Serves 4.*

PENNY PINCHER'S RICE CASSEROLE

3 cups cooked rice
1 can (1 pound) cut green beans, drained
1 can (12 ounces) whole kernel corn, drained
½ cup chopped onion
½ cup chopped green pepper
1½ cups grated Cheddar cheese
2 tablespoons butter or margarine, melted
1 egg, beaten
1 cup tomato juice
1½ teaspoons salt
¼ teaspoon pepper
½ teaspoon garlic powder
1 pound frankfurters

Combine rice, vegetables, 1 cup cheese, and butter. Blend egg with tomato juice and seasonings. Stir into rice mixture. Spoon into buttered 3-quart casserole. Top with frankfurters that have been cut in ½-inch slices diagonally almost through to bottom. Sprinkle with remaining cheese. Bake at 350°F. for 25 minutes. *Serves 6–8.*

DELMONICO RICE

3 cups cooked rice
⅓ cup chopped green pepper
3 hard-cooked eggs, chopped
1 can (10½ ounces) cream of celery soup
1 cup milk
¼ teaspoon pepper
buttered bread crumbs

Combine rice, green pepper, eggs, soup, milk, and pepper. Turn into a buttered casserole. Top with buttered bread crumbs. Bake at 350°F. for 20 to 25 minutes. *Serves 6.*

8.
Main Dishes

MUSHROOM SAUSAGE SKILLET DINNER

½ pound bulk pork sausage shaped into 1" balls
1 medium onion, chopped
1 can (4 ounces) sliced mushrooms
1 cup uncooked long-grain rice
2 chicken bouillon cubes
3 cups hot water
½ cup frozen green peas (1 cup if desired)
1 can (2 ounces) pimiento, diced

Cook onion and sausage balls in skillet until onion is tender and sausage is lightly browned. Drain off excess fat. Add next 4 ingredients. Heat to boiling, cover; reduce heat, simmer 20 minutes. Add peas and pimiento, cover, simmer 5–10 minutes longer. Taste for seasonings. Some salt and pepper may be needed depending on seasonings in sausage. *Serves 4–6.*

SPACE-AGE BEEF STROGANOFF

3 tablespoons margarine or butter
1 pound tenderized veal cutlets, cut in 1" squares
½ cup chopped green onions
1 can (4 ounces) sliced mushrooms
1 beef bouillon cube
2 tablespoons brown gravy mix

⅓ cup mayonnaise
3½ cups cooked (1 cup uncooked) long-grain rice
¼ teaspoon dried dill

In electric skillet or heavy iron skillet, heat margarine or butter. Add meat and brown lightly. When meat is almost ready, add green onions, mushrooms, dried dill, and beef bouillon cube, crushed. Mix well. Stir in brown gravy mix and mayonnaise and heat until mixture begins to bubble; do not allow to boil or cook further. Serve on hot rice. *Serves 4–6.*

RICE-CHOPPED BEEF STROGANOFF

1 pound chopped beef
1 medium onion, diced
1 stalk celery, diced
½ cup sliced water chestnuts
¼ teaspoon dried dill
1 beef bouillon cube, crushed
1 3-ounce can button mushrooms and liquid
1 10½-ounce can cream of mushroom soup, undiluted
1 cup sour cream
3½ cups cooked (1 cup uncooked) long-grain rice

Sauté chopped beef in moderately hot skillet until beef loses red color. Add vegetables and water chestnuts and continue to cook until vegetables are limp. Stir in seasonings, mushrooms, and soup. Simmer until all ingredients are heated and blended. Just before serving, stir in sour cream and heat but *do not boil.* Serve over hot cooked rice. *Serves 4–6.*

BARBECUED BEEF PATTIES

2 cups oven-toasted rice cereal
¾ cup catsup
3 tablespoons vinegar
3 tablespoons honey
1 tablespoon prepared mustard
⅛ teaspoon liquid pepper sauce
1 egg, slightly beaten

  2 tablespoons finely chopped onions
  1½ teaspoons salt
  ¼ teaspoon pepper
  1½ pounds lean ground beef

Measure oven-toasted rice cereal, then crush to 1 cup. Set aside.
Mix together catsup, vinegar, honey, mustard, and pepper sauce.
Set aside. Next, combine egg, rice cereal, onions, salt, pepper, and
¼ cup catsup mixture. Add meat. Mix well. Shape into 6 patties,
¾ inch thick. Broil 3 inches from heat about 8 minutes first side
and 5 minutes second side. Baste occasionally with remaining
sauce. Serve with parsley garnish. *Makes 6.*

HOPPIN' JOHN

  1 cup dried black-eyed peas
  1 medium ham hock
  1 medium onion, chopped
  ¾ cup chopped celery
  1 small bay leaf
  2–3 cups water
  ¼ teaspoon pepper
  ½ teaspoon salt
  1 cup uncooked rice

In saucepan combine all ingredients except rice. Simmer until
peas are tender, about two hours. Meanwhile, cook rice as package
directs. Combine cooked peas, cooked rice, ham cut from the
bone, and some of the liquid from peas. Simmer several minutes
to blend flavors. *Serves 8.*

JAMBALAYA

  2 cups cooked ham, cut in bite-size pieces
  1 tablespoon margarine
  ½ cup finely chopped onion
  ½ cup finely chopped green pepper
  1 clove garlic, minced
  One 1-pound can stewed tomatoes
  ¼ teaspoon Tabasco sauce

1 cup water
1 cup uncooked rice

Brown ham lightly in margarine. Stir in onion, green pepper, garlic; cook 5 minutes, stirring occasionally. Blend in tomatoes, Tabasco sauce, water, and rice. Cover and simmer about 30 minutes or until rice is done. *Serves 6.*

GREEK BEEF AND RICE

1 tablespoon oil
1 medium onion, chopped
1 clove garlic, minced
1 pound ground beef
1 8-ounce can tomato sauce
1 teaspoon salt
¼ teaspoon black pepper
½ teaspoon dried mint
⅛ teaspoon cinnamon
2 tablespoons dried parsley
¼ cup margarine
2 tablespoons flour
2 cups milk
2 eggs, well beaten
¼ cup Parmesan cheese
3 cups cooked rice

In skillet, cook in oil the onion, garlic, and ground meat until meat loses its red color. Now add tomato sauce, salt, pepper, mint, cinnamon, and parsley. Cover and simmer 5 minutes. In a medium saucepan over low heat, melt margarine, stir in flour. Off the heat, gradually stir in milk, keeping smooth. Cook over moderately low heat until smooth and thickened. Stir a small amount hot mixture into beaten eggs, then stir eggs into sauce. Add ½ teaspoon salt, ⅛ teaspoon pepper, and the Parmesan cheese. Arrange half the rice in a greased baking dish. Sprinkle lightly with pepper. Spread meat mixture over rice, then add remaining rice. Pour sauce over entire dish. Bake at 375°F. about 30 minutes. *Serves 6.*

FIESTA GRANDE

¾ pound ground beef
½ cup chopped onion
¼ cup chopped green pepper
1 clove garlic, chopped
¾ teaspoon salt
⅔ cup grated American cheese
1 teaspoon chili powder
1 15-ounce can kidney beans, pinto beans,
    or chili beans
1½ cups cooked rice
1 8-ounce can tomato sauce
½ cup water
1 15-ounce can enchiladas, sliced crosswise

Brown the ground beef, onion, green pepper, and garlic. Spoon off excess grease. Stir in the salt, beans, rice, tomato sauce, and water. Pour the mixture into a large baking dish; bake at 350°F. for 15 minutes. Remove from oven. Garnish with enchiladas and cheese. Continue cooking for 10 minutes. *Serves 6.*

SPANISH RICE CREOLE WITH MEATBALLS

1 pound ground meat
2¼ teaspoons salt
1 cup plus 2 tablespoons uncooked rice
¼ cup butter or margarine
1 small onion, chopped
1 medium green pepper, chopped
dash of Tabasco
1 cup water
1 can (16 or 17 ounces) tomatoes
1 can (4 ounces) mushrooms and juice

Combine meat, 1 tablespoon salt, 2 tablespoons uncooked rice. Shape into small balls. In large skillet, brown meat in butter, remove. Add remaining rice, onion, and green pepper. Stir while cooking until vegetables are tender and lightly browned. Add meatballs, rest of salt, water, Tabasco, tomatoes, and mushrooms with juice. Heat to boil, cover tightly, reduce heat. Simmer without lifting lid for 30 minutes. *Serves 6–8.*

BEEFY ACAPULCO RICE

¼ cup cooking oil
1 cup uncooked rice
1 pound ground beef
1 medium onion, finely chopped
1 small garlic clove, finely minced
1 tablespoon finely minced green chili pepper
1 cup canned tomatoes
1 tablespoon chili powder
2 teaspoons salt
1½ cups water

Heat 2 tablespoons of the oil in a heavy skillet; add the rice and brown lightly. Remove rice to absorbent paper to drain. Add the remaining oil, ground beef, onion, garlic, and chili pepper and cook over heat until meat loses its red color. Drain off the excess drippings. Stir in the rice and remaining ingredients; bring to a boil. Pour into a greased 2-quart casserole, cover, and bake in a moderate oven (350°F.) for 30 minutes or until the rice is tender. *Serves 6.*

PORK CHOP PACIFICA

4 pork chops
2 cups boiling water
2 chicken bouillon cubes
1 cup uncooked rice
3 green onions, sliced
1 large tomato, peeled and chopped
½ green pepper, chopped
1 teaspoon salt
paprika

Season pork chops as desired. Brown well on both sides; put in shallow baking dish. In boiling water, dissolve bouillon cubes; pour over chops. Add rice, onion, tomato, and green pepper.

Sprinkle with salt and paprika. Cover tightly with lid (or foil, sealed well). Bake at 350°F. for one hour. *Serves 4.*

ORIENTAL CHOPS AND RICE

> 4 thick pork chops
> salt
> pepper
> ginger
> 1 tablespoon oil
> 1 cup rice
> 2 cups water
> 2 tablespoons soy sauce
> 1 teaspoon salt
> 1/4 teaspoon ginger
> 1/2 cup sliced green onion
> 1/2 cup chopped celery
> 1/2 cup slivered green pepper

Season pork chops to taste with salt, pepper, and ginger. In skillet, brown chops on both sides in oil. Stir in rice, water, soy sauce, salt, and ginger. Cover and simmer 20 minutes. Add chopped vegetables. Cover and simmer 10 more minutes. *Serves 4.*

GOLDEN RICE BEEFBURGER PIE

Beefburger Filling:
> 2 tablespoons butter or margarine
> 3/4 cup chopped celery
> 3/4 cup chopped onions
> 1/2 cup chopped green pepper
> 1 pound lean ground beef
> 2/3 cup tomato sauce
> 1 tablespoon bottled barbecue sauce
> 1 can (4 ounces) sliced mushrooms
> 1 teaspoon salt
> 1/4 teaspoon pepper
> Golden Rice

Golden Rice:
> 2 cups cooked rice (cook in beef broth or bouillon)

2 tablespoons minced parsley
2 tablespoons diced pimiento
1 tablespoon prepared mustard
2 eggs, beaten
½ teaspoon salt
dash of pepper

Melt butter in skillet. Add celery, onions, and green pepper; cook until tender but not brown. Remove from heat. Add remaining ingredients *except* rice. Mix well. Turn into a 1½-quart baking dish. Blend rice ingredients and rice, spread over meat. Cover and bake at 400°F. for 30 minutes. *Serves 6.*

MEXICAN RICE

fat for browning rice
½ cup rice, uncooked
¼ cup onion, minced
¼ cup green peppers, chopped fine
¾ cup water
3 tablespoons tomato sauce (canned)
½ teaspoon salt

Brown rice in deep fat until golden brown. Pour fat through strainer and let rice drain thoroughly in strainer. Combine onions, green pepper, water, tomato sauce, and salt in a one-quart saucepan. Bring to a boil; add browned rice. Stir once. Cover with a tight-fitting lid and simmer over low heat for 30 minutes. Remove lid and allow mixture to dry for 10 minutes. *Serves 2.*

SUGGESTION: Rice must be handled gently to prevent grains from mashing.

RICE BEEF STEW

2½ pounds beef
½ cup flour
1 teaspoon salt
½ teaspoon pepper
6 tablespoons fat

½ medium onion
2 cloves garlic, minced
4 cups boiling water
3 cups tomatoes
2 tablespoons salt
1 teaspoon Worcestershire sauce
18 small onions, peeled and quartered
7 carrots, peeled and cut into 2-inch
    strips
2 cups peas, frozen or canned
1 cup uncooked rice

Cut meat into 1½-inch cubes. Combine flour, salt, and pepper; coat meat with flour mixture. Melt fat in Dutch oven; add meat and brown. Add diced onions, garlic, boiling water, tomatoes, salt, and Worcestershire sauce. Cover and simmer meat about 2 hours or until tender. Add onions and carrots and cook 20 minutes. Add peas and uncooked rice; cook 15 minutes longer. *Serves 8.*

RICE AND CABBAGE ROLLS

1 pound ground round steak
3 tablespoons Parmesan cheese
½ teaspoon salt
¼ teaspoon pepper
1 egg
2 slices bread
½ cup uncooked rice
12 large cabbage leaves
½ teaspoon salt
½ teaspoon chili powder
1 cup tomato sauce

Place ground meat in large mixing bowl; add Parmesan cheese, salt, pepper, egg, and bread that has been placed in water, then well drained. Add uncooked rice. Mix well. Divide into 12 equal parts and shape into cones. Wilt cabbage leaves by steaming in hot water. Remove from water and drain. Place a cone-shaped meat roll into each cabbage leaf. Roll tight and place close together, open edge down, in a 2-quart casserole, so as not to come apart. Sprinkle ½ teaspoon salt and ½ teaspoon chili powder over rolls. Mix tomato sauce and 1 cup water together and pour over cabbage rolls. Cover and bake in 375°F. oven for 75 minutes. *Serves 6.*

SPANISH RICE AU GRATIN

½ cup uncooked rice
1 cup water
½ cup chopped onions
⅓ cup chopped green peppers
½ cup chopped celery
1½ tablespoons butter or margarine
1 cup tomatoes (stewed or canned)
½ teaspoon salt
1 teaspoon sugar
1 teaspoon chili powder
½ teaspoon Worcestershire sauce
1 cup grated Cheddar cheese

Combine rice, water, and salt. Bring to a boil. Stir; cover and reduce heat. Simmer for 14 minutes. Meanwhile, cook onions, green pepper, and celery in butter. Add tomatoes, salt, sugar, chili powder, and Worcestershire sauce. Add cooked rice and simmer until thick. Pour into a buttered casserole and top with cheese. Place under broiler and melt. *Serves 6.*

RICE AU GRATIN

3 cups hot cooked rice
¾ cup grated Cheddar cheese
3 tablespoons butter or margarine
½ teaspoon curry powder
1 slice bread, cut in small cubes

Spoon half the rice into a greased baking dish. Sprinkle with part of the cheese. Add remaining rice and cheese. Bake at 350°F. until the cheese melts. *Meanwhile:* melt butter in a small skillet;

stir in curry. Add bread cubes and brown lightly. Sprinkle over the baked rice. *Serves 5.*

HASHED BROWN RICE

3 cups cooked rice
3 tablespoons flour
1/4 cup milk
2 tablespoons butter or margarine
1/2 cup chopped onion

Combine the rice, flour, and milk. Heat butter in a 10-inch skillet. Add onions and cook until tender. Spread the rice mixture evenly in the skillet; press it down firmly with a spatula. Cook over medium heat until bottom is golden brown. Turn out onto serving dish, brown side up. *Serves 4.*

PAELLA

3 tablespoons vegetable oil
1 2-pound chicken, unjointed
1 pound pork, cut in half-inch cubes
1 onion, chopped
1 clove garlic, minced
3 ripe tomatoes, peeled and diced
2 cups rice, uncooked
4 cups chicken stock, hot
1/4 teaspoon pepper
1 pound raw, shelled, deveined shrimp

Heat oil in frying pan. Brown chicken parts. Drain and set aside. While oil is still hot, add pork and cook until well-seared. Add onion and garlic. Cook until tender but not brown. Add tomatoes and cook for 5 minutes, stirring constantly. Pour in rice and cook 5 minutes more. Add broth and seasonings. Pour into baking pans. Place chicken parts on top. Cover with a tight lid or foil. Place in a 350°F. oven and bake for 15 minutes. Remove from oven and add shrimp. Recover and return to the oven for another 15 minutes. *Serves 8.*

SUGGESTION: If parboiled rice is used, bake 35 minutes before adding the shrimp.

GREEN RICE

¾ cup green onions, thinly sliced
3 tablespoons salad oil
1 cup rice, uncooked
½ cup green peppers, minced
¼ cup parsley, minced
2 cups stock, chicken
1 teaspoon salt
¼ teaspoon pepper

Cook onions (use tops as well as white part) in salad oil until soft but not browned. Add remaining ingredients. Pour into a 2-quart baking pan with cover. If no cover is available, use foil. Bake in 350°F. oven about 30 minutes, or until rice is tender. Toss lightly with a fork before serving. *Serves 6.*

CHINESE FRIED RICE

3 tablespoons butter
½ cup green onions and tops
1 cup celery, diced
1 cup mushrooms, sliced
2½ cups cooked rice
2 tablespoons soy sauce
1 egg, slightly beaten
10 slices crisp bacon

Heat butter in skillet. Add onions and celery. Cook until almost tender. Add mushrooms, rice, and soy sauce. Cook 10 minutes on low heat, stirring occasionally. Stir in beaten egg and cook only until egg is done. Sprinkle with crumbled bacon and serve. *Serves 8.*

SUGGESTION: Extra soy sauce may be served with rice.

QUICK SKILLET BARBECUE

2 cups onion soup
½ cup all-purpose barbecue sauce
2 tablespoons butter
¼ teaspoon salt
1⅓ cups packaged enriched pre-cooked rice
1 cup cooked peas
8 frankfurters, sliced

In large skillet, heat soup, ¼ cup of the barbecue sauce, butter, and salt. Stir in rice. Bring quickly to a boil. Reduce heat. Cover; simmer 5 minutes. Stir in peas. Push rice mixture to sides of skillet. Place sliced frankfurters in center of skillet; add remaining barbecue sauce. Cook until heated—about 5 minutes. *Serves 4.*

STUFFED PEPPERS ESPAÑOL

1 package (6 ounces) Spanish rice mix
6 medium green peppers
1½ cups cold cooked veal, pieces or cubes
⅓ cup chopped onion
2 tablespoons Worcestershire sauce
½ cup grated Parmesan cheese

Cook rice according to package directions. Meanwhile, cut tops off green peppers, remove seeds and membranes. Cook in boiling salted water for 5 minutes; drain. Sprinkle inside of peppers with desired seasonings. Combine all remaining ingredients with cooked. rice. Stuff peppers; stand upright in foil-lined 9x9x2-inch baking pan. Bake uncovered in 350°F. oven 25 minutes or until hot. Sprinkle with more cheese, if desired. *Serves 6.*

CURRY RICE

1 package curry-flavored rice mix
5-pound crown roast of lamb, about 14 ribs
seasoned salt and pepper
1 pound ground lamb

   ½ teaspoon seasoned salt
   ⅛ teaspoon ground black pepper
   ½ cup diced green pepper
   ⅓ cup seedless raisins
   ½ cup chicken broth or bouillon
   2 tablespoons lemon juice

Sprinkle roast with seasoned salt and pepper. Place on rack in shallow roasting pan and roast at 325°F. slow oven, for 2½ hours. *Meanwhile,* prepare rice as directed on package, using only 2¼ cups water. Brown around lamb in skillet and drain off fat. Add cooked rice, ½ teaspoon seasoned salt, ⅛ teaspoon pepper, green pepper, raisins, broth, and lemon juice. Fill center of roast with rice mixture after lamb has cooked for 1½ hours. Cover with foil. Any leftover stuffing may be cooked in a separate uncovered casserole along with the roast. *Serves 6–8.*

RED BEANS AND RICE

   1 pound red beans (kidney or others)
   ½ pound salt pork, sliced
   1 small onion, sliced
   salt and pepper to taste
   garlic and Tabasco or chili powder (if desired)
   1 tablespoon minced parsley (if desired)
   1 cup uncooked parboiled rice

Pick through and wash beans. Cover with water, add pork, and simmer. After 1 hour of cooking, add onion and seasonings to taste. Continue cooking until beans are tender, adding water as necessary. Meanwhile, cook rice according to package directions. Serve beans over cooked rice. *Serves 6.*

BUSY-DAY DINNER

   2 tablespoons minced onion
   1 tablespoon butter or margarine
   1½ cups chopped leftover (or canned) meat—ham, chicken,
                                 sausage, beef
   3 cups cooked parboiled rice

1 can (10½ ounces) cream of mushroom soup
salt, if needed
grated cheese, optional

Sauté onion in butter or margarine in skillet until tender. Add
meat, cooked rice, cream of mushroom soup, and salt, if needed.
If extra moistness is desired, add small amount of water or milk.
Cover and simmer over very low heat about 20 minutes. Serve
from a skillet—or turn onto a warm platter—and sprinkle with
grated cheese if desired. *Serves 4.*

SUGGESTION: To make a meal, serve with a tossed green salad; add
any leftover cooked vegetables the refrigerator may harbor; add
garlic bread, apples or other fruit with cheese wedges for dessert.

SKILLET STROGANOFF
(One-Pan Recipe)

1½ pounds sirloin steak, cut in thin strips
2 tablespoons all-purpose flour
¾ teaspoon salt
⅛ teaspoon pepper
2 tablespoons salad oil
¾ cup finely chopped onions
½ pound fresh mushrooms, sliced (about 3 cups), *or* 1 can
　　　　　　　(6 ounces) sliced mushrooms, drained
2 teaspoons Worcestershire sauce
1 can (10½ ounces) condensed cream of celery soup
1 cup sour cream
1 bouillon cube
1⅓ cups boiling water
½ teaspoon salt
2 tablespoons chopped parsley (optional)
1⅓ cups enriched pre-cooked rice

Dust meat with mixture of flour, ¾ teaspoon salt, and pepper.
Brown quickly in oil in a skillet over high heat. Add onions and
mushrooms. Sauté over low heat until lightly browned and tender.
Blend in Worcestershire sauce, soup, and sour cream. Then bring
just to a boil. *Meanwhile,* dissolve bouillon cube in boiling water.
Add ½ teaspoon salt, parsley, and rice. Make a well in the center

of meat mixture and pour in rice mixture. Bring to a boil, cover tightly, and simmer about 5 minutes, or until rice is tender. Makes 4 cups. *Serves 4.*

PEPPER STEAK AND RICE

2 tablespoons cornstarch
dash of pepper
2 tablespoons water
1 tablespoon soy sauce
3 tablespoons salad oil
1 pound flank steak, sliced diagonally into thin strips
2 medium green peppers, cut in 1-inch squares
1 small clove garlic, crushed
¼ teaspoon salt
1½ cups boiling water
1⅓ cups enriched pre-cooked rice

Combine cornstarch, pepper, 2 tablespoons water, soy sauce, and 1 tablespoon of the oil in bowl. Stir in steak strips and let stand to marinate for 2 or 3 hours. *Next:* heat 1 tablespoon oil in a skillet. Sauté green peppers in oil until just tender, but still slightly crisp. Remove from skillet. Add remaining 1 tablespoon oil to skillet. Sauté garlic in oil until golden brown. Add meat mixture. Cook 1 minute without stirring. Then cook and stir the mixture just until the meat is medium rare. *Meanwhile:* warm a shallow 1½-quart serving dish or casserole. Stir salt, boiling water, and peppers into meat mixture. Pour over rice in warmed dish. Mix just to moisten all rice. Cover and let stand 5 minutes. *Serves 4.*

NO-BAKE STUFFED PEPPERS

6 medium green peppers
boiling salted water
1 pound ground beef
¼ cup chopped onion
2 tablespoons butter
2¼ cups water
½ cup barbecue sauce, any flavor
1½ teaspoon salt

1⅓ cups enriched pre-cooked rice
1 cup cubed process American cheese

Remove stem ends and seeds from peppers; cook in boiling salted water 10 minutes or just until almost tender. Meanwhile, brown beef and onion in butter in deep skillet. Add 1½ cups of the water, ¼ cup barbecue sauce, salt, and rice. Bring to a boil. Then cover and simmer 5 minutes. Add cheese. *Next:* drain cooked peppers. Fill with rice mixture. Place upright in skillet. Pour remaining water and barbecue sauce around peppers. Cover and simmer 5 minutes. To serve, spoon sauce in skillet over peppers. *Serves 6.*

HAM AND RICE TIMBALES

¼ cup chopped onion
1 can (4 ounces) mushroom pieces, drained
1 cup diced cooked ham
2 tablespoons butter
1⅓ cups enriched pre-cooked rice
1⅓ cups water
½ teaspoon salt
dash of pepper
½ cup sliced Brazil nuts *or* chopped pecans
3 eggs, slightly beaten
Mustard Sauce

Sauté onion, mushrooms, and ham in butter until onion is transparent. Stir in remaining ingredients except eggs and sauce. Bring quickly to a boil. Remove from heat, cover and let stand 5 minutes. Stir in eggs. Pack into 6 well-greased custard cups. Place in a large shallow skillet or pan. Pour ½ inch hot water around cups. Cover and simmer for 15 to 20 minutes, or until firm. To unmold, loosen around edges, invert, and let stand 1 minute before removing cups. Serve with Mustard Sauce. Makes 3 cups. *Serves 6.*

MUSTARD SAUCE

Melt 2 tablespoons butter; mix in 3 tablespoons all-purpose flour. Gradually stir in 2 cups milk. Add 1 teaspoon salt and a dash of pepper. Cook and stir until thickened. Remove from heat; stir in 2 tablespoons prepared mustard. *Makes 2 cups.*

HAWAIIAN SUPPER

2½ cups slivered cooked ham or pork
2 tablespoons butter
1 medium green pepper, cut in strips
1 can (13½ ounces) pineapple chunks
4 teaspoons vinegar
2 tablespoons cornstarch
2 tablespoons brown sugar
1 teaspoon salt
pepper
2 teaspoons prepared mustard
1⅓ cups hot water
2 tablespoons chopped scallions or chives
1⅓ cups enriched pre-cooked rice

Sauté ham in butter until brown; then stir in green pepper. Meanwhile, drain pineapple, measuring syrup and adding water to make 1⅓ cups. Blend syrup mixture, vinegar, cornstarch, brown sugar, ½ teaspoon salt, dash of pepper, and mustard. Add to ham; cook and stir until sauce is thickened and transparent. Cover and simmer 10 minutes; then add pineapple. *Next:* combine hot water, ½ teaspoon salt, dash of pepper, scallions, and rice. Make a well in center of ham mixture; pour in rice mixture. Bring to a boil, cover, and simmer for 5 minutes or until rice is tender. Makes 3⅔ cups ham mixture plus rice. *Serves 4.*

LOUISIANA RICE BAKE

½ pound bulk pork sausage
¾ cup chopped onion
¼ cup chopped green pepper
¾ cup chopped celery
¼ cup chopped parsley
1 cup cornbread crumbs
2 eggs, lightly beaten
1¼ cups chicken broth

½ teaspoon dried sage
½ teaspoon dried thyme
½ teaspoon salt
¼ teaspoon pepper
3 cups cooked parboiled rice

Brown sausage lightly in skillet. Pour off most of the accumulated fat. Add onion, green pepper, and celery; sauté lightly. Combine with remaining ingredients; mix well. Turn into a lightly greased casserole. Cover and bake in 350°F. oven 20 minutes. Remove cover; continue baking 15 minutes. *Serves 6.*

DUTCH CABBAGE ROLLS

1 small head green cabbage
2½ cups cooked parboiled rice
1 pound ground beef
2 tablespoons finely diced onion
1 teaspoon salt
⅛ teaspoon pepper
1 egg, beaten
1½ cups tomato juice

Wash and drain cabbage. Cook in boiling salted water until leaves are tender and pliable. Drain and remove outer leaves, reserving 6 large ones. Combine rice, beef, onion, seasonings, and egg, stirring to blend. Shape into 6 rolls and place each in center of cabbage leaf; fold or roll and fasten with toothpicks. Place seam side down in casserole. Add tomato juice. Cover and bake in a moderate 350°F. oven for 1 hour. Serve hot with tomato sauce. *Serves 6.*

RICE CALIFORNIAN

5 slices bacon, diced
½ cup diced celery (optional)
¼ pound mushrooms, sliced (about 1½ cups)
1½ cups water
1 cup canned tomatoes (or 1 can, 8 ounces stewed tomatoes)
1 package dehydrated onion soup mix

1⅓ cups enriched pre-cooked rice
¾ cup grated Cheddar cheese

Fry bacon in a skillet over low heat until crisp. Pour off all except 2 tablespoons drippings. Then add celery and mushrooms and sauté just until tender. Pour into a 1½-quart baking dish. Stir in water, tomatoes, soup mix, rice, and ½ cup of the cheese. Sprinkle with remaining cheese. Cover and bake at 375°F. for 20 minutes, or until rice is tender. Makes about 4½ cups. *Serves 4.*

PEPPY FRANKS WITH RICE

4 cups cooked rice
2½ cups prepared barbecue sauce
2 pounds frankfurters, sliced diagonally in 1-inch pieces

Prepare rice according to package directions. Combine barbecue sauce and franks. Cover and simmer 15 to 20 minutes. Serve over beds of hot fluffy rice. *Serves 8.*

QUICK SUPPER SKILLET

1 large green pepper, cut in strips
2 medium onions, sliced
1 can (4 ounces) mushrooms, drained (optional)
2 tablespoons butter
1 can (7 ounces) shrimp, drained
2 cans (4½ ounces each) deviled ham
1 can (10½ ounces) condensed cream of celery soup
½ cup water
1⅓ cups enriched pre-cooked rice
¼ cup pimiento strips

Sauté green pepper, onions, and mushrooms in butter until lightly browned. Add shrimp and ham; cook until ham is lightly browned. Stir in remaining ingredients. Bring to a boil. Then cover and simmer 5 minutes. Garnish with additional pimiento or green pepper, if desired. *Serves 4–5.*

CAMPFIRE STEW

⅔ cup enriched pre-cooked rice
1½ cups canned tomatoes
1 can (1 pint, 2 ounces) tomato juice
4 teaspoons instant minced onion *or* onion flakes
1½ teaspoons sugar
1 teaspoon salt
pinch of basil
3 frankfurters, sliced
1 tablespoon butter
parmesan cheese

Combine rice, tomatoes, tomato juice, onion, sugar, salt, and basil in a saucepan. Bring quickly to a boil over high heat. Cover and cook gently 5 minutes. Meanwhile, sauté frankfurters in butter until browned. Add to rice mixture. Remove from heat; stir. Sprinkle with cheese before serving. *Serves 4.*

SKILLET GUMBO

1 cup diced cooked ham (canned luncheon meat may be
substituted)
½ cup chopped green pepper
½ cup chopped onion
¼ pound okra, cut in one-inch pieces
1 cup canned tomatoes
½ cup water
¾ teaspoon salt
dash of pepper
½ cup uncooked rice

Combine all ingredients *except* the rice in a heavy skillet. Bring to a boil. Cover and simmer for 10 minutes. Stir in rice. Replace lid and simmer 20 minutes or until rice is tender. *Serves 2.*

PONCHO RICE

1 cup uncooked rice
3 tablespoons cooking oil

1¾ cups water
½ cup minced onion
½ cup chopped green pepper
¼ cup tomato sauce
1 teaspoon salt
1 teaspoon chili powder
green pepper ring, onion rings, or
    pimiento strips for garnish

In a heavy 2-quart saucepan, brown rice in oil until golden. Add water, onion, green pepper, tomato sauce, salt, and chili powder. Heat to boiling; stir. Cover and simmer over low heat for 30 minutes. Remove cover and allow mixture to dry over low heat for 10 minutes. Fluff rice with a fork before serving. *Serves 4–6.*

9.
Seafood

SHRIMP AND RICE GLORIOSA

¼ pound butter or margarine
2 pounds shrimp, shelled and deveined
2 medium onions, chopped
1 green pepper, cut in 1" squares
½ pound fresh mushroom caps, sliced
2 medium tomatoes cut in wedges
salt and ground white pepper to taste
6 cups cooked (2 cups uncooked) long-grain rice

Heat margarine or butter in skillet. Sauté onions and green peppers until just tender. Add mushrooms and shrimp; sauté 2–3 minutes until shrimp are opaque. Stir in tomatoes and heat slightly. Season with salt and pepper. Serve on cooked rice. *Do not overcook. Serves 4–6.*

RICE AND OYSTERS ORIENT EXPRESS

¼ pound butter or margarine
1 12-ounce jar oysters, drained
½ cup celery, sliced
½ cup green onions, chopped
1½ cups uncooked long-grain rice
3¾ cups boiling water
2 chicken bouillon cubes

1½ teaspoons salt
¼ teaspoon ground white pepper
⅛ teaspoon thyme
½ cup water chestnuts, sliced and drained
1 tablespoon lemon juice
½ cup slivered almonds

Sauté oysters in butter about 5 minutes. Remove. Sauté vegetables 2–3 minutes until limp. Remove. Add rice, water, seasonings, and bouillon cubes. Cover and cook about 20 minutes. Add sautéed oysters and vegetables and water chestnuts to rice and reheat. Mix in lemon juice. Garnish with toasted almonds. Serve with soy sauce. *Serves 4–6.*

CRAB À LA SWISS

⅓ cup regular margarine or butter
1 cup oven-toasted rice cereal
¼ cup chopped onions
¼ cup chopped green pepper
¼ cup regular all-purpose flour
1 teaspoon salt
2 cups cooked rice
2 packages (12 ounces) frozen crabmeat,
    thawed and drained
2 cups (8 ounces) grated process Swiss cheese
1 can (4 ounces) sliced mushrooms, drained
⅓ cup pitted, sliced ripe olives
¼ cup slivered almonds, toasted

Melt margarine in medium-size saucepan; remove 1 tablespoon and toss with rice cereal. Set aside. Cook onions and green pepper in remaining margarine over low heat until tender, stirring occasionally. Mix in flour and salt. Add milk, stirring until smooth. Increase heat to medium and cook until bubbly and thickened, stirring constantly. Stir remaining ingredients into sauce and spread in 2-quart baking dish. Sprinkle with rice cereal. Garnish with paprika and green pepper strips. Bake in moderate oven (325°F.) about 30 minutes or until thoroughly heated. *Serves 8.*

TUNA RICE LOUISIANA

3 cups cooked rice
1 6½-ounce can tuna fish, drained
   and flaked
1 cup grated cheese
2 tablespoons diced pimiento
1 teaspoon prepared mustard
½ teaspoon salt
1 8-ounce can English peas,
   including liquid
½ cup evaporated milk
½ cup water
1 tablespoon butter or margarine

Mix all ingredients and pour into a greased 1½-quart baking dish. Bake for 20 minutes at 400°F. *Serves 6.*

TUNA-RICE PEPPERS

1 cup boiling water
6 medium green bell peppers
1 6½-ounce can chunk-style tuna
3 cups cooked rice
2 tablespoons grated onion
¾ cup grated American cheese
¾ cup milk
½ teaspoon salt
¼ teaspoon Tabasco sauce
⅓ cup water

Preheat oven to 350°F. Remove stems from green peppers, making large hole in top. Scoop out seeds and membranes. Cook peppers in boiling water about 10 minutes; drain well. Break tuna up. Stir in rest of ingredients *except* water. Mix well and pack into peppers. Place stuffed peppers in shallow baking dish. Pour water around peppers. Bake in a moderate oven for 30 minutes. If desired, serve with tomato sauce. *Serves 6.*

PILAF OF SEAFOOD

2 tablespoons vegetable oil
½ cup finely diced onion
½ cup finely chopped celery
3 cups cooked rice
One 1-pound can stewed tomatoes
1 bay leaf
½ teaspoon salt
¼ teaspoon paprika
1 cup grated American Cheese
1 7-ounce can crabmeat, drained
    and flaked

In medium-sized skillet, sauté onion and celery in oil until limp. Stir in remaining ingredients and heat until cheese is melted. Pour into a greased 2-quart casserole and bake, covered, in a 350°F. oven about 25 minutes. *Serves 6.*

SUGGESTION: This may also be made with chicken livers rolled in seasoned flour and browned in bacon fat until done.

TUNA HI-RICE

1 can (10½ ounces) cream of mushroom soup
1 can (7 ounces) tuna, drained and flaked
2 cups cooked rice
2 tablespoons grated onion
2 tablespoons diced pimiento
2 tablespoons chopped parsley
½ cup grated cheese
4 egg yolks, slightly beaten
4 egg whites, stiffly beaten

In a saucepan, combine soup, tuna, rice, onion, pimiento, and parsley. Heat thoroughly. Remove from heat and stir in cheese. Gradually stir beaten egg yolks into soup mixture. Gently fold in beaten egg whites. Pour into an ungreased 2-quart casserole; set in pan of water. Bake at 350°F. for 30–35 minutes or until firm. *Serves 6.*

SHRIMP CURRY IN A HURRY

½ cup chopped onion
1 tablespoon butter
1 can frozen condensed cream of
   shrimp soup, undiluted
1 cup dairy sour cream, at room
   temperature
½ teaspoon curry powder
1 cup cleaned and cooked shrimp
3 cups hot, cooked rice
paprika

In a heavy saucepan, sauté onion in butter until tender. Add soup, stirring until smooth. Blend in sour cream, curry powder, and shrimp; heat slowly to serving temperature, keeping heat low and being careful *not* to boil. Serve over hot, cooked rice. Sprinkle with paprika and serve with condiments such as chutney, salted nuts, chopped onions, crumbled crisp bacon, or toasted coconut. *Serves 4.*

CRAB-STUFFED MUSHROOMS WITH GOLDEN RICE

Crab and Mushroom Mixture:
6–8 large mushrooms
2 tablespoons finely chopped green onion
2 tablespoons finely chopped green pepper
1 medium garlic clove, finely minced
2 tablespoons butter
1 can (6½ ounces) white crabmeat,
   drained and removed of shell
1 egg, well beaten
½ cup soft bread crumbs
1 teaspoon dehydrated parsley
1 envelope instant chicken broth
2 teaspoons lemon juice
¼ teaspoon Tabasco sauce

Rice:
2 cups water

2 envelopes instant chicken broth
1 tablespoon chopped mushroom stems
1 tablespoon finely chopped green onion
1 tablespoon butter
1 teaspoon dehydrated parsley
½ teaspoon salt
¼ teaspoon Tabasco sauce
1 cup rice

Sauce:

1 can (10½ ounces) cream of mushroom
    soup
½ cup sour cream
1 cup grated cheddar cheese

Wash mushrooms and remove stems. Chop stems finely and reserve one tablespoon for use in rice. Sauté remaining stems with
green onion, green pepper, and garlic in butter about 5 minutes;
combine with remaining ingredients of "crab and mushroom
mixture." Mold about 2 tablespoons of this onto each mushroom
cap. Place mushrooms upright in well-buttered 2-quart casserole.
Add ½ cup water or broth to cover bottom of casserole. Bake at
425°F. for 20–25 minutes. SUGGESTION: To be sure that everything
will be ready at the same time, place casserole in oven after the
rice has begun to cook. In a 3-quart saucepan, bring to boil the
water, broth, mushrooms stems, onion, butter, parsley, salt, and
Tabasco. Stir in the rice. Cover the saucepan, lower the heat, and
simmer 20 minutes or until the rice is tender and all the water
is absorbed. MEANWHILE: Prepare the sauce by blending the soup,
sour cream, and cheese. Heat gently. To serve, arrange the stuffed
mushrooms on a bed of rice and spoon the sauce over all.
Serves 3–4.

SWISS TUNA RICE PIE

2 cups hot cooked rice
1½ tablespoons butter or margarine
1 egg, slightly beaten
3 tablespoons stuffed olives, chopped fine
¾ cup scalded milk
2 eggs, slightly beaten

1 7-ounce can tuna fish
3 tablespoons chopped green onions with tops
¼ teaspoon salt
dash of pepper
dash of nutmeg
1 cup grated Swiss cheese

Combine rice and butter. Stir in one slightly beaten egg and olives. Spread evenly over bottom and sides of a greased 9-inch pie pan to make a shell. Gradually stir milk into two slightly beaten eggs. Add tuna fish, green onions and seasonings. Pour into rice-lined pan. Sprinkle cheese over the top. Bake at 400°F. for 15 minutes. Reduce heat to 350°F. and bake 15 minutes longer. *Serves 6.*

SHRIMP à la NEWBURG

2 cups shelled cooked shrimp
½ cup sherry
3 tablespoons butter or margarine
2 tablespoons flour
1 cup cream
4 hard-cooked egg yolks
1 teaspoon salt
¼ teaspoon nutmeg
dash of pepper
4 cups hot cooked rice

Marinate shrimp in sherry in a shallow dish for one hour. Melt butter in saucepan. Stir in flour, then cook and stir over low heat until thickened. Press egg yolks through a sieve; mash to a paste. Stir into hot sauce. Add seasonings, shrimp, and sherry. Heat through. Serve over hot cooked rice. *Serves 4.*

SHRIMP AND RICE MOUSSE

1 pound shrimp
3 cups water
2 teaspoons salt
¼ teaspoon peppercorns

1 small bay leaf
2 tablespoons unflavored gelatin
½ cup water, cold
¾ cup mayonnaise
2 tablespoons lemon juice
1 cup whipping cream
3 cups cold cooked rice
½ cup thinly sliced cucumbers, quartered
½ cup thinly sliced green onions

Clean and devein raw shrimp. Bring shrimp, water, salt, pepper-corns, and bay leaf to boil; simmer 10 minutes, or until shrimp are tender. Drain, reserving 2 cups of the shrimp broth. Slice shrimp and chill thoroughly. Soften gelatin in cold water. Dissolve over boiling water. Combine dissolved gelatin, mayonnaise, shrimp broth, and lemon juice. Stir until smooth. Chill until almost set. Set in bowl of ice water. Whip until light and fluffy. Beat cream until stiff. Fold in gelatin mixture together with rice, cucumbers, onions, and shrimp. Pour into a 2-quart mold. Chill until firm. Unmold onto a bed of endive. Garnish with additional shrimp and cucumbers. *Makes 8 one-cup servings.*

CATALINA SHRIMP AND RICE

1 cup pancake mix
1 cup milk
1 jar (1½ ounces) sesame seeds
1 pound cleaned shrimp
fat for frying
1 cup rice, uncooked
2 cups water
⅓ cup soy sauce
¼ teaspoon salt

Make a batter of pancake mix, milk, and sesame seed. Dip shrimp into batter and deep fry at 375°F. for about 5 minutes. Cook rice, water, soy sauce, and salt according to package directions. Serve with Golden Fruit Sauce. *Serves 4–6.*

GOLDEN FRUIT SAUCE

Combine a 12-ounce can of apricot nectar, $\frac{1}{16}$ teaspoon salt, and 2 tablespoons prepared mustard. Thicken mixture with 1 tablespoon cornstarch. Add 1 tablespoon lemon juice to the hot sauce. Serve with Catalina Shrimp and Rice.

PILAF OF SEAFOOD

1 medium-sized onion, chopped
2 tablespoons shortening
2 cups cooked rice
2 cups (1-pound can) tomatoes
3 stalks celery, diced
$\frac{1}{2}$ teaspoon salt
$\frac{1}{4}$ teaspoon paprika
$\frac{1}{2}$ bay leaf, crumbled
$\frac{1}{4}$ cup grated cheese
1 cup cooked shrimp or crabmeat

Cook onion in shortening until browned. Stir in rice. Combine tomatoes, celery, salt, paprika, bay leaf, and cheese in saucepan. Heat until cheese is melted. Fold in rice and seafood. Pour into a greased casserole. Cover. Bake in moderately slow oven (325°F.) about 25 minutes. *Serves 6.*

SHRIMP AND RICE ROLLS

$\frac{1}{2}$ cup tomato juice
1 egg, well beaten
$\frac{1}{2}$ cup dry bread crumbs
1 cup cooked rice
dash of pepper
1 teaspoon chopped parsley
$\frac{1}{2}$ teaspoon celery salt
1 5-ounce can shrimp, mashed
12 slices bacon, cut in half

Mix tomato juice and egg. Add crumbs, rice, seasoning, parsley, celery salt, and shrimp. Mix thoroughly. Roll into finger lengths;

wrap each roll with ½ slice bacon and fasten with toothpicks. Broil, turning frequently, to brown evenly. Makes about 30 rolls.

SUGGESTION: These may be prepared the day before and chilled. They seem to hold together better. These were made to be served as hors d'oeuvres.

SHRIMP CREOLE

2 tablespoons butter or margarine
1 tablespoon flour
1 bay leaf
2 onions
2 green sweet peppers
1 clove garlic
1 tablespoon parsley and thyme, minced
3 shallots, minced
salt and pepper to taste
2 pounds peeled, deveined, raw shrimp
7 tomatoes, quartered
1 cup water
2 drops Tabasco sauce
6 cups cooked rice

Melt butter and cook with flour to make a dark syrup. Add bay leaf, onions, peppers, garlic, minced parsley, thyme, shallots, salt, and pepper. Then add the raw shrimp and mix well. Let color nicely and then add the tomatoes and one cup water. Cook about 30 minutes, stirring often, until sauce is thickness of light cream. Add the Tabasco sauce. Serve the shrimp and the sauce over 1 cup of boiled rice. *Serves 6.*

SPEEDY JAMBALAYA

1 package (6 ounces) saffron-flavored rice mix
¼ cup butter or margarine
½ cup diced onion
½ cup diced green pepper
2 cups diced cooked ham (½-inch cubes)

1 can (4½ ounces) medium-size shrimp,
drained
1 can (16 ounces) whole tomatoes, well-
drained and cut up

Cook rice according to package directions; cook 20 minutes.
Meanwhile, melt butter in skillet. Add onion and green pepper;
sauté until golden but not browned. Add ham and shrimp; cook
over low heat until ham is lightly browned and shrimp are pink.
Add tomatoes and hot cooked rice. Mix well. Cover and simmer
about 5 minutes or until mixture is heated through thoroughly.
Serves 4–6.

FISH FOR A KING

1 package chicken-flavored rice mix
2 1½-pounds boned fish *or* 2 packages
frozen fish fillets
1 cup chopped celery
1 cup chopped onion
¼ cup butter or margarine
4 hard-boiled eggs, chopped
1 teaspoon green hot sauce
¼ teaspoon pepper
2 tablespoons butter

Cook chicken-flavored rice mix according to package directions.
Sauté celery and onions in butter until tender. Combine celery
mixture with rice, eggs, green hot sauce, and pepper. Season fish
with salt and pepper. Melt butter in saucepan. Stuff fish and
brush with butter. Bake on a rack in a pre-heated 425°F. oven for
20 minutes. *Serves 4.*

SUGGESTION: Stuffing is also delicious as side dish with barbecued
hot dogs.

LOUISIANA GUMBO

½ cup chopped onion

½ cup chopped green pepper
½ cup chopped celery
1 clove garlic, minced
1 package (10 ounces) cut okra, frozen
1 can (1 pound) tomatoes
1 can (12½ ounces) chicken broth
1 teaspoon salt
½ teaspoon sugar
dash of pepper
pinch of thyme
1 small bay leaf
½ pint shucked oysters
½ pound (about 1 cup) halved cleaned
    shrimp
1⅓ cups enriched pre-cooked rice

Sauté onion, green pepper, celery, and garlic in butter in a large skillet until lightly browned. Add okra, tomatoes, broth, and seasonings. Drain oysters, adding the liquid to mixture in skillet. Cover and simmer 30 minutes, stirring occasionally. Add shrimp and cook 5 minutes. Then add oysters and cook 1 minute, or just until edges of oysters curl. Before serving, discard bay leaf. *Meanwhile,* prepare pre-cooked rice according to package directions. *To serve:* spoon rice into soup bowls and ladle gumbo over rice. *Or,* if desired, combine rice and gumbo in a tureen or large bowl before serving. *Serves 6.*

CURRIED SHRIMP-RICE SUPPER

1 can (10½ ounces) condensed cream of
    mushroom soup
2 cups water
1½ teaspoons curry powder
1 teaspoon salt
1⅓ cups (about) coconut flakes, shredded
1⅓ cups enriched pre-cooked rice
1 pound cleaned shrimp

Bring soup, water, curry powder, salt, and 1 cup of coconut to a boil. Stir in rice and shrimp. Simmer over low heat, stirring occasionally, until rice is tender—5 to 8 minutes. Garnish with remaining coconut. *Serves 6.*

TUNA-RICE DELIGHT

2 tablespoons butter
1 can (7 ounces) tuna,* drained
1 tablespoon chopped chives or scallions
1⅓ cups enriched pre-cooked rice
1½ cups hot water
1 cup cooked sliced carrots
1 can (10½ ounces) condensed cream of
    mushroom soup
½ teaspoon salt
dash of pepper
2 teaspoons lemon juice
¼ teaspoon Worcestershire sauce
2 drops Tabasco sauce

Melt butter in skillet. Add tuna and chives. Heat and stir about 3 minutes. Remove from heat. Stir in remaining ingredients. Cover and cook over low heat until liquid is absorbed, stirring occasionally—about 10 minutes. Garnish with additional chives, if desired. *Serves 3–4.*

---

* Or use 1 can (5 or 7½ ounces) lobster or crab meat, drained.

TUNA-RICE PIE

1⅓ cups enriched pre-cooked rice
1⅓ cups water
½ teaspoon salt
1½ teaspoons butter
1 egg, slightly beaten
1 cup grated process American *or*
    Swiss cheese
1 can (7 ounces) tuna, drained
¾ cup milk, scalded
2 eggs
½ teaspoon salt
⅛ teaspoon nutmeg

⅛ teaspoon pepper

Measure rice into a 9-inch pie pan. Bring water, ½ teaspoon salt, and butter to a boil. Stir into rice, cover and let stand 5 minutes. Then blend in beaten egg. Press against bottom and sides—not above rim—of pan. Sprinkle ½ cup cheese into rice crust; top with half of the tuna. Repeat layers. Blend remaining ingredients; pour over tuna. Bake at 400°F. for 25 minutes. If desired, top pie with seasoned tomato wedges or cooked asparagus 5 minutes before it has finished baking. *Serves 6.*

TUNA-RICE LOAF

1⅔ cups (14½-ounce can) evaporated milk
⅓ cup water
2 cans (7 ounces each) tuna, drained and
   flaked
2 cups enriched pre-cooked rice
¼ cup butter, melted
1 tablespoon minced parsley
¾ teaspoon salt
dash of pepper
2 eggs, slightly beaten
Souper Cheese Sauce

Combine milk and water; bring just to boiling point. Meanwhile, combine remaining ingredients except sauce in a bowl. Add milk mixture and blend well. Grease bottom and sides of a 9-x-5 inch loaf pan, line bottom with wax paper, and grease paper. Pour rice mixture into pan. Bake at 350°F. for 10 minutes; then pour ½ cup cheese sauce over loaf and bake another 10 to 15 minutes, or until firm. Unmold on platter and remove paper. Serve with remaining cheese sauce that has been reheated. Garnish loaf and sauce with additional parsley, if desired. *Serves 5–6.*

SOUPER CHEESE SAUCE

Combine 1 can (11 ounces) condensed Cheddar cheese soup and ¼ cup milk in saucepan; bring just to a boil. Add ½ cup grated Cheddar cheese and stir over medium heat until cheese melts—about 1 minute. *Makes about 2 cups of sauce.* SUGGESTION: For 3 cups sauce, omit grated cheese and use 2 cans of soup and ½ cup milk.

FIVE-MINUTE PAELLA

1⅓ cups enriched pre-cooked rice
2 tablespoons minced onion
1 cup bouillon
⅛ teaspoon saffron
1 can (7½ ounces) minced clams
1 can (7 ounces) small oysters
1 can (4½ ounces) shrimp
4 pimientos, quartered

Combine all ingredients in a saucepan. Cover and bring to a boil. Then simmer 5 minutes. *Serves 4–6.*

SUGGESTION: If desired, 1 can (1 pound) tomatoes may be substituted for the bouillon, omitting saffron and pimientos.

CHICKEN-SEAFOOD PAELLA: Prepare as for Five-Minute Paella, increasing bouillon to 1½ cups, substituting 1 can (6 ounces) boned chicken for the oysters, and adding ½ teaspoon salt.

TUNA CHOP SUEY

1 tablespoon cooking oil
2 stalks celery, slant cuts
½ small onion, sliced
¾ cup parboiled rice
2 tablespoons soy sauce
1 teaspoon sugar
dash pepper
2 cups water
1 7-ounce can tuna, drained
lettuce, shredded
tomato, diced

Heat oil in skillet. Lightly sauté celery and onion. Remove from heat. Add rice, seasonings, and water. Bring to a boil. Stir, cover, and lower heat. Cook 20–25 minutes or until rice is tender and liquid is absorbed. Fold in tuna and remove from heat. Mound lettuce and tomato on top; sprinkle with additional soy sauce if desired. Cover 3 minutes. Serve from skillet. *Serves 4–5.*

TUNA-IN-SKILLET

1 tablespoon oil from tuna
  (or other fat)
1 small onion, sliced
2½ cups canned tomatoes
1 bay leaf
salt, pepper
1 cup parboiled rice
1 can (6½ ounces) tuna

Cook onion in oil in skillet until tender. Stir in tomatoes, seasonings, uncooked rice. Add tuna and cover tightly. Cook over low heat for about 25 minutes until rice is tender and liquid absorbed. (Use more water during cooking if needed.) *Serves 4–6.*

SUGGESTION: For a different flavor treat, use this same recipe for canned salmon.

QUICK SALMON BECHAMEL

1 can (10½ ounces) condensed cream of mushroom soup
½ cup liquid from salmon (part water or milk, if necessary)
dash nutmeg
1 can (1 pound) salmon
4 cups hot cooked parboiled rice

Blend cream of mushroom soup, liquid, and nutmeg. Heat thoroughly. Break salmon into chunks, remove bones, and stir into a sauce. Heat and serve over hot, fluffy rice. *Serves 4.*

RICE AND TUNA CROQUETTES

1 cup cooked parboiled rice

1 can (6½ ounces) tuna, flaked
1 egg, separated
2 tablespoons minced onion
1 teaspoon lemon juice
½ teaspoon salt
⅛ teaspoon pepper
¾ cup bread crumbs
shortening *or* oil for deep frying

Combine slightly beaten egg yolk with flaked tuna. Add rice and seasonings; chill. Just before shaping, fold in stiffly beaten egg white. Shape into 8 patties or cones. Roll in bread crumbs and fry in deep fat. Serve hot with tomato or cream sauce. *Serves 4.*

RICE-STUFFED BAKED FISH

¼ cup chopped onion
¼ cup butter or margarine, melted
¼ cup dry bread crumbs
2 cups cooked rice
1½ teaspoon salt
½ teaspoon pepper
½ teaspoon basil
¼ teaspoon dried dill weed
1 tablespoon chopped parsley
2 tablespoons lemon juice
1 bass, trout, or whitefish (3–4 pounds)
paprika

Cook onion in 2 tablespoons butter until tender. Add to bread crumbs, rice, ½ teaspoon salt, ¼ teaspoon pepper, basil, dill weed, parsley, and 1 tablespoon lemon juice. Mix well. Clean and dress fish, cut fish almost through on under side. Fill with rice dressing. Fasten opening with skewers and thread. Season fish with remaining salt and pepper. Combine remaining butter and lemon juice. Brush over fish. Sprinkle with paprika. Bake at 400°F. 10 minutes per pound, basting frequently with the lemon butter. Serve garnished with lemon slices and watercress or parsley. *Serves 6.*

BAKED FISH FILLETS WITH CHEESE SAUCE

2 pounds fish fillets
salt and pepper
2 tablespoons lemon juice
2 tablespoons butter or margarine
2 cups chopped green onions with tops
   (optional)
2 cans (10½ ounces) Cheddar cheese soup
½ cup milk
1½ teaspoons curry powder
4 cups cooked rice
¼ teaspoon paprika

Season fish fillets with salt and pepper; sprinkle with lemon juice. Set aside. *Next:* melt butter in skillet; add onions and cook until tender. Combine soup, milk, onions, and curry powder. Butter a shallow baking dish; spread rice over bottom of dish and place fillets on top. Pour sauce over fish; sprinkle with paprika. Bake at 400°F. for 20 to 30 minutes, or until fish flakes easily when tested with a fork. *Serves 6.*

RICE AND TUNA MEDLEY

¼ cup butter or margarine
¾ cup chopped onion
¾ cup diced celery
2 medium unpeeled apples, diced
2 cans (6½ ounces each) tuna
2 cups cooked rice
1½ cans (10 ounces each) cheese
   soup, undiluted
1 teaspoon salt
¼ teaspoon pepper
⅔ cup crushed rice cereal
⅓ teaspoon curry powder (optional)

Melt half of butter in large skillet. Add onion, celery, and apples; cook until tender but not brown. Stir in tuna, rice, soup, salt, and pepper; mix thoroughly. Turn into a buttered 1½-quart casserole. Melt remaining butter and stir into rice cereal with curry powder. Sprinkle seasoned crumbs over top of rice mixture. Bake at 450°F. for 15 minutes. If preferred, rice and fish mixture may be heated through in large skillet, then turned into serving dish and topped with seasoned crumbs before serving. *Serves 6.*

SHRIMP GUMBO

1 pound ground salt pork *or* ⅓ cup salad oil
4 cups chopped onions
2 green peppers, chopped
2 cups chopped celery
3 No. 2½ cans tomatoes
1 teaspoon dry mustard
1 teaspoon oregano
1 teaspoon thyme
1 teaspoon salt
½ teaspoon crushed chilies
½ teaspoon pepper
1½ pounds okra *or* 2 packages frozen okra, sliced
2 tablespoons vinegar
3 pounds raw shrimp, shelled and deveined
1 pint *or* 2 6½-ounce cans crabmeat
6 cups hot cooked rice

In a large saucepan, cook pork until crisp or heat salad oil. Add onions, green peppers, and celery. Sauté until tender. Add tomatoes and bring to the simmering point. Add dry mustard, oregano, thyme, salt, chilies, and pepper. Cover and simmer slowly for 1 hour. Add okra and vinegar and cook until okra is tender. Add shrimp and crabmeat and cook until shrimp are pink and tender, 5 to 8 minutes. Serve over beds of hot rice. *Serves 12–14.*

SUGGESTION: Half the recipe may be frozen for another meal.

10.
Poultry

RICE-TURKEY PAELLA

4 tablespoons butter
3 cups uncooked turkey breast, diced
2 stalks celery, thinly sliced
1 large onion, thinly sliced
1 medium green pepper, diced
1 cup uncooked long-grain rice
2–3 cups boiling water
1 chicken bouillon cube
1 teaspoon salt
½ teaspoon ground white pepper
½ teaspoon poultry seasoning
½ pound snow peas (optional)
2 medium tomatoes, diced
½ cup ripe olives
½ cup cashew nuts

Sauté turkey dice in melted butter until opaque. Remove from pan. Sauté vegetables until limp; remove. Return meat to skillet with rice, crushed bouillon cube, seasonings, and water. Cover and bring to boil. Reduce heat and simmer about 20 minutes. Add sautéed vegetables and remaining ingredients. Cook about one minute. Stir in cashews. *Serves 4–6.*

RICE AND CHICKEN SUPERB

¼ pound butter or margarine
3 pounds breast of chicken
1 cup chopped green onions
2 medium green peppers cut in 1″ squares
1 cup sliced celery
1 can (3 ounces) sliced mushrooms
1 chicken bouillon cube, crushed
1 jar (2 ounces) pimientos
½ cup whole cashews
salt and pepper to taste
6 cups cooked long-grain rice (*2 cups uncooked*)

Using heavy skillet or electric skillet, sauté in butter the boned and diced chicken until opaque. Add and sauté next four ingredients to tender crisp stage. Stir in pimientos, bouillon cube, and cashews. Adjust seasonings. Serve on cooked rice with soy sauce, if desired. *Serves 6.*

CHICKEN à la KING

2 cups or 1 13-ounce can chicken broth
½ cup chopped green pepper
½ cup sliced celery
2 tablespoons chopped onion
¼ cup non-fat dry milk
¼ cup flour
2 cups diced cooked chicken
2 tablespoons diced pimiento
½ teaspoon salt
⅛ teaspoon white pepper
½ teaspoon soy sauce
3 cups hot cooked rice

Combine chicken broth, green pepper, celery, and onion in a large saucepan. Bring to a boil, lower heat, and simmer over medium heat 15 minutes or until vegetables are tender. Blend non-fat dry milk, flour, and water or wine. Stir into hot broth mixture; simmer until thickened. Add chicken, pimiento, and seasonings. Heat thoroughly about 10 minutes. Serve over bed of hot cooked rice, following package directions. *Serves 4–6.*

GOLDEN CHICKEN 'N' RICE

¼ cup chopped onion
¼ cup chopped green pepper
2 tablespoons butter or margarine
1 can (10½ ounces) cream of chicken soup, undiluted
½ cup milk
¼ teaspoon Tabasco sauce
2 cans (5 ounces each) boned chicken, diced
3 cups cooked rice
1 can (3½ ounces) onion rings

Sauté onion and green pepper in butter until tender. Stir in soup, milk, Tabasco sauce, chicken, and rice. Pour into buttered 3-quart casserole. Sprinkle with canned onion rings. Bake for 10 minutes at 450°F. *Serves 6.*

SUNNY CHICKEN

⅓ cup flour
1 teaspoon salt
⅛ teaspoon pepper
1 frying chicken (2–2½ pounds) cut into serving portions
½ cup oil
⅓ cup sliced onion
¼ cup water
½ can (6 ounces) frozen orange juice, undiluted
3 cups hot cooked rice

Preheat oven to 350°F. Combine flour, salt, and pepper in a small paper bag. Put in chicken, piece at a time; shake until coated. Heat oil in heavy skillet; brown chicken on all sides. Remove chicken and drain; place in 1½-quart casserole. In the same skillet, sauté onion until tender. Remove and drain; place on top of chicken. Pour off the drippings. Add the water; bring to a boil and pour over chicken. Add orange juice concentrate, cover, and bake at 350°F. for one hour until tender. Serve over hot cooked rice. *Serves 4.*

CHICKEN DINNER BAKE

2 tablespoons salad oil
2 pounds chicken breasts (or a 2½-pound frying chicken, cut into serving portions)
1 can (16 ounces) cut green beans
1 can (10½ ounces) condensed cream of chicken soup, undiluted
¼ teaspoon salt
1 tablespoon chopped pimiento
2 cups cooked rice

Season chicken as desired; in skillet, brown on all sides in oil. Remove chicken and place in 2-quart casserole. Drain remaining oil from skillet. Drain green beans, saving ½ cup liquid. In skillet, combine this liquid with soup and salt. Heat, stirring, until smooth; pour over chicken. Bake, uncovered, at 375°F. for 45 minutes. Combine beans, pimiento, and cooked rice; spoon into casserole around chicken. Cover and bake 15 more minutes. *Serves 4–6.*

PECAN RICE STUFFING FOR POULTRY

1 cup butter or margarine
1 cup chopped onion
1 cup chopped celery
¼ cup minced parsley
8 cups cooked rice (cooked in chicken broth)
2 cups chopped pecans
2 teaspoons thyme
1½ teaspoons salt
1 teaspoon sage
1 teaspoon celery seed
½ teaspoon ground cloves
½ teaspoon pepper
½ teaspoon nutmeg

Melt butter or margarine in a Dutch oven. Add onion, celery, and parsley. Sauté over low heat until tender, stirring constantly. Add cooked rice, pecans, and seasonings. Toss together lightly. Makes enough stuffing for a 12- to 16-pound turkey.

RISOTTO WITH CHICKEN AND MUSHROOMS

1 cup uncooked rice
4 tablespoons butter or margarine
2 cups chicken broth
1 cup diced cooked chicken
1 can (2 ounces) sliced mushrooms
½ cup grated cheese
½ teaspoon salt
⅛ teaspoon paprika
dash of cayenne

Sauté rice in butter for one minute. Add chicken broth. Bring to a boil, stir once, reduce heat, cover, and simmer 15 minutes or until rice is tender. Add remaining ingredients and cook 5 minutes longer. *Serves 4.*

SUGGESTION: Cooked beef, lamb, pork, crab, shrimp, or tuna may be substituted for chicken.

TURKEY AND RICE CASSEROLE

½ 10-ounce can cream of mushroom soup
¼ cup milk
1½ teaspoons lemon juice
½ teaspoon salt
dash of pepper
1 tablespoon chopped pimiento
1 7-ounce can turkey, diced
1½ cups cooked rice
⅓ cup buttered cereal crumbs

Pour soup into a saucepan; add milk slowly, stirring constantly until smooth. Add lemon juice, salt, pepper, pimiento, and turkey. Heat thoroughly. Remove from heat. Fold in rice. Pour into a greased one-quart casserole. Sprinkle with buttered cereal crumbs. Bake in a 350°F. oven for 20 to 25 minutes or until thoroughly heated and crumbs are brown. *Serves 2.*

EIGHT BOY CHICKEN CURRY*

1 5–6-pound stewing hen, cut up
6 cups water
3 medium-sized onions, chopped
2 apples, minced
8 stalks celery, minced
¼ cup olive oil
¼ cup curry powder
¼ teaspoon pepper
½ teaspoon ginger
½ teaspoon Tabasco sauce
¼ cup flour
2 cups heavy cream
3 egg yolks, slightly beaten
½ cup sherry
salt to taste
6 cups hot cooked rice

Simmer chicken in water in covered pan until tender. Cook onions, apples, and celery in olive oil until browned, stirring frequently. Add curry powder and simmer 5 minutes. Add 4 cups of the broth from the chicken and seasonings; simmer 20 minutes. Blend in flour smoothly and cook until thickened, stirring constantly. Bone and dice chicken. Add to sauce and let stand at least 3 hours. When ready to serve, add cream, egg yolks, sherry, and salt to taste. Heat thoroughly. Serve over hot rice. *Serves 6.*

Serve the Following Foods, Each in a Separate Dish:
4 hard-cooked eggs, chopped
2 cups chutney
1 fresh coconut, grated
2 green peppers, chopped

---

* Eight Boy Chicken Curry is so named from the number of condiments served with it. Traditionally, each is served by a separate houseboy carrying the bowls in white-gloved hands. Number of condiments may be varied from two up.

½ pound bacon, fried and chopped
½ cup currant jelly
½ cup pickles, chopped
½ pound salted peanuts, chopped

CHICKEN CACCIATORE

½ cup butter or margarine
2 cups celery, chopped
1 cup green onions, minced
1 cup parsley, chopped
1 clove garlic, minced
3 cups Italian peeled tomatoes
¼ teaspoon red pepper
¼ teaspoon thyme
½ teaspoon marjoram
2½ teaspoons salt
½ teaspoon black pepper
1½ pounds chicken giblets, cooked and chopped
2 cups rice, uncooked
1 quart chicken broth
Parmesan cheese

Heat butter in large skillet or Dutch oven. Add celery, onions, parsley and garlic. Sauté until tender. Add remaining ingredients; simmer, covered, 20 to 30 minutes or until tender. Cook rice in chicken broth, covered, and simmer 14 minutes. Serve chicken over beds of fluffy rice. Sprinkle with Parmesan cheese. *Serves 8.*

CREAMED TURKEY FLORENTINE

1 package (6 ounces) long-grain and wild rice mix
1 package (10 ounces) frozen chopped spinach
2 tablespoons butter or margarine
¼ pound mushrooms, sliced, *or* 1 can (4 ounces) sliced mushrooms
1 can (10½ ounces) cream of chicken soup
2 cups sliced or cubed cooked turkey (or chicken)
⅓ cup dry white wine
1 tablespoon parsley flakes

Cook long-grain and wild rice and spinach according to package directions. Meanwhile, melt butter in skillet. Add mushrooms; sauté until tender. Stir in soup, turkey, wine, parsley flakes; simmer until mixture begins to bubble. Spread hot cooked rice in bottom of shallow baking dish. Spread spinach in wide strip down center of rice. Pour creamed turkey mixture over spinach. To serve, garnish with parsley, if desired. *Serves 4–6.*

CHICKEN ACAPULCO

1 package (6 ounces) Spanish rice mix, cooked according to package directions
2 cups cooked chicken, cubed
1 teaspoon salt
1 can (10¾ ounces) chicken gravy
1 tablespoon prepared mustard
1 tablespoon instant minced onion
12 cherry tomatoes, cut in half
½ avocado, cut into short strips (optional)

Season chicken with salt. Add chicken gravy, mustard, and onion; stir until smooth. Cover and cook over medium heat 5 minutes. Add tomatoes and avocado; toss lightly. Cover and continue cooking 2 minutes. Serve over Spanish rice. *Serves 6.*

CHICKEN LIVERS GONE WILD

1 package long-grain and wild rice mix
1 medium-size onion, chopped
4 tablespoons butter or margarine
1 pound chicken livers cut in pieces
3 tablespoons butter
¼ cup Parmesan cheese

Cook rice according to package directions. Sauté onion in butter until golden, add chicken livers, and cook 4 minutes. Combine mixture and rice in a 1½-quart covered casserole. Dot with remaining butter and sprinkle with cheese. Cover and bake in a preheated 350°F. oven for 15 minutes. *Serves 6.*

CAN-CAN CHICKEN

1 can (10½ ounces) condensed cream of chicken soup
1 can (10½ ounces) condensed cream of celery soup
1 can (1⅓ cups) water
1⅓ cups enriched pre-cooked rice
1 can (12 ounces) boned or 1½ cups diced cooked chicken
1 can (3 ounces) chow mein noodles, *or* use 1 can (3½ ounces)
            French fried onions and heat as directed on can.

Combine all ingredients except noodles in a large skillet. Bring quickly to a boil. Cover and simmer 7 minutes. To serve, top with chow mein noodles. *Serves 4–6.*

GOLDEN RICE-AND-CHICKEN

1. Cook 2 tablespoons minced onion in ¼ cup butter or margarine until soft. Stir in ⅓ cup flour, 1 teaspoon salt, ⅓ teaspoon pepper, ¼ teaspoon poultry seasoning.
2. Dissolve 2 chicken bouillon cubes in 1¼ cups water. Gradually add to butter mixture with ½ cup milk. Cook, stirring, until mixture bubbles and thickens.
3. Combine 2 cups parboiled rice (already cooked) with 2 cups minced or finely diced chicken, ¼ cup chopped green pepper, ¼ cup chopped pimiento.
4. Add eggs, slightly beaten, to rice mixture. Fold in sauce. Butter a 10x6x2-inch baking pan and pour in rice-chicken mixture. Top with buttered crumbs.
5. Bake in 350°F. oven about 30 minutes or until set. Meanwhile, sauté ½ pound mushrooms, sliced, in 2 tablespoons butter or margarine. Stir in 1 can condensed tomato soup.
6. Add ¼ cup milk. Heat through. Cut baked chicken mixture into squares, top each serving with a spoonful of sauce. *Serves 6.*

SUGGESTION: Turkey may be substituted for chicken.

CHICKEN CONTINENTAL

3 pounds frying chicken pieces
⅓ cup seasoned all-purpose flour

¼ cup butter
1 can (10½ ounces) condensed cream of chicken soup
2½ tablespoons grated onion
1 tablespoon chopped parsley
1 teaspoon salt
½ teaspoon celery flakes
⅛ teaspoon thyme
dash of pepper
1⅓ cups water
1⅓ cups enriched pre-cooked rice

Roll chicken in seasoned flour. Sauté in butter in a skillet until golden brown. Remove chicken from skillet. Combine soup, onion, and seasonings in skillet. Gradually stir in water. Bring to a boil over medium heat, stirring constantly. Pour rice into a shallow 1½-quart casserole. Stir in all except ⅓ cup soup mixture. Top with chicken and pour reserved soup mixture over chicken. Cover with aluminum foil and bake at 375°F. about 30 minutes, or until chicken is tender. Sprinkle with paprika and garnish with additional chopped parsley, if desired. *Serves 4.*

GINGER CHICKEN AND RICE

2 pounds frying chicken pieces
2 teaspoons salt
⅛ teaspoon pepper
1 tablespoon butter
1 small clove garlic, crushed
⅓ cup chopped celery
½ cup corn syrup*
1½ teaspoons ground ginger*
2 tablespoons lemon juice
1 can (12½ ounces) chicken broth or consommé
1⅓ cups enriched pre-cooked rice

Sprinkle chicken with salt and pepper. Sauté in butter until browned. Add garlic and celery and sauté until garlic is lightly browned. Blend corn syrup, ginger, lemon juice, and 1 cup of the consommé; pour over chicken. Bring to full boil; then cover and

---

* Or use 1 tablespoon chopped preserved ginger and ¼ cup of the syrup in which it is packed.

simmer until tender—about 15 minutes. Remove chicken; add remaining consommé to mixture in pan. (If desired, refrigerate chicken and consommé mixture separately until about 30 minutes before serving.) *Next:* place rice in shallow 2½-quart baking dish. Bring consommé mixture to boil. Stir into rice. Top with chicken. Cover and bake at 400°F. for 25 minutes. *Serves 4.*

SUNSHINE CHICKEN

1⅔ cups thinly sliced carrots
2 tablespoons butter
¼ cup chopped onion
1⅓ cups orange juice
⅔ cup water
1 teaspoon salt
½ teaspoon grated orange rind
½ teaspoon poultry seasoning
⅛ teaspoon pepper
1½ cups diced cooked chicken
1⅓ cups enriched pre-cooked rice

Sauté carrots in butter in large skillet over medium heat until almost tender—about 5 minutes—turning frequently. Add onion and sauté until lightly browned. Add remaining ingredients except chicken and rice. Bring to a boil, then stir in chicken and rice. Cover and simmer 8 minutes. *Serves 4.*

BRAZILIAN CHICKEN

3 pounds frying chicken pieces
3 tablespoons butter
½ cup chopped onion
1 clove garlic, crushed
1 jar (2½ ounces) dried beef, diced
2 chicken bouillon cubes
3⅓ cups hot water
1⅓ cups enriched pre-cooked rice
½ cup sliced ripe olives

1 hard-cooked egg, finely chopped
2 tablespoons finely chopped parsley
2 tablespoons grated Parmesan cheese

Sauté chicken in butter in a large deep skillet until golden brown. Add onion, garlic, and dried beef; sauté until onion is transparent. Dissolve bouillon cubes in hot water. Add 1½ cups bouillon to chicken mixture. Bring to a boil; cover and cook gently until chicken is almost tender—30 minutes. *Meanwhile:* stir rice and olives into remaining bouillon in a saucepan. Bring to a boil. Then cover, remove from heat, and let stand 5 minutes. Mix egg, parsley, and cheese. Place on a platter, top with chicken, and sprinkle with egg mixture. *Serves 4–5.*

CHICKEN LUZON

¼ cup lime juice
2 tablespoons soy sauce
½ teaspoon salt
⅛ teaspoon pepper
3 pounds frying chicken pieces
⅓ cup salad oil
1 lime, sliced
1⅓ cups water
½ teaspoon salt
1⅓ cups enriched pre-cooked rice
1 tablespoon soy sauce
2 tablespoons lime juice
1 tablespoon chopped scallions or chives

Combine ¼ cup lime juice, 2 tablespoons soy sauce, ½ teaspoon salt and pepper. Pour over chicken and refrigerate about 12 hours to marinate. Then drain, reserving marinade. Sauté chicken in oil, turning to brown evenly. Add reserved marinade and lime slices. Cover and cook gently 20 to 40 minutes, or until chicken is tender. *Meanwhile:* bring water and ½ teaspoon salt to a boil. Stir in remaining ingredients. Cover, remove from heat, and let stand 5 minutes. Toss lightly with a fork. Arrange on serving platter and top with chicken. *Serves 4.*

CURRIED CHICKEN DELUXE

1 cup chopped onions
½ cup chopped green pepper
¼ cup butter
¾ cup unsifted all-purpose flour
5 cups chicken broth*
1½ teaspoons salt
2 tablespoons curry powder
4 cups diced cooked chicken
½ cup slivered blanched almonds
2 tablespoons butter
2⅔ cups water
⅓ cup dried currants
1 teaspoon salt
2⅔ cups enriched pre-cooked rice

Sauté onions and green pepper in ¼ cup butter in skillet until tender. Stir in flour. Gradually blend in chicken broth, 1½ teaspoons salt, and curry powder. Cook until thickened, stirring occasionally. Then add chicken and cook until thoroughly heated. *Meanwhile:* sauté almonds in 2 tablespoons butter in a saucepan until golden brown. Add water, currants, and 1 teaspoon salt. Bring to a boil. Stir in rice. Then cover, remove from heat, and let stand 5 minutes. Fluff with fork before serving. Serve curry over rice—almonds and currants in rice eliminate the need for condiments but chutney may be served, if desired. *Serves 8.*

---

* Or use 3 cans (12½-ounces each) chicken broth

CHICKEN-RICE ORIENTAL

1 small clove garlic, minced
3 tablespoons salad oil
1½ cups diced cooked chicken (or ham, pork, or beef)
1⅓ cups enriched pre-cooked rice
⅛ teaspoon pepper
2 cups water
1½ cups shredded lettuce, escarole, or spinach
2 tablespoons soy sauce

Sauté garlic in oil just until golden brown. Add chicken, rice, pepper, and water; mix just to moisten rice. Bring to a boil over high heat. Then cover, remove from heat, and let stand 5 minutes. Just before serving, add lettuce and soy sauce; toss lightly. *Serves 4.*

CHICKEN AND RICE ALEXANDRIA

1 cup milk
¼ cup unsifted all-purpose flour
1½ cups water
1 cup chicken broth
¼ cup butter
¼ cup sherry (optional)
¼ teaspoon Worcestershire sauce
1½ teaspoons salt
dash of pepper
1⅓ cups enriched pre-cooked rice
1½ cups diced cooked chicken
1 can (4 ounces) sliced mushrooms
3 tablespoons finely chopped pimiento
2 tablespoons chopped parsley
2 teaspoons butter, melted
½ cup dry bread crumbs

Blend milk into flour in large saucepan; add water, broth, and ¼ cup butter. Cook and stir over medium heat until mixture comes to a boil and is thickened—4 to 5 minutes. Then add sherry, Worcestershire sauce, salt, and pepper; blend. Stir in rice, chicken, mushrooms, pimiento, and parsley. Pour into a greased 2-quart casserole. Mix melted butter and crumbs; sprinkle over rice mixture. Bake at 450°F. for 15 minutes. Garnish with additional pimiento or parsley just before serving, if desired. *Serves 4–6.*

WILD RICE, CHICKEN LIVERS

1 package (6 ounces) long-grain and wild rice
1 pound chicken livers, halved
1 tablespoon minced onion
2 tablespoons chopped parsley
¼ cup butter or margarine

Cook contents of rice according to package directions. Sauté livers, onion, and parsley in butter or margarine. During last 5 minutes of rice cooking time, add sautéed mixture to rice; cover and continue cooking until rice is tender and liquid is absorbed, about 5 minutes. *Serves 4–6.*

ARROZ CON POLLO (Spanish Chicken and Rice)

2–3 pounds frying chicken pieces
¼ cup seasoned all-purpose flour
3 tablespoons butter
½ clove garlic
½ cup sliced onion
¼ pound fresh mushrooms, sliced (about 1½ cups)
1 can (1 pound, 12 ounces) tomatoes or 2 cans (8 ounces each) tomato sauce
1½ cups chicken broth or bouillon
½   bay leaf
1 teaspoon salt
⅛ teaspoon saffron (optional)
1⅓ cups enriched pre-cooked rice
½ cup cooked peas
¼ cup sliced green pepper
1 tablespoon chopped parsley

Roll chicken in seasoned flour. Sauté in butter in skillet until golden brown. Place chicken in a large saucepan. Sauté garlic, onion, and mushrooms in butter remaining in skillet until tender; add to chicken with tomatoes, broth, bay leaf, salt, and saffron. Mix well. Cover and simmer about 30 minutes, or until chicken is tender, stirring occasionally. Then stir in remaining ingredients. Simmer 5 to 10 minutes longer. Before serving, remove and discard bay leaf and garlic. *Serves 4.*

BAKED CHICKEN LOAF

1 cup milk
1 cup chicken broth (or 1 chicken bouillon cube dissolved in 1 cup hot water)

Rice Ranchero

Fresh Spinach and Rice Salad Bowl

Sky-High Rice Salad

Delmonico Rice

Skillet Gumbo

Poncho Rice

Rice Stuffed Baked Fish

Baked Fish Fillets with Cheese Sauce

Rice and Tuna Medley

Shrimp Gumbo

Rice and Chicken Supreme

Chicken and Rice Creole

Baked Rice with Cheese

Golden Rice Loaf

Rice, Green Beans, and Sour Cream

Zesty Rice Stuffed Acorn Squash

Spicy Steak and Rice Supper

Apricot Ham Rolls

Creamy Rice Pudding

Calas

Glorified Lemon Rice

Rice and Vegetable Dressing

  2 tablespoons butter
  3 eggs, slightly beaten
  2 cups finely diced cooked chicken
  1 tablespoon minced parsley
  1 teaspoon grated onion
  ¾ teaspoon salt
  dash of pepper
  1 teaspoon Worcestershire sauce
  ½ teaspoon poultry seasoning
  1⅓ cups enriched pre-cooked rice
  1 can (10½ ounces) condensed cream
     of mushroom soup

Bring milk, ½ of the broth, and butter almost to boiling point. *Meanwhile:* combine remaining ingredients except remaining broth and soup; add milk mixture and mix well. Butter bottom and sides of a 9 x 5 loaf pan, line bottom with wax paper, and butter the paper. Pour rice mixture into pan. Bake at 350°F. for 30 minutes, or until firm. *Next,* combine remaining ½ cup broth and the soup; heat thoroughly, stirring frequently. Unmold baked loaf on serving platter and remove paper. Serve soup mixture as sauce with the loaf. *Serves 4–6.*

ZESTY CHICKEN SALAD

  ¾ cup mayonnaise
  2 tablespoons lemon juice
  1½ cups cubed cooked chicken
  1 cup cold cooked parboiled rice
  ½ cup chopped celery
  2 tablespoons grated onion
  ½ cup chopped cucumber pickle
  ¼ cup diced ripe pitted olives

Mix mayonnaise and lemon juice. Combine other ingredients. Toss with mayonnaise-lemon mixture. *Serves 4–6.*

SUGGESTIONS: To make a meal, serve cold clam-and-tomato juice spiked with lemon, artichoke hearts and cherry tomatoes marinated in a little oil and white-wine vinegar, hot rolls, and lemon mousse with lady fingers for dessert.

CHICKEN VERMOUTH WITH RICE

1 frying chicken (2½ to 3 pounds)
  cut into serving pieces
2½ teaspoons salt
½ teaspoon pepper
3 medium carrots, sliced
2 ribs celery, thinly sliced
1 medium onion, thinly sliced
12 cloves garlic, peeled*
2 tablespoons chopped parsley
⅓ cup dry white vermouth
¼ cup sour cream
3 cups hot cooked rice (cooked in
  chicken broth)

Sprinkle chicken with salt and pepper. Place all ingredients *except* sour cream and rice in a 2-quart covered casserole. Cover with double thickness of foil. Place casserole lid over foil. Bake 1½ hours at 375°F. without removing cover. Stir in sour cream. Serve over hot fluffy rice. *Serves 4.*

* That's right—12. And it's great!

PATIO CHICKEN SALAD DELUXE

1 package (10 ounces) frozen green peas
1 teaspoon curry powder
½ teaspoon salt
1½ cups pineapple juice
1⅓ cups enriched pre-cooked rice
½ cup chopped dill pickles (or use ½ cup
  toasted slivered almonds)
1 teaspoon grated onion
⅛ teaspoon pepper
1½ cups diced cooked chicken
½ cup diced celery
¾ cup mayonnaise

Cook peas as directed on package; drain. Meanwhile, combine salt, curry powder, and pineapple juice in a saucepan. Bring to a boil. Stir in rice. Cover, remove from heat, and let stand 5 minutes. Then add peas, pickles, onion, and pepper; mix lightly with a fork. Chill. Before serving, add chicken, celery, and mayonnaise. Toss lightly. Serve on crisp salad greens and garnish with tomato wedges, if desired. *Serves 6.*

RICE AND CHICKEN SUPREME

1 can (10½ ounces) mushroom soup
¼ cup water
1 can (2½ ounces) deviled ham
1 teaspoon minced onion
2 tablespoons diced pimiento
1½ cups diced cooked chicken
2 packages (10 ounces each) frozen
    broccoli, cooked
3 cups hot cooked rice
Garnish: hard-cooked egg slices or
    pimiento strips

In a saucepan, combine soup, water, ham, and onion; stir over medium heat until smooth and hot. Fold in pimiento and chicken. Arrange broccoli on serving platter. Top with rice. Spoon sauce over rice. Garnish with eggs or pimiento strips. *Serves 4.*

CHICKEN AND RICE CREOLE

1 frying chicken, cut in serving pieces
¼ cup flour
2 teaspoons salt
¼ teaspoon pepper
3 tablespoons butter or margarine
1 onion, sliced
3 green onions, chopped
1 green pepper, slivered
3 tomatoes, quartered
3 cups chicken consommé
1 bay leaf
2 tablespoons minced parsley

1 cup rice, uncooked
½ cup ham, slivered
¼ cup sherry

Dredge chicken in flour seasoned with salt and pepper. Brown on all sides in butter or margarine in a large skillet. Lay chicken parts to one side, add all onions and green pepper, and cook 5 minutes. Place chicken to fit in pan. Add tomatoes, consommé, bay leaf, and parsley. Cover tightly and cook for 20 minutes over low heat. Add rice, ham, and sherry; cover and continue to cook 30 minutes longer. *Serves 6.*

11.

Egg and Cheese

RICE FRANKLY

1 can (10½ ounces) condensed cheese
    soup, undiluted
¼ cup milk
¼ teaspoon Tabasco sauce
¼ cup finely chopped onion
3 tablespoons chopped green pepper
3 cups cooked rice
1 pound frankfurters, sliced in half
    lengthwise
½ cup grated cheddar cheese

Combine first 5 ingredients; stir into cooked rice. Spoon half of
this mixture into buttered, 2-quart, oblong or oval baking dish;
top with half the frankfurter slices. Cover with rest of rice mixture. Place remaining frankfurters on top. Bake at 375°F. for
20 minutes. Sprinkle grated cheese over top. Continue baking
5 minutes. *Serves 6.*

RICE AHOY

1 cup rice
8 ounces processed American cheese, cut in cubes
½ cup milk
¼ teaspoon Tabasco sauce

1 can (7 ounces) salmon, drained and flaked
½ cup stuffed olives, sliced

Cook rice as package directs. Meanwhile, put cheese, milk, and Tabasco sauce into double boiler. Heat and stir until melted and smooth. Alternate layers of cooked rice, salmon, olive slices, and cheese sauce in a buttered 1½-quart casserole. Bake uncovered at 350°F. for 30 minutes. Garnish with more olive slices, if desired. *Serves 6.*

RICE ROMANOFF

3 cups cooked rice
¼ cup finely chopped green onion
1 cup cream-style cottage cheese
1 cup sour cream
¼ cup milk
1 clove garlic, finely minced
¼ teaspoon Tabasco sauce
2 envelopes instant chicken broth
½ cup grated Cheddar cheese

Combine rice and green onion. Blend cottage cheese with sour cream, milk, garlic, Tabasco sauce, and chicken broth. Stir into rice mixture. Pour into a buttered 1½-quart casserole. Sprinkle with Cheddar cheese. Bake at 350°F. for 25 minutes. *Serves 6.*

CHEESE AND RICE SOUFFLÉ

2 tablespoons butter or margarine
3 tablespoons flour
¾ cup milk
½ pound sharp cheese, grated
4 eggs, separated
½ teaspoon salt
dash of cayenne
1 cup cooked parboiled rice

Combine butter and flour in a saucepan, stir over low heat until smooth. Gradually add milk; cook, stirring, until thickened. Add cheese, salt, and cayenne; cook, stirring occasionally, until thick. Beat egg yolks lightly with a fork. Add slowly to cooking mixture, stirring constantly. Remove from heat and stir in rice. Beat egg whites until stiff but not dry. Gently fold in cheese-rice mixture. Turn into a greased 1½-quart casserole. Bake, uncovered, in a 325°F. oven for 40 minutes. Then serve at once. *Serves 5–6.*

SUGGESTION: Serve this easy, puffy wonder as soon as it is done. The same applies to all soufflés.

RICE RAREBIT

1 pound sharp Cheddar cheese,
   shredded or cubed
½ cup milk
2 teaspoons prepared mustard
dash of Worcestershire sauce
12 slices bacon
4 cups hot cooked parboiled rice
3 tomatoes, cut into 4 slices each

Place cheese, milk, mustard, and Worcestershire in the top of a double boiler. Cook over hot (not boiling) water, stirring frequently, until melted. Meanwhile, fry the bacon and drain. Divide the rice into six portions on plates. On each portion, place 2 slices of tomato. Pour cheese sauce over. Top each portion with two criss-crossed slices of bacon. *Serves 6.*

CHEDDAR-RICE LOAF

¼ cup butter or margarine
1 cup milk
2 cups cooked parboiled rice
1½ cups grated sharp Cheddar cheese
½ cup fine dry bread crumbs
3 eggs, slightly beaten
¼ cup chopped celery
¼ cup minced onion
1 tablespoon dehydrated parsley
½ cup chopped green pepper

1 teaspoon salt
½ teaspoon prepared mustard

Heat butter with milk until melted. Add rice, cheese, and crumbs to eggs; stir in hot milk. Add celery, onion, parsley, green pepper, and seasonings. Turn into a greased loaf pan, 8¼ x 4½ x 2¾, that has been lined in bottom with greased aluminum foil. Bake in a 350°F. oven for 1 hour and 15 minutes. Unmold on platter; accompany with hot Mushroom Sauce. *Serves 6.*

MUSHROOM SAUCE

1 can (10½ ounces) cream of mushroom soup
½ cup water
1 can (3 or 4 ounces) sliced mushrooms

Blend soup with water until smooth; heat with canned mushrooms and their liquid.

COTTAGE CHEESE-RICE BAKE

1⅓ cups water
½ teaspoon salt
1⅓ cups enriched pre-cooked rice
2 cups (1 pound) cream-style cottage cheese
3 eggs, slightly beaten
1½ cups milk
2 tablespoons butter, melted
1½ teaspoons salt
⅛ teaspoon pepper
1 tablespoon minced parsley
1 tablespoon grated onion
¼ cup grated carrot

Bring water and ½ teaspoon salt to a boil. Stir in rice. Cover, remove from heat, and let stand 5 minutes. *Meanwhile:* add cottage cheese to eggs and beat only enough to break up curds. Blend in milk, butter, 1½ teaspoons salt, and pepper. Add rice, parsley, onion, and carrot. Pour into a greased 8-inch square pan.

Place in a pan of hot water and bake at 375°F. for 1 hour, or until knife inserted near center comes out clean. Remove from water. Cut into center and serve. *Serves 9.*

CHEESE VEGETABLE RICE

1 cup chopped onion
½ cup chopped green pepper
2 tablespoons butter or margarine
1 can (12 ounces) whole kernel corn
1 can (8 ounces) tomato sauce
½ cup chicken broth *or* water
3 cups cooked parboiled rice
1 teaspoon salt
¼ teaspoon pepper
3–4 drops hot Tabasco
½ pound shredded Cheddar cheese

Cook onion and green pepper in butter until tender. Add corn, tomato sauce, chicken broth, rice, and seasonings. Heat thoroughly. Add cheese and stir until cheese is melted. Serve hot. *Serves 8.*

SUGGESTIONS: To make a meal, serve cold roast beef (or pork or lamb or chicken). This dish complements almost any meat flavor. Add a tossed green salad with red onion rings, club rolls, and a homemade jelly roll for dessert.

EGG-RICE BAKE

6 eggs, well beaten
2 tablespoons milk
1 teaspoon salt
dash of pepper and Tabasco
1½ cups cooked parboiled rice
paprika *or* grated cheese

Blend milk and seasonings with eggs. Add cooked rice. Pour into flat, buttered baking dish; sprinkle with paprika or cheese. Bake in pan with water at 325°F. for about 30 minutes until eggs are set and top is browned. Serve immediately with cheese, tomato, or other favorite sauce. *Serves 4–6.*

SUGGESTION: Cooked vegetables, such as asparagus or spinach, may be placed in the baking dish before the eggs.

BAKED RICE WITH CHEESE

1 tablespoon butter or margarine
½ cup chopped onion
1 cup uncooked rice
¼ teaspoon garlic powder
2 teaspoons Worcestershire sauce
1 tablespoon minced parsley
1½ cups chicken broth
⅔ cup dry white wine
1 cup cubed sharp Cheddar cheese

Melt butter in a skillet; add onions and cook until tender. Stir in rice and continue cooking until rice is golden. Add garlic powder, Worcestershire sauce, parsley, chicken broth, and wine. Heat to boiling. Stir in cheese. Turn into a buttered 1½-quart casserole. Cover casserole and bake in a 350°F. oven for 35 to 40 minutes. Serve hot as meat accompaniment. *Serves 6.*

GOLDEN RICE LOAF

½ cup flour
1¼ teaspoons salt
⅛ teaspoon pepper
½ teaspoon dry mustard
¼ teaspoon sage
2½ cups milk
2 cups grated sharp Cheddar cheese
1 tablespoon grated onion
3 cups cooked rice
3 eggs, slightly beaten
3 hard-cooked eggs

Combine flour, salt, pepper, mustard, sage, and about ⅓ cup of the milk; stir until smooth. Stir in remaining milk. Cook until thickened, stirring frequently. Add cheese and stir until cheese is melted. Remove from heat. Fold in onions and rice. Stir in slightly beaten eggs. *Next:* line bottom of greased 8½ x 4½ inch loaf pan with waxed paper. Put about half of the rice-cheese mixture in bottom of pan. Arrange hard-cooked eggs lengthwise in center. Cover with remaining rice-cheese mixture. Set in pan of hot water. Bake at 350°F. about 1 hour or until set. Let stand in pan about 5 minutes before unmolding. Slice to warm. *Serves 6–8.*

12.

Gourmet Cookery with Rice

GINZA SUKIYAKI

1 package beef-flavored rice mix
¼ cup butter or margarine
1 medium onion, chopped
1 pound sirloin steak cut in strips
½ cup diced celery
1 can bean sprouts
½ pound fresh white mushrooms, sliced
2 tablespoons soy sauce
½ pound fresh washed and drained spinach

Cook rice according to package directions. Sauté onion in melted butter. Add beef strips to onion and brown on all sides. Add celery, bean sprouts, mushrooms, and soy sauce and cook for 8 minutes. Add spinach and cook for 2 minutes. Serve over the beef rice. *Serves 6.*

BAKED HERB PILAF

1 can (12½ ounces) chicken broth
1 cup enriched pre-cooked rice
1 teaspoon instant minced onion or onion flakes
1 teaspoon chopped parsley or parsley flakes
1 teaspoon celery seed or celery flakes
1 teaspoon salt

¼ teaspoon oregano
1 tablespoon butter (optional)

Measure broth and add water to make 2 cups. Combine all ingredients in a shallow 1-quart baking pan or casserole. Cover with aluminum foil. Bake at 350°F. for 20 minutes, or until liquid is absorbed. *Serves 6.*

SWEDISH RICE MEATBALLS

1 cup enriched pre-cooked rice
1 pound ground beef
1 egg, slightly beaten
2 tablespoons minced onion
1 tablespoon chopped parsley
1½ teaspoons salt
¼ teaspoon nutmeg
dash of pepper
½ cup milk
1 can (10½ ounces) condensed cream of
    mushroom *or* cream of celery soup
⅔ cup water
1 teaspoon lemon juice

Combine rice, beef, egg, onion, parsley, salt, nutmeg, pepper, and milk, mixing lightly. Shape into 24 small balls. Place in skillet. Blend soup with water and lemon juice. Pour over meatballs and bring to a boil. Cover and simmer 10 minutes, basting occasionally. Garnish with chopped parsley, if desired. *Serves 6.*

HAWAIIAN MEATBALLS AND RICE

16 small meatballs
1 clove garlic, minced
2 tablespoons salad oil
2½ tablespoons pre-cooked tapioca *or*
    cornstarch
½ cup sugar
1 teaspoon salt
1 tablespoon soy sauce (optional)

⅓ cup vinegar
1 cup broth or water
1 cup sliced green peppers
1⅓ cups boiling water
1⅓ cups enriched pre-cooked rice
Orange sections (optional)

Prepare meatballs, using favorite recipe. Sauté garlic in oil. Add meatballs and sauté until evenly browned. Combine tapioca, sugar, salt, soy sauce, vinegar, and broth; add to meatballs. Heat and stir until sauce thickens. Make a well in center of mixture and add green peppers and boiling water; stir rice into water. Cover and simmer 10 minutes, or until rice is tender. Garnish with orange sections. *Serves 4.*

TRADITIONAL CHOP SUEY

2 cups water
3 tablespoons cornstarch
1 tablespoon soy sauce
1 teaspoon salt
dash of pepper
1 cup chopped onions
¼ cup butter or other shortening
2 cups celery strips
1 can (1 pound) bean sprouts or chop suey vegetables, drained
2 cups cooked pork, cut in thin strips
1⅔ cups enriched pre-cooked rice

Blend water into cornstarch; add soy sauce, salt, and pepper. Sauté onions in butter in a large skillet until golden brown. Stir in cornstarch mixture, celery, bean sprouts, and pork. Bring quickly to a boil; then cover and simmer 5 minutes, stirring occasionally. *Meanwhile:* prepare rice as per package directions. Serve chop suey over rice. Sprinkle with chow mein noodles or toasted slivered blanched almonds and serve with additional soy sauce, if desired. *Serves 4–6.*

SUGGESTION: To use fresh pork in the Traditional Chop Suey, brown 1 pound lean pork, cut in thin strips, in the butter before adding onions and omit the cooked pork.

SKILLET CHOP SUEY
(One-Pan Recipe)

1 large clove garlic, minced
1½ cups celery strips
1 large onion, cut into 8 wedges
1 medium green pepper, cut in strips
3 tablespoons salad oil
2 tablespoons cornstarch
1 cup cold water
1 tablespoon soy sauce
1½ teaspoons salt
1 cup diced cooked pork or other meat (or use 1 can, 9¼ ounces
                              tuna, drained and flaked)
1⅓ cups boiling water
1⅓ cups enriched pre-cooked rice

Sauté garlic, celery, onion, and green pepper in oil until tender but crisp. Blend cornstarch with 2 tablespoons cold water. Add remaining cold water and soy sauce to vegetables. Gradually stir in cornstarch. Add 1 teaspoon salt and meat. Cook and stir until mixture is thickened. *Next:* form a well in center; pour in 1 cup boiling water. Sprinkle in rice and ½ teaspoon salt. Pour remaining boiling water over rice; stir to moisten rice. Cover, remove from heat, and let stand 5 minutes. Serve meat mixture over rice. Garnish with toasted almonds or chow mein noodles, if desired. *Serves 4.*

SAVORY RICE AND LAMB KEBABS

¼ cup salad oil
2 tablespoons vinegar
1 package dehydrated onion soup mix
2 cloves garlic, split
1 pound boned lamb, cut in 1-inch cubes
2 cups water
1⅓ cups enriched pre-cooked rice
1½ cups cooked peas
2 small tomatoes, cut in wedges

Combine oil, vinegar, 1 tablespoon of the soup mix, and 1 clove garlic in bowl. Add meat and stir to coat on all sides. Let stand to marinate at least 3 hours. (To marinate meat longer than 3 hours, refrigerate.) Then place meat on skewers and broil or grill until of desired doneness. *Meanwhile,* combine marinade, remaining soup mix, 1 clove garlic, and water. Bring to a boil. Discard garlic. Stir in rice, peas, and tomatoes. Cover and bring again to a boil; then simmer 5 minutes. Serve rice with the lamb kebabs. Makes about 5⅓ cups rice mixture plus lamb kebabs. *Serves 4–5.*

CHICKEN IN WHITE WINE SAUCE

2 pounds small white onions, peeled
8 small carrots
½ teaspoon salt
3 cups boiling water
2 broiling chickens, quartered
½ cup butter
1 cup dry white wine
1 cup heavy cream
1½ teaspoons salt
pepper
2 tablespoons all-purpose flour
1 egg yolk, beaten
2 cups enriched pre-cooked rice

Add onions, carrots, and ½ teaspoon salt to water and cook about 10 minutes. Drain. Meanwhile, brown chicken lightly in butter in a Dutch oven or a large kettle. Add wine, cream, onions and carrots, 1½ teaspoons salt, and pepper. Cover and simmer for 35–40 minutes, or until chicken is tender. Place chicken, onions, and carrots on a warm serving dish or platter. *Next:* pour off and reserve all except about ¾ cup liquid in kettle. Gradually blend flour with liquid in kettle, stirring until smooth. Then gradually add reserved liquid. Cook and stir until gravy thickens. Stir a little hot gravy into egg yolk. Add egg yolk to hot gravy and cook about 2 minutes or until thick. *Meanwhile:* prepare rice according to package directions. To serve, spoon gravy over rice and chicken. *Serves 4–6.*

SAVORY SAUCE

¼ cup butter
3 tablespoons all-purpose flour
1 teaspoon salt
⅛ teaspoon pepper
dash of nutmeg
2 tablespoons chopped parsley (optional)
2 cups milk

Melt butter in saucepan. Blend in flour, salt, pepper, nutmeg, and parsley. Gradually stir in milk. Bring to a boil over medium heat, stirring constantly. Then cook mixture gently, stirring constantly, until thickened and well blended—about 3–5 minutes. *Makes 2¼ cups sauce.*

CURRY SAUCE: Prepare as for Savory Sauce, adding ¼ teaspoon lemon juice and ½ teaspoon curry powder with the flour and other seasonings.

ALMOND SAUCE: Prepare as for Savory Sauce, adding ¼ cup chopped or slivered toasted almonds just before serving.

OLIVE SAUCE: Prepare as for Savory Sauce, omitting nutmeg and adding ¼ cup chopped stuffed olives with flour and seasonings.

RICE WITH A PLUS-FLAVOR

Prepare 4 servings (1⅓ cups) enriched pre-cooked rice as per package directions, adding *one* of the suggestions below as directed. If more or fewer servings of rice are desired, adjust these amounts accordingly.

APPLE RICE: Add 1½ cups finely diced unpeeled red apples to the water before bringing to a boil.

ALMOND RICE: Add ¼ cup slivered or chopped almonds (or other nuts) to the rice just before serving.

CELERY RICE: Sauté ½ cup chopped celery in the butter until tender; then add water and salt and bring to a boil.

CHEESE RICE: Add ¾ to 1 cup grated Cheddar or process American cheese to rice and mix lightly just before serving.

CHIVE RICE: Add 2 tablespoons finely chopped chives to rice and mix lightly just before serving.

CURRANT OR RAISIN RICE: Add ¼ cup dried currants or raisins to water before bringing to a boil.

LEMON RICE: Add 1½ teaspoons grated lemon rind when you stir the rice into the water.

MINTED RICE: Add 2 tablespoons chopped fresh mint when you stir in rice. If desired, also add ½ teaspoon sugar.

OLIVE RICE: Add ¼ cup chopped stuffed olives when you stir in the rice.

PARSLEY RICE: Add 2 tablespoons chopped parsley when you stir rice into the water.

PIMIENTO RICE: Add 2 tablespoons chopped pimiento when you stir the rice into the water.

FLORENTINE RICE

¼ cup chopped onion
3 tablespoons butter
1⅓ cups water
1 teaspoon salt
dash of pepper
1⅓ cups enriched pre-cooked rice
½ cup cooked chopped spinach (or use finely chopped raw
                              spinach)
½ cup grated Cheddar or Parmesan cheese

Sauté onion in butter over medium heat until golden brown. Add water, salt, and pepper; bring to a boil. Then stir in rice and spinach. Cover, remove from heat, and let stand 5 minutes. Before serving, fluff lightly with a fork and sprinkle with cheese. *Serves 4–5.*

BRANDIED FRUIT RICE

1 cup chopped candied fruit
2 tablespoons brandy
1 cup milk
½ cup water

½ teaspoon salt
1⅓ cups enriched pre-cooked rice
½ cup milk
½ cup sugar
4 egg yolks, beaten
1 teaspoon vanilla
1 cup heavy cream
⅓ cup pecan halves

Combine candied fruit and brandy in a small bowl; set aside. Combine 1 cup milk, water, and salt, in a saucepan. Cover and bring to a boil. Stir in rice, cover, remove from heat, and let stand 10 minutes. *Meanwhile:* combine ½ cup milk, sugar, egg yolks, and vanilla in top of double boiler. Cook over boiling water, stirring constantly, until thick—about 6 minutes. Combine with rice and chill. Whip the cream and fold into chilled rice mixture with fruit mixture and pecans. Chill until thickened. *Serves 8–10.*

CUSTARD SAUCE

2 egg yolks, slightly beaten
2 tablespoons sugar
1½ cups milk
½ teaspoon vanilla (or ½ teaspoon grated lemon rind)

Combine egg yolks, sugar, and milk in a saucepan. Cook and stir over low heat until mixture is thickened and coats a dry metal spoon. Cool thoroughly; then stir in vanilla. Chill, if desired. Makes about 1½ cups sauce.

RISOTTO RICE ROMA

2 tablespoons fat
1 small onion
1 cup parboiled rice
2½ cups meat stock or broth
grated cheese (if desired)

Heat the fat and brown the chopped onion and rice in it. Add the stock or broth and cook until the rice is tender and the liquid has been absorbed. Taste and add salt if necessary. Just before serving, a little grated cheese may be stirred in. *Serves 6.*

GREEK PILAF

2½ cups chicken stock *or* chicken bouillon
1 tablespoon lemon juice
1½ teaspoons salt
1 bay leaf
¼ teaspoon white pepper
¼ to ½ cup butter or margarine
1 cup parboiled rice

Heat chicken stock, lemon juice, salt, bay leaf, white pepper, and half the butter or margarine in top of double boiler. Add rice. Cover and cook 35 minutes over boiling water, stirring occasionally. Remove from heat; turn into a well-buttered casserole, 1½-quart size; top with remaining butter, cover, bake in a moderate oven, 350°F., 10 minutes. Serve hot. *Serves 6.*

PICADILLO

3 tablespoons chopped green pepper
1 cup chopped onions
1 clove garlic, chopped
1½ pounds ground beef
2 tablespoons salad oil
1½ cups diced cooked ham
1 can (1 pound) kidney beans
1 can (1 pound) tomatoes
1 teaspoon salt
1 teaspoon chili powder
2⅔ cups enriched pre-cooked rice

Sauté green pepper, onions, garlic, and beef in oil until lightly browned. Stir in ham, beans, tomatoes, salt, and chili powder. Simmer about 30 minutes, stirring occasionally. (If mixture becomes too thick, gradually add ¼ cup water.) Meanwhile, prepare rice according to package directions. Arrange rice in a ring on serving platter. Fill center of rice ring with meat and bean mixture. Arrange Sautéed Bananas around rice as garnish, if desired. *Serves 6.*

SAUTÉED BANANAS

Slice 3 or 4 firm bananas in half lengthwise, or cut in 1-inch pieces. Sauté in 2 tablespoons butter just until thoroughly heated. Serve warm with any highly seasoned entrée. *Serves 4–6.*

GOLDEN PEANUT RICE

½ cup raisins
¼ teaspoon curry powder
3 tablespoons butter *or* margarine, melted
⅓ cup finely chopped parsley
¼ cup finely chopped peanuts
¼ teaspoon salt
4 cups hot cooked parboiled rice

Soak raisins in hot water until soft; drain. Blend curry powder into butter. Mix all ingredients into hot rice. *Serves 6.*

MINCEMEAT RICE

½ cup chopped onion
2 tablespoons butter or margarine
3 cups cooked rice
⅔ cup brandied mincemeat

Cook onion in butter until tender. Add rice and mincemeat. Blend and heat thoroughly. Serve as accompaniment to meat or poultry. *Serves 6.*

BEEFED-UP RICE

½ cup diced green pepper
2 tablespoons butter or margarine
1 cup uncooked rice

> 2 cups beef broth
> 1 teaspoon salt
> ½ cup chopped pimiento

Cook green pepper in butter until tender. Add rice, broth, and salt. Heat to boiling; stir once. Cover, reduce heat, and simmer for 14 minutes, or until liquid is absorbed. Remove from heat and toss lightly with pimiento. Serve hot. *Serves 4.*

RICE, GREEN BEANS, AND SOUR CREAM

> 1 can (4½ ounces) sliced mushrooms
> ¼ cup chopped onions
> 2 tablespoons butter or margarine
> 1 can (1 pound) green beans
> 1½ cups cooked rice
> 1 can (2 ounces) pimiento, chopped
> ½ teaspoon salt
> ¼ teaspoon pepper
> ½ cup sour cream

Cook mushrooms and onion in butter until tender. Add beans, rice, pimiento, and seasonings. Fold in sour cream and heat slowly. *Serves 6.*

ORIENTAL RICE

> 3 tablespoons butter or margarine, melted
> ¼ teaspoon curry powder
> 4 cups hot cooked rice
> ⅓ cup finely chopped parsley
> 1 teaspoon salt
> ¼ cup finely chopped peanuts

Blend curry powder into butter; mix into rice with remaining ingredients. *Serves 6.*

EASY DOES IT RICE

> 1⅓ cups water
> 2 teaspoons butter (optional)

1⅓ cups enriched pre-cooked rice
1 tablespoon dehydrated salad dressing mix, any flavor

Bring water and butter to a boil. Stir in rice and dehydrated salad dressing mix. Cover, remove from heat, and let stand 5 minutes. Fluff with a fork before serving. Serve with steak and other entrées. Makes 2⅔ cups. *Serves 4.*

TANGY ORANGE RICE

1 cup diced celery
3 tablespoons chopped onion
¼ cup butter
1⅓ cups enriched pre-cooked rice
1 cup water
½ cup orange juice
1½ teaspoons salt
½ teaspoon sugar
1–2 teaspoons grated orange rind

Sauté celery and onion in butter until tender but not browned. Stir in rice, water, orange juice, salt, and sugar. Bring quickly to a boil over high heat. Cover, remove from heat, and let stand 5 minutes. Add grated orange rind and fluff with a fork before serving. Serve with ham, duck, or chicken. *Serves 4–5.*

SAVORY LEMON RICE

½ clove garlic, minced
2 tablespoons butter
1⅓ cups enriched pre-cooked rice
1⅓ cups chicken broth (or use 1 chicken bouillon cube
                     dissolved in 1⅓ cups hot water)
½ teaspoon salt
2 tablespoons chopped parsley
1 tablespoon lemon juice
1 teaspoon grated lemon rind

Sauté garlic in butter until golden brown. Stir in rice, broth, and salt. Bring quickly to a boil over high heat. Cover, remove from heat, and let stand 5 minutes. Add parsley, lemon juice, and rind and fluff with a fork before serving. Serve with seafood or chicken. *Serves 4.*

TUNA-RICE PUFF

1. Melt ⅓ cup butter or margarine. Add ¼ cup flour, 1 tablespoon salt, ¼ teaspoon pepper. Gradually add 1½ cups of milk. Cook, stirring.

2. Beat 2 egg yolks slightly. Stir a little of this hot sauce into yolks, then add yolks to cooking sauce and mix thoroughly. Cook 2 minutes longer, stirring constantly.

3. Remove from heat. Fold in 1 can (7 ounces) tuna, flaked; add 2 tablespoons grated onion, 1 tablespoon lemon juice, 2 cups cooked parboiled rice.

4. Beat 2 egg whites until stiff but not dry. Fold into mixture. Pour mixture into ungreased 1½-quart casserole. Cut 3 slices process American cheese in half, diagonally.

5. Arrange cheese slices around edge of casserole in an attractive pattern. Set casserole in a pan of hot water. Bake in 350°F. oven about 40 minutes or until firm.

6. *To make a meal:* serve with frosty tomato juice to start, sautéed zucchini and yellow squash, rye bread, fresh strawberry-rhubarb tarts for dessert. *Serves 6.*

13.

Vegetable Dishes

LUNCHEON-IN-ONE-DISH

2 cups enriched pre-cooked rice
1½ cups milk
½ teaspoon salt
¼ teaspoon pepper
1¼ cups grated Swiss cheese
¼ cup Parmesan cheese
1 can (10½ ounces) asparagus spears, drained
½ to 1 pound cooked ham, cut in strips

Combine rice, milk, salt, and pepper and bring to a boil. Add
½ cup Swiss cheese and the Parmesan cheese. Cook until mixture
thickens. Pour into buttered 9-inch pie plate. Arrange asparagus
on top, with tips pointing toward center. Place strips of ham
between. Sprinkle with remaining Swiss cheese. Cover and bake
15 minutes in 350°F. oven. Remove cover and bake until brown,
about 10 minutes. *Serves 4–6.*

GARDEN JAMBALAYA

½ cup diced celery
⅓ cup thinly sliced onion
3 tablespoons butter
2 cups thinly sliced cucumber*
1 tomato, peeled and cut into wedges*

    1 cup green pepper strips*
    2 cups hot bouillon
    1 teaspoon salt
    ⅛ teaspoon pepper
    1 tablespoon lemon juice
    1 tablespoon cornstarch
    2 tablespoons water
    1⅓ cups enriched pre-cooked rice

Sauté celery and onion in butter in a large skillet until tender. Stir in vegetables, 1 cup of the bouillon, salt, pepper, and lemon juice. Mix cornstarch and water until smooth. Gradually stir into vegetables. Make a well in the center of the vegetables; pour in rice. Carefully pour remaining 1 cup bouillon over rice, moistening rice evenly. Cover and simmer 5 minutes, or until rice is tender. *Serves 6.*

* Or use 4 cups assorted seasonal fresh vegetables.

ZESTY RICE-STUFFED ACORN SQUASH

    3 acorn squash
    2 tablespoons melted butter or margarine
    1½ teaspoons salt
    ½ teaspoon pepper
    ½ cup sour cream
    1 teaspoon prepared mustard
    ½ teaspoon celery salt
    3 cups cooked rice
    ¼ cup chopped green onions
    5 slices bacon, cooked and crumbled

Wash and cut acorn squash in half lengthwise; discard seeds and stringy fiber. Brush with melted butter; season with salt and pepper. Turn flat side down on greased baking pan. Bake at 375°F. until tender, 30–45 minutes. Blend sour cream with mustard and celery salt. Fold in rice, green onion, and crumbled bacon and heat through. Spoon into baked acorn squash shells. *Serves 6.*

VEGETABLES AND RICE

1 package (10 ounces) frozen mixed garden vegetables
2 tablespoons finely chopped onion
2 tablespoons butter
1⅓ cups water
½ teaspoon salt
dash of pepper
1⅓ cups enriched pre-cooked rice

Prepare mixed vegetables as directed on package. Meanwhile, sauté onion in butter in a saucepan. Then add water, salt, and pepper; bring to a boil. Stir in rice. Cover, remove from heat, and let stand 5 minutes. Add drained cooked vegetables and mix lightly with a fork. *Serves 6.*

RICE ITALIENNE

¼ cup chopped onion
1 clove garlic, crushed
2 tablespoons butter or salad oil
2 small tomatoes, cut into wedges
1½ cups chicken broth or bouillon
½ teaspoon salt
1⅓ cups enriched pre-cooked rice
2 tablespoons grated Parmesan cheese

Sauté onion and garlic in butter for 2–3 minutes. Add tomatoes and sauté about 1 minute. Then add broth and salt. Cover and bring to a boil. Stir in rice. Cover, remove from heat, and let stand 5 minutes. Add cheese and fluff with fork. Serve with steak. *Serves 4–5.*

MEXICAN VEGETABLE MEAL

1 cup enriched pre-cooked rice
2½ cups chicken broth
1 teaspoon seasoned salt
3 avocados, peeled, diced

1 teaspoon grated onion
2 medium tomatoes, finely diced
1½ teaspoons salt
1 tablespoon lemon juice
2 tablespoons mayonnaise
¼ teaspoon Tabasco sauce

Combine rice, chicken broth, and seasoned salt in a saucepan. Bring to a boil, stir once. Cover and reduce heat. Simmer for 25 minutes or until rice is tender and liquid absorbed. Chill. Mix avocados with onion, tomatoes, salt, lemon juice, mayonaise, and hot pepper sauce. Cover and chill. When ready to serve, toss both mixtures together gently. Mound on vegetable leaves. *Serves 6.*

SPANISH PICNIC VEGETALA

2 cups cold cooked enriched pre-cooked rice
½ cup cold cooked cubed carrots
½ cup cold cooked cauliflower
⅓ cup olive oil
1 tablespoon lemon juice
1 teaspoon onion juice
2 teaspoons wine vinegar
1 teaspoon celery seed
½ teaspoon dry mustard
dash of coarse-ground black pepper
2 tablespoons drained capers

Combine rice and vegetables. Make a Sauce Vinaigrette by combining oil, lemon juice, onion juice, vinegar, celery seed, dry mustard, salt, and pepper. Use enough of this just to hold salad together. Sprinkle capers over top. *Serves 6.*

SUGGESTION: Many things can be added to extend this salad—tuna fish, sardines, anchovies, or diced cold meat or poultry. Use a bit more Sauce Vinaigrette.

GOLD-AND-WHITE BAKE

3 cups cooked parboiled rice

2 packages (10½ ounces each) frozen
yellow squash, cooked
½ teaspoon salt
2 tablespoons instant-minced onion
1 can (10½ ounces) condensed cream
of chicken soup
2 tablespoons chopped pimiento
⅛ teaspoon pepper
1 cup grated Cheddar cheese

Combine all ingredients except cheese and heat. Turn into a
greased casserole. Top with grated cheese. Bake in 375°F. oven
15–20 minutes or until cheese is melted. *Serves 6–8.*

IMPERIAL VEGETABLE RICE

4 cups enriched pre-cooked rice
3 tomatoes, cut in thin strips
1 green pepper, cut in strips
¼ cup slivered pimiento
4 scallions, very finely sliced
1 can (8 ounces) peas
1 can (4 ounces) black olives, chopped
3 tablespoons wine vinegar
1 teaspoon dry mustard
salt, pepper
1 clove garlic, mashed

Cook rice according to package directions. Combine remaining
ingredients; toss with rice to mix. Chill before serving; mound on
platter. Garnish with watercress, tomato strips, black olives, cucumber slices, if desired. *Serves 4–5.*

SUGGESTION: To make a meal, serve with king crab cocktail, cold
Vitello Tonnato, salt sticks, and chocolate mousse for dessert.

RICE-AND-PEAS

2 cups enriched pre-cooked rice
1⅔ cups water

1 teaspoon salt
¾ cup Italian salad dressing
½ teaspoon fresh-ground black pepper
1 tablespoon grated onion
½ cup chopped pimiento
1½ cups diced celery
1½ cups cooked green peas

Combine rice, water, and salt in a saucepan. Heat to boiling; cover and simmer about 5 minutes or until the water is absorbed. Blend salad dressing and pepper; toss gently with warm rice. Stir in onion and pimiento and cool. Add celery and peas to cooled rice mixture. Chill. *Serves 4–5.*

14.

Rice and Meat

PEPPER STEAK

1–1½ pounds lean round or sirloin steak,
    cut in thin pieces (strips across the
    grain)
salt and pepper, according to taste
2 tablespoons oil
½ cup chopped onion
1 clove garlic, minced
1 cup water
1 envelope beef broth
One 1-pound can stewed tomatoes
1 green pepper, cut in strips
½ cup water
1 tablespoon cornstarch
1 tablespoon soy sauce
3 cups hot, cooked rice

Season strips of steak to taste with salt and pepper. Brown in oil
over medium high heat. Add onions and garlic; sauté until tender.
Stir in 1 cup water and beef broth. Bring to boil, then lower heat
and simmer 20 minutes. Add tomatoes and green pepper. Cover
and simmer 10 more minutes. Blend remaining ingredients and
stir into meat mixture. Heat until sauce becomes thickened and
shiny. *Serves 6.*

BEEFED-UP RICE

1½ cups diced celery
¼ cup minced onion
2 tablespoons butter or margarine
2 cups cooked rice
1 teaspoon salt
1 pound ground beef
¼ cup water
1 can (10½ ounces) condensed tomato
  soup, undiluted
⅓ cup grated Parmesan cheese

In skillet, sauté celery and onion in butter until tender. Spread cooked rice in buttered 1½-quart casserole; top with celery-onion mixture. Add salt to beef and brown in skillet; spoon into casserole. Mix water with soup; pour over beef. Bake at 375°F. for 30 minutes. Sprinkle cheese over top and return to oven 5 to 10 minutes. *Serves 6.*

RICE AND BEEF de ROMA

1 pound ground beef
½ cup chopped onion
¼ cup diced green pepper
1 garlic clove, minced
1 teaspoon salt
1 teaspoon parsley flakes
½ teaspoon leaf oregano
½ teaspoon basil
¼ teaspoon black pepper
1 can (8 ounces) tomato sauce
1 can (1 pound) stewed tomatoes
3 cups cooked rice
1 pound cream-style cottage cheese
⅓ cup Parmesan cheese

Brown ground beef in skillet. Drain off excess fat. Stir in onion, green pepper, and garlic and sauté until tender. Add seasonings, tomato sauce, and tomatoes. Simmer 5 minutes to blend flavors. Into buttered 3-quart baking dish, layer the rice, cottage cheese, and meat sauce. Bake, uncovered, at 350°F. for 30 minutes. Remove and sprinkle with Parmesan cheese. Bake additional 10 minutes. *Serves 8.*

RICE AND HAM SNACKS

3 cups hot cooked rice
3 tablespoons butter or margarine
1 egg, beaten
¼ cup pickle relish
1 tablespoon chopped parsley
8 slices boiled ham (4 x 4 inches)
8 slices American cheese (4 x 4 inches)
16 paper-thin onion slices
8 slices tomato
2 tablespoons grated Parmesan cheese

Combine hot rice and butter. Stir in egg, pickle relish, and parsley. Mix well and spoon into a greased sheet pan, 15½ x 10½ inches. Spread evenly. Bake at 350°F. for 10 minutes. *Meanwhile:* arrange ham, cheese, onion, and tomato slices in eight stacks. Sprinkle tomatoes with Parmesan cheese. Arrange the stacks on the baked rice. Make sure all the rice is covered. Broil just long enough to melt the cheese. Cut into squares and serve immediately. *Serves 8.*

SPEEDY BEEF STROGANOFF

½ cup uncooked rice
2 cups water
1 1½-ounce envelope onion soup mix
½ teaspoon salt
2 cups cubed cooked beef
1 4-ounce can sliced mushrooms
2 pimientos, chopped
1 cup sour cream
2 tablespoons ketchup
2 tablespoons sherry

Combine rice, water, soup mix, and salt in a saucepan. Bring to a boil. Stir. Cover and cook over low heat 15 minutes, or until rice is tender. Add remaining ingredients and heat through. *Serves 4.*

CALICO RICE IN FRANKFURTER CROWN

¼ cup salad oil
2 tablespoons vinegar
2 tablespoons prepared mustard
1½ teaspoons salt
⅛ teaspoon pepper
4½ cups hot cooked rice (1½ cups rice cooked in 3 cups chicken broth)
2 hard-cooked eggs, diced
1¼ cups sliced ripe olives
1 cup diced celery
¾ cup chopped green onions
½ cup chopped sour pickle
½ cup crumbled crisp bacon
1 tablespoon celery seed
1½ pounds frankfurters

Blend salad oil with vinegar, mustard, salt, and pepper. Pour over hot rice; mix well. Add hard-cooked eggs, olives, celery, green onions, pickle, bacon, and celery seed; toss together. Cut frankfurters in half crosswise, and stand them on end in a casserole to form a crown. Fill with rice mixture. Cover and bake at 450°F. for 15 minutes. *Serves 8.*

SKILLET GUMBO

1 cup cooked ham, diced (canned luncheon meat may be substituted)
½ cup green pepper, chopped
½ cup onion, chopped
¼ pound okra, cut in one-inch pieces
1 cup canned tomatoes
½ cup water
¾ teaspoon salt
dash of pepper

½ cup rice, uncooked

Combine all ingredients *except* the rice in a heavy skillet. Bring to a boil. Cover and simmer for 10 minutes. Stir in rice. Replace lid and simmer 20 minutes or until rice is tender. *Serves 2.*

SOUR CREAM MEATBALLS ON RICE

Meatballs:

> ½ pound beef, ground
> ¼ cup tomato sauce (canned)
> 1 tablespoon grated onion
> ½ cup bread crumbs
> 1 egg
> ½ teaspoon salt
> dash of pepper
> 2 tablespoons butter or margarine

Sauce:

> 2 tablespoons chopped green pepper
> 1 tablespoon flour
> 1 cup canned tomatoes
> 1½ cups hot cooked rice
> ½ cup sour cream
> ½ teaspoon salt
> dash of pepper
> ½ teaspoon Worcestershire sauce

Combine all ingredients in step one except butter and mix thoroughly. Form into 2-inch balls. (Makes approximately 6 balls.) Melt butter in saucepan and sauté meatballs until partly done. Remove from pan and sauté green pepper. Add flour and brown. Mix in tomatoes, breaking them up by stirring with fork. Add sour cream and seasonings. Return meatballs to sauce and simmer for 15 minutes. Serve over beds of hot fluffy rice. *Serves 2.*

RICE AND HAM SNACKS

> 3 cups hot cooked rice
> 3 tablespoons butter or margarine
> 1 egg, beaten

1 tablespoon chopped parsley
6 slices boiled ham (4 x 4 inches)
6 slices American cheese (4 x 4 inches)
12 paper thin onion slices
6 slices tomato
6 stuffed olives, sliced

Combine hot rice, butter, egg, and parsley. Mix well and spread into a greased sheet pan (12 x 8 inches). Bake for 10 minutes in a 350°F. oven. *Meanwhile:* as rice is cooking, make 6 snacks of 1 slice ham, then cheese; place onion slices on top, add a tomato slice, and top with 3 slices of stuffed olives on each. Remove rice crust from oven and place the 6 snacks on the rice crust, being sure that all the rice is covered with the snacks. Broil under the broiler just long enough to melt the cheese. Slice and serve immediately. *Serves 6.*

RICE MEDLEY

2 tablespoons butter or margarine
½ cup diced celery
2 cups cooked rice
1 4¼-ounce can deviled ham
1 egg, beaten
¼ teaspoon salt
dash of pepper
½ cup Cheddar cheese, grated
crumbled bacon

Melt butter in skillet; sauté celery until tender but not brown. Add rice, ham, egg, salt, and pepper. Heat thoroughly, stirring constantly. Pour into buttered casserole. Top with cheese and bacon. Place under broiler only until cheese is melted. *Serves 4.*

LAMB AND OLIVES ON RICE

1 egg, slightly beaten
¼ cup fine dry crumbs
2 cups water
2 teaspoons salt

¼ teaspoon pepper
1½ pounds lean ground lamb
¼ cup flour
2 tablespoons shortening
1 teaspoon paprika
3 tablespoons brown sugar
2 tablespoons lemon juice
¾ cup sliced stuffed olives
3 cups hot cooked rice

Blend together egg, crumbs, ½ cup of the water, 1½ teaspoons of the salt, and pepper. Add meat and mix thoroughly. Shape into 18 small balls; roll in 2 tablespoons of the flour. Brown meatballs in shortening and remove from pan. Pour off drippings, reserving 2 tablespoons. In same pan, blend drippings and remaining 2 tablespoons flour. Add remaining salt, paprika, brown sugar, and lemon juice. Cook until thickened, stirring constantly. Add meatballs to sauce; Cover pan. Simmer about 20 minutes, stirring occasionally. Add olives and cook uncovered about 5 minutes, stirring frequently. Serve over the hot rice. *Serves 6 (3 meatballs for each serving)*.

PORCUPINE MEATBALLS

1 pound ground beef
½ cup uncooked rice
1 teaspoon salt
⅛ teaspoon pepper
1 small onion, sliced
½ green pepper, sliced
1 tablespoon shortening
2½ cups tomato juice
dash of nutmeg
salt and pepper to taste

Combine ground beef, rice, salt, and pepper. Pour into small balls about 1½ inches in diameter. Place in baking dish. In a skillet, brown onions and green pepper in shortening. Add tomato juice, nutmeg, and salt and pepper to taste. Pour over meatballs. Cover baking dish. Bake in moderate oven (350°F.) about 1 hour or until rice is very tender. *Makes 8 porcupines.*

RICE PICADILLO
(Beef Tips with Spanish Olives and Rice)

½ cup flour
2 teaspoons salt
½ teaspoon pepper
2 pounds round steak, cut thin
4 tablespoons butter or margarine
2 cups beef bouillon or water
1 cup milk
¾ cup sliced green olives
4 cups cooked rice

Combine flour, salt, and pepper. Cut round steak in strips and roll in seasoned flour. Melt butter in Dutch oven; add meat and sauté until brown. Add bouillon; cover and simmer about 45 minutes or until meat begins to be tender. Add milk and olives; cover and simmer another 30 minutes. Serve over beds of hot fluffy rice. *Serves 8.*

HAM AND RICE CROQUETTES

½ medium onion, chopped
2 teaspoons parsley, minced
2 teaspoons butter or margarine
2 tablespoons flour
½ cup milk
½ teaspoon salt
½ teaspoon pepper
½ teaspoon prepared mustard
½ teaspoon lemon juice
2 cups ground ham
1 cup cooked rice
1 teaspoon celery salt
1 egg
2 tablespoons water
fat for frying

Chop onion and parsley fine. Melt butter in small saucepan. Add flour and mix until smooth. Add milk and cook, stirring constantly until sauce thickens. Add salt, pepper, mustard, and lemon juice. Combine sauce with ham, chopped onion, parsley, celery salt, and cooked rice. Mix well. Chill. Shape into balls or cones. Beat eggs slightly, add water; place crumbs on waxed paper. Roll croquettes in bread crumbs then in egg mixture, then again in bread crumbs. Heat enough fat to reach a depth of about 2 to 2½ inches at 390°F. Fry croquettes for about 3 minutes or until golden brown. Drain on paper toweling. *Makes 10 croquettes.* Serve with Sharp Cheese Sauce.

SHARP CHEESE SAUCE

    2 tablespoons butter or margarine, melted
    1½ tablespoons flour
    1 cup milk
    ½ cup grated sharp cheese
    1 cup green peas
    2 hard-cooked eggs, chopped
    1 tablespoon pimiento, chopped

Melt butter and blend in flour. Add milk and cook until slightly thickened over low heat. Add cheese and stir until smooth. Add peas, eggs, and pimiento. Serve over Ham and Rice Croquettes.

LAMB TERRAPIN ON HERB RICE

    1 package (6 ounces) herb-flavored rice mix
    2 cups cut-up cooked lamb
    2 hard-cooked eggs, chopped
    2 tablespoons lemon juice
    2 tablespoons butter or margarine
    2 tablespoons flour
    1 teaspoon salt
    1½ teaspoons dry mustard
    ⅛ teaspoon pepper
    2 cups milk (substitute with juices from roast lamb)
    1 teaspoon Worcestershire sauce
    ⅓ cup chopped parsley

Cook rice according to package directions. Meanwhile, combine cut-up lamb and hard-cooked eggs; sprinkle with lemon juice. In saucepan melt butter. Blend in flour, salt, dry mustard, and pepper. Stir in milk and Worcestershire sauce. Cook, stirring constantly, until mixture thickens and comes to a boil. Add lamb, egg, and lemon juice; heat thoroughly. Combine hot cooked herb-flavored rice mix with parsley. Serve with creamed lamb mixture. *Serves 4–6.*

QUICKIE BEEF STROGANOFF

1 package (6 ounces) beef-flavored rice mix
2 cups cold cooked beef, cut into strips
1 can (3 ounces) sliced or chopped mushrooms
½ to ¾ cup sour cream

Put rice on to cook according to package directions; cook 20 minutes. Add remaining ingredients. Cover and simmer 5 minutes longer. *Serves 4–6.*

HAPPY HAM KABOBS

1 package (6 ounces) curry-flavored rice mix
2 green peppers, cut into squares
2 cups cold cooked ham cubes (about 1-inch square)
1 can (13¼ ounces) pineapple chunks
1 can (6 ounces) mushroom caps
5 or 6 12-inch skewers

Cook rice according to package directions. Meanwhile, cook green pepper squares in boiling salted water for 5 minutes; drain. Alternate ingredients on skewers. Brush kabobs generously with Tangy Tomato Sauce. Broil kabobs 5 minutes on each side. Serve with hot cooked curry-flavored rice. *Serves 5–6.*

TANGY TOMATO SAUCE

1 can (8 ounces) tomato sauce
2 tablespoons vinegar
2 tablespoons molasses
1 tablespoon Worcestershire sauce

Combine all ingredients. Brush generously on kabobs during broiling. *Makes 1 cup.*

SWEET AND PUNGENT PORK

1 package (6 ounces) chicken-flavored rice mix
½ cup vinegar
¼ cup brown sugar
1 cup water, divided
1 tablespoon molasses
1 cup pineapple cubes
1 green pepper, cut into ¾-inch pieces
2 tablespoons cornstarch
2 cups cooked pork, cut into thin strips

Cook rice according to package directions. Meanwhile, combine vinegar, brown sugar, ¾ cup water, molasses, pineapple cubes, green pepper in large saucepan; heat to boiling. Combine remaining ¼ cup water with cornstarch. Pour slowly into heated liquid in saucepan; stir constantly until mixture thickens and begins to boil. Add pork; continue cooking about 5 minutes. Serve sweet and sour mixture over hot cooked chicken-flavored mix. *Serves 4–6.*

FILL-YOU-UP MEATBALLS

1 package herb-flavored rice mix
2 pounds ground round steak
1 can cream of mushroom soup
½ cup milk
1 tablespoon butter or margarine
¼ teaspoon oregano (optional)

Cook rice according to package directions. Cool. Combine cooked rice, raw ground beef. Form into 1½ inch meat balls. Melt butter in skillet and brown meatballs. Combine soup with milk and pour over meatballs. Top with oregano if desired. Cover and simmer 45 minutes. *Makes 12–16 meatballs.*

ORIENTALIA FRIED RICE

2 small pork chops
2 tablespoons fat

⅔ cup chopped onion
1 cup parboiled rice
1 egg, beaten (optional)

Remove meat from chop bones and dice. Brown in fat in a skillet. Meanwhile, cook rice according to package directions. Remove meat from pan and brown onions in remaining fat. Return pork to pan and add cooked rice. Toss lightly until brown. Add egg, if desired, and cook briefly. Serve in individual bowls. Garnish, if desired, with chopped green onions. *Serves 4–6.*

RICE AND BEEF À LA DEUTSCH

1 egg
½ cup milk
1 cup soft bread crumbs
1 pound ground beef
2 tablespoons chopped onion
1 tablespoon chopped parsley
1½ teaspoons salt
⅛ teaspoon pepper
1 can (10½ ounces) condensed onion soup
1 cup water
1 tablespoon sugar
1 tablespoon cornstarch
1 teaspoon salt
¼ teaspoon ginger
⅛ teaspoon pepper
2 tablespoons vinegar
1 tablespoon butter
1 cup cooked peas and carrots, peas or carrot slices
1⅓ cups enriched pre-cooked rice

Blend egg and milk in mixing bowl. Stir in bread crumbs. Let stand until milk is absorbed. Then add beef, onion, parsley, 1½ teaspoons salt, and ⅛ teaspoon pepper; mix well. Combine remaining ingredients except vegetables and rice. Spread vegetables in a shallow 1½-quart baking dish. Spread rice over vegetables; then pour on soup mixture. Spoon meat mixture over top, placing spoonfuls close together to cover soup mixture entirely. Bake at 350°F. for 35 to 40 minutes, or until meat is browned. *Serves 4–6.*

RICE MEATBALLS

2 cans (8 ounces each) tomato sauce (or use 2½ cups tomato
                    juice instead of sauce and water)
½ cup water
1 cup enriched pre-cooked rice
1 pound ground beef
1 egg, slightly beaten
2 teaspoons grated onion
2 teaspoons salt
⅛ teaspoon marjoram (optional)
dash of pepper
½ teaspoon sugar

Mix tomato sauce and water. Combine rice, beef, egg, onion,
salt, marjoram, pepper, and ½ cup tomato mixture, mixing
lightly. Shape into 18 balls. Place in skillet. Blend sugar with
remaining tomato mixture; pour into skillet. Bring to a boil; then
cover and simmer about 15 minutes, basting occasionally with
the tomato mixture in skillet. *Serves 6.*

MEAT-CRUST RICE PIE

1 pound ground beef
½ cup dry bread crumbs
¼ cup grated onion
¼ cup chopped green pepper
1½ teaspoons salt
⅛ teaspoon oregano
⅛ teaspoon pepper
2 cans (8 ounces each) tomato sauce
1 cup water
1⅓ cups enriched pre-cooked rice
½ teaspoon salt
1 cup grated Cheddar cheese
4–6 tomato slices (optional)

Combine beef, bread crumbs, onion, green pepper, 1½ teaspoons
salt, oregano, pepper, and ½ cup of the tomato sauce; mix well.
Pat meat mixture into bottom and sides of a greased 9-inch pie
pan. *Next:* Combine remaining 1½ cans tomato sauce, water, rice,

½ teaspoon salt, and ½ cup of the cheese. Spoon into meat shell. Cover with aluminum foil. Bake at 350°F. for 25 minutes. Uncover, top with tomato slices and sprinkle with remaining cheese. Bake uncovered 10 to 15 minutes longer. To serve, cut in wedges. *Serves 5-6.*

APRICOT HAM ROLLS

1 can (12 ounces) apricot nectar
1 tablespoon prepared mustard
½ teaspoon salt
1 cup enriched pre-cooked rice
2 tablespoons finely chopped parsley
1 tablespoon butter
6–8 slices ham *or* spiced luncheon meat
1 tablespoon maple syrup

Combine 1⅓ cups of the apricot nectar, mustard, and salt in a skillet. Bring to a boil. Stir in rice. Cover and simmer 5 minutes. Add parsley and butter. Fluff lightly with a fork. Spoon rice mixture onto the slices of ham. Fold two opposite corners of ham over one another and attach with a toothpick (this leaves 2 ends open). Combine remaining apricot nectar and syrup in a skillet. Bring just to a boil. Add ham rolls and simmer over low heat, basting occasionally, until thoroughly heated—about 5 minutes. Makes 6–8 rolls. *Serves 3-4.*

APRICOT-RICE PORK ROAST

1 can (1 pound, 13 ounces) apricot halves
2¾-pound loin of pork roast
½ cup chopped celery
¼ cup butter
1⅓ cups water
¼ cup raisins
⅛ teaspoon ginger
½ teaspoon salt
1⅓ cups enriched pre-cooked rice

Drain apricot halves, reserving syrup. Roast pork at 350°F. about

2½ hours, or until meat thermometer registers 180°F., basting occasionally with drained apricot syrup. *Next:* cut apricot halves in half. Sauté celery in butter about 2 minutes. Add apricots, water, raisins, ginger, and salt. Bring to a boil. Stir in rice. Cover, remove from heat, and let stand 5 minutes. *Next:* remove pork from pan, place on heated platter, and keep warm. Drain fat from drippings in pan. Add rice mixture to the drippings in pan and return to oven for 15 minutes. To serve, cut between the chops of roast and stuff with some of the rice mixture; then arrange remainder around roast. *Or* serve the rice mixture as a side dish with the pork. Makes 3¾ cups rice mixture. *Serves 6.*

SUGGESTION: Serve this rice mixture with other meats, fish, or poultry.

SWISS VEAL ROLLS

1 package (8 ounces) sliced Swiss cheese
4 slices boiled ham
8 slices (about 12 ounces) veal scallopini
2 tablespoons all-purpose flour
1 teaspoon salt
⅛ teaspoon pepper
3 tablespoons butter
¼ cup minced onion
2 cups hot water
1 tablespoon lemon juice
1 can (4 ounces) mushrooms
1⅓ cups enriched pre-cooked rice

Cut 2 slices of cheese into 4 strips each. Cut ham slices in half. Place 1 strip of cheese and 1 piece of ham in the center of each slice of veal. Fold over edges of veal and fasten each roll with a toothpick. Combine flour, salt, and pepper. Roll the veal rolls in flour, and reserve remaining flour mixture. Sauté veal rolls in butter until golden brown on all sides. Remove from skillet and set aside. *Next:* add onion to butter remaining in skillet; sauté until transparent. Stir in remaining flour mixture. Gradually stir in hot water, blending until smooth. Add lemon juice and mushrooms. Bring to a boil. *Meanwhile:* cut remaining cheese into narrow strips. Combine with rice in a shallow 2½-quart baking dish. Pour hot mushroom mixture over rice. Top with veal rolls. Cover and bake at 400°F. for 20–25 minutes. Garnish with lemon wedges, if desired. Makes 8 veal rolls plus rice. *Serves 4.*

VEAL PIZZAIOLA

1 pound veal scallopini
3 tablespoons olive or salad oil
3 large cloves garlic
2 cans (1 pound, 12 ounces each) tomatoes
½ cup tomato juice or water
1 tablespoon sugar (optional)
2–3 teaspoons salt
1½ teaspoons oregano
⅛ teaspoon pepper
1⅓ cups enriched pre-cooked rice
4 slices Mozzarella *or* process American cheese, cut in strips

Sauté veal quickly in oil until lightly browned on both sides. Remove from skillet and keep warm. Reduce heat; sauté garlic in oil until golden brown. Add tomatoes, stirring gently and breaking tomatoes slightly. Stir in tomato juice and seasonings. Simmer for about 20 minutes. *Next:* remove garlic and bring mixture to a boil. Press rice into mixture around edge of skillet. Arrange veal in center. Cover, remove from heat, and let stand 5 minutes. Then place cheese on veal and broil just until lightly browned and bubbly. Makes 3½ cups rice plus veal. *Serves 4–6.*

SUGGESTION: If veal scallopini (Italian-style veal cutlets) are unavailable, use a 1-pound veal steak, ½-inch thick. Cut steak into 2-inch squares and split each by slicing almost to edge. Spread slices apart and pound flat.

LAMB CURRY

2½ pounds boned lamb shoulder, cut in 1¼-inch cubes
3 tablespoons all-purpose flour
2 teaspoons salt
⅛ teaspoon pepper

½ cup chopped onion
1 clove garlic, minced
1 tablespoon curry powder
1 can (1 pound) tomatoes
1 cup water
1 tablespoon butter
1 teaspoon lemon juice
2 cups enriched pre-cooked rice

Heat a few pieces of fat trimmed from lamb in a large skillet. Meanwhile, dust meat with mixture of flour, salt, and pepper. Remove pieces of fat from skillet; quickly brown the lamb in the drippings. Pour off any excess drippings; then add onion and garlic and sauté until transparent. Stir in curry powder, tomatoes, water, butter, and lemon juice. Bring to a boil. Cover and cook gently for 1 hour, or until meat is tender. *Next:* About 10 or 15 minutes before serving, prepare rice according to package directions. Serve curry over rice with condiments, such as chutney, coconut, peanuts, and crumbled crisp bacon, if desired. *Serves 5–6.*

MIDDLE EASTERN LAMB STEW

2 pounds boned lamb shoulder, cut in 1-inch cubes
¾ cup finely chopped onions
1 clove garlic, sliced
1 can (6 ounces) tomato paste
1 teaspoon salt
⅛ teaspoon pepper
1 cup Burgundy wine *or* unsweetened grapefruit juice
1½ cups water
¾ cup whole cranberry sauce
¼ teaspoon ginger
¼ teaspoon oregano
Lemon Rice

Heat several pieces of fat trimmed from lamb in large skillet; then remove pieces of fat and brown lamb in the drippings. Pour off excess drippings. Add onions, garlic, tomato paste, salt, pepper, wine, and water. Cover and simmer for 45 minutes. Add cranberry sauce, ginger, and oregano. Cook another 45 minutes or until meat is tender. More water may be added during cooking, if necessary. Serve with Lemon Rice. *Serves 4–6.*

LEMON RICE

Add 1½ teaspoons grated lemon rind when you stir the rice into the water.

STEAK 'N' RICE

1 cup uncooked rice
2 cups water
2 chicken bouillon cubes
1 tablespoons butter or margarine
1 teaspoon salt
½ teaspoon rosemary
½ teaspoon marjoram
½ teaspoon thyme

Combine all ingredients in a saucepan. Bring to a boil and stir well. Cover and cook over very low heat for 14 minutes or until rice is tender and the liquid is absorbed. Serve with your favorite steak. *Serves 4.*

STUFFED TOMATOES WITH RICE AND CHIPPED BEEF

6 tomatoes
1½ cups cooked rice
⅔ cup diced celery
½ medium onion, chopped
1 can (2½ ounces) dried beef, diced
½ cup sour cream
¼ teaspoon dill

Peel tomatoes. Scoop out center pulp and dice. Add cooked rice, celery, onions, and diced beef to tomato pulp. Mix in sour cream and season with dill. *Serves 6.*

DELICIOUS MEATBALLS

½ cup parboiled rice
1½ pounds ground beef
¼ cup finely diced onion
¼ cup finely diced green pepper
1½ teaspoons salt
⅛ teaspoon pepper
3 tablespoons fat
¼ cup milk
1 can (10½ ounces) condensed tomato soup
1 soup can water

Mix uncooked rice with all ingredients except soup and water. Shape into balls. Place in greased baking dish; cover with tomato soup and water. Bake in 300°F. oven for 90 minutes, covered. *Serves 6.*

HAM 'N' EGGS 'N' RICE

1 can (10¾ ounces) condensed Cheddar cheese soup
1 tablespoon chili sauce
1 can (4 ounces) sliced mushrooms, drained
1 cup diced cooked ham
1 teaspoon curry powder
¼ teaspoon garlic salt
4 hard-cooked eggs, cut in quarters
3 cups cooked parboiled rice

Combine cheese soup, chili sauce, mushrooms, ham, and seasonings. Heat thoroughly. Fold in eggs. Serve over mounds of hot rice. *Serves 4–5.*

VEAL ROLLS WITH MUSHROOM RICE

½ pound fresh mushrooms
2 tablespoons butter
6 slices boiled ham, cut in half
12 veal cutlets, pounded very thin

    3 tablespoons butter
    1 package (7 ounces) chicken-flavored rice mix
    1¾ cups hot water
    2 tablespoons butter
    ¼ cup Marsala wine
    2 tablespoons chopped parsley

Chop mushroom stems and some caps to make 2 cups. Slice remaining mushroom caps. Sauté chopped mushrooms in 1 tablespoon butter in a large skillet until softened. Remove from heat. Place a half slice of ham on each veal cutlet. Place about a tablespoon of mushroom mixture along one edge. Roll up. Repeat with remaining veal, ham, and mushroom filling to make 12 rolls. Set aside. *Next:* sauté sliced mushroom caps in 3 tablespoons butter until lightly browned; add rice mixture, stirring constantly until lightly browned. Remove from heat. *Slowly* stir in hot water and contents of seasoning packet. Bring to a full boil. Cover and remove from heat. Let stand 7 minutes. *Meanwhile:* brown veal rolls on all sides in 2 tablespoons of butter. Add wine. Cover and simmer 5 minutes. To serve, stir rice mixture and place in center of serving platter; surround with veal rolls. Sprinkle with chopped parsley. Garnish with lemon wedges, if desired. *Serves 6.*

HAM ROLL-UPS

Sauté ½ cup each—minced green pepper and onion—in 2 tablespoons butter for 5 minutes. Mix with 4 cups hot cooked rice (cook in chicken consommé instead of water). Spread 6 slices of boiled ham with mustard; spoon on rice. Roll. Bake, open side down, in a low pan for 15 minutes at 400°F. *Serves 4–6.*

RICE 'N' MEAT in WALNUT-STUFFED PEPPERS

    2 cups cooked rice
    6 green peppers
    1 cup chopped walnuts
    1½ cups chopped cooked meat
    3 tablespoons melted fat

2 tablespoons salt
1½ cups tomato sauce
½ cup cold water

Remove stems and seeds from the peppers. Place in boiling salted water, cook 10 minutes, drain and rinse with cold water. Mix cooked rice with chopped walnuts, salt, meat and melted fat, also part of the tomato sauce (½ cup) and the cold water. Fill the pepper shells with this mixture and stand them in baking dish. Pour around them 1 cup tomato sauce and bake in moderate oven (350°F.) 30 minutes. During baking, baste with the tomato sauce. *Serves 4–6.*

SPICY STEAK AND RICE SUPPER

1½ pounds round or loin steak (one inch thick) cut in
thin strips
1 large green pepper, sliced
1 large onion, sliced
Marinade
3 medium tomatoes, peeled and cut into wedges
1 tablespoon butter or oil
2 tablespoons cornstarch
3 cups hot cooked rice

Combine meat, pepper, onion, and marinade. Refrigerate several hours or overnight, stirring occasionally. Add tomatoes an hour before cooking. Drain meat and vegetables (saving marinade) and brown in oil over high heat. Mix cornstarch with marinade and add to meat. Cook 5 to 10 minutes longer. Serve over hot, fluffy rice. *Serves 6.*

MARINADE

Mix thoroughly the following ingredients: 2 tablespoons brown sugar, 1 teaspoon dry mustard, ½ teaspoon ginger, ½ teaspoon garlic powder, 1 teaspoon salt, 2 tablespoons vegetable oil, 1 tablespoon vinegar, 6 tablespoons soy sauce, ¾ cup water. Combine with sauce from drained meat and vegetables and use as marinade.

HAM-IT-UP SKILLET

1½ cups cooked ham strips (or 1 can of luncheon meat, cut
in narrow strips)
2 tablespoons salad oil
1 can (10½ ounces) condensed onion soup
1½ cups enriched pre-cooked rice
2 tablespoons chopped parsley
2 tablespoons chopped stuffed olives

Sauté ham in oil. Blend water into soup; add to meat. Stir in
rice. Cover and simmer 5 minutes. Just before serving, stir in
chopped parsley and chopped olives. Garnish with additional
stuffed olives, if desired. *Serves 3–4.*

PINEAPPLE-SAUSAGE SKILLET

1 package (8 ounces) brown 'n' serve sausages
½ cup thinly sliced scallions
1 can (8¾ ounces) pineapple tidbits
1 tablespoon brown sugar
¾ teaspoon salt
¼ teaspoon dry mustard
dash of each: pepper and ginger
1⅓ cups enriched pre-cooked rice

Brown sausages in skillet. Pour off all except 1 tablespoon drippings. Add scallions and sauté briefly, stirring frequently. Meanwhile, drain pineapple, measuring syrup and adding water to
make 1⅓ cups. Add syrup mixture, brawn sugar, salt, mustard,
pepper, ginger, and pineapple to skillet. Bring mixture to a boil.
Cover and simmer 5 minutes. *Serves 4.*

SAUSAGE-RICE SCRAMBLE

1 package (8 ounces) brown 'n' serve sausages, halved
⅓ cup chopped onion
1 tablespoon salad oil
1⅔ cups beef bouillon
¼ teaspoon basil

½ teaspoon salt
1 package (10 ounces) frozen mixed garden vegetables *or* frozen peas and carrots
¼ cup barbecue sauce
1⅓ cups enriched pre-cooked rice

Sauté sausages and onion in oil in skillet until browned. Add
bouillon to skillet with basil, salt, and vegetables. Bring to a
boil; then cover and simmer 5 minutes. Stir in barbecue sauce
and rice. Cover and simmer 5 minutes. *Serves 4–5.*

CORNED BEEF WITH RICE

⅔ cup minced onion
1½ tablespoons bacon drippings or shortening
2 cans (12 ounces each) corned beef, flaked
2 cups cooked rice
2 tablespoons mustard
4 eggs

Cook onions in drippings until tender. Add corned beef, rice,
and mustard; heat through. With back of large spoon, make four
indentations in meat mixture. Break an egg into each indentation.
Cover pan and cook over low heat about 20 minutes or until
eggs are done. *Serves 4.*

15.
Cakes, Desserts, Puddings

FRUITED-RICE PUDDING

2 cups homogenized milk
1 package vanilla pudding mix (3¼ ounces)
2 tablespoons granulated sugar
1 teaspoon vanilla
½ teaspoon cinnamon
⅓ cup currants (plumped and drained)
⅓ cup pineapple preserves
2 cups cooked long-grain rice

Heat milk to boiling over moderate heat. Quickly stir in vanilla pudding mix and bring to boil. Remove from heat. Stir in cinnamon dissolved in vanilla, sugar, currants, and pineapple or favorite flavor preserves. Stir in rice and blend. Chill. May be served with whipped cream, if desired. *Serves 4–6.*

DATE-NUT CUSTARD

2 eggs, well beaten
2 cups milk
2 cups cooked rice
3 tablespoons sugar
1 tablespoon melted butter
 or margarine
¼ cup chopped dates

1/4 cup chopped pecans
1/4 cup raisins
1/8 teaspoon nutmeg
1 teaspoon vanilla

Combine all ingredients and mix well. Pour into buttered 1½-quart baking dish or custard cups. Set in pan of hot water, about 1" deep. Bake at 350°F. for 1 hour (about 40 minutes for individual cups), or until a knife inserted near the center of custard comes out clean. *Serves 6* (about ½ cup each).

RICE RAISIN MERINGUE

2 cups milk
2 cups cooked rice
2 egg yolks, well beaten
½ cup sugar
1/4 teaspoon salt
½ cup raisins
1/4 teaspoon vanilla

In the top of a double boiler, heat milk to scalding point. Add cooked rice. Beat egg yolks with sugar and salt. Into this, gradually stir hot milk and rice. Return mixture to double boiler and simmer until thick, about 30–35 minutes. Fold in raisins and vanilla. Pour into buttered casserole and cover with meringue.

MERINGUE

2 egg whites
1/4 cup sugar
1/4 teaspoon vanilla

Beat egg whites until frothy. Gradually add sugar and vanilla; continue to beat until meringue stands in peaks. Bake at 350°F. for 12–15 minutes or until lightly browned. *Serves 6.*

DUTCH APPLE RICE

Rice Mixture:
3 cups hot, cooked rice

1 can (1 pound) applesauce
½ cup packed brown sugar
¼ cup raisins
2 tablespoons butter or margarine
½ teaspoon cinnamon

Crumb Mixture:

1 cup graham cracker crumbs
¼ cup packed brown sugar
¼ cup chopped pecans
2 tablespoons butter or margarine
¼ teaspoon cinnamon

Combine the ingredients of the Rice Mixture. In a separate bowl, combine the ingredients of the Crumb Mixture. Into a buttered 3-quart baking dish, sprinkle ¾ cup of the Crumb Mixture. Pour in all the Rice Mixture. Sprinkle with remaining crumbs. Bake at 350°F. for 30 minutes. Serve warm with whipped cream, if desired. *Serves 8.*

GOURMET RICE PUDDING

½ cup rice
3 cups boiling water
½ teaspoon salt
1 can (15 ounces) sweetened
  condensed milk
½ cup raisins, if desired
¼ cup margarine
1 tablespoon vanilla extract

Measure rice, boiling water, and salt into top of double boiler. Cook over rapidly boiling water until rice is tender, about 40 minutes. Stir in sweetened condensed milk, margarine, and raisins. Cook, stirring frequently over boiling water, until slightly thickened, about 20 minutes. Remove from heat and stir in vanilla. Serve warm or cold. *Serves 8.*

TROPICAL FRUIT DELIGHT

Drain one No. 2 can crushed pineapple. Add water to pineapple liquid to make 2 cups. Heat to boiling. Dissolve one 3-ounce package lemon-flavored gelatin in the hot liquid. Cool until the consistency of egg whites. Stir in 1 cup cooked rice (flavored with 1 teaspoon walnut extract), pineapple, and 2 mashed bananas. Whip 1 cup of whipping cream and fold into fruit-rice mixture. Turn into an attractive 1½-quart mold. Chill until firm. *Serves 8.*

TOASTED PECAN RICE BAVARIAN

½ cup broken pecans
1 tablespoon unflavored gelatin
¾ cup dark brown sugar
¼ teaspoon salt
¾ cup water
½ cup evaporated milk
2 cups cold cooked rice
½ pint whipping cream
1 teaspoon vanilla flavoring

Toast pecans in a moderate oven (350°F.) for 5 minutes. Mix gelatin, sugar, and salt in a saucepan. Add water and stir over low heat until gelatin dissolves. Add evaporated milk. Chill until partially set. Fold rice and pecans into gelatin mixture. Whip cream with vanilla. Fold into mixture. Pour into 1½-quart mold. Chill till firm. *Serves 8.*

STRAWBERRY RICE FLUFF PIE

1 package (8 ounces) cream cheese, room temperature
½ cup sugar
1 package (1 pound) frozen strawberries, thawed and drained
⅓ cup juice drained from strawberries
1½ tablespoons unflavored gelatin
1 cup cold cooked rice
1 cup heavy cream, whipped
1 baked 9-inch pie shell

Beat cheese with sugar until light and fluffy. Add strawberries. Soften gelatin in ⅓ cup juice drained from strawberries. Heat over hot water until dissolved. Cool. Combine with cheese mixture and rice. Mix well. Fold whipped cream into rice mixture. Turn into pie shell. Chill until firm. *Serves 6.*

SUGGESTION: Garnish with fresh or frozen strawberries for added tasty color.

FRUITED RICE DELIGHT

> 1 cup heavy cream
> 1/3 cup sugar
> 1½ cups cool cooked rice
> 1 teaspoon rum extract
> *Strawberry Topping:*
> 1 (10-ounce) package frozen strawberries, thawed
> 10 ladyfingers
> ½ cup chopped walnuts
> *Peach Topping:*
> 1 can (1 pound, 4 ounces) sliced peaches
> 1/3 cup toasted almonds or macaroon crumbs

Whip cream and sweeten with sugar. Fold in rice and rum extract. Chill until time to use. Serve with strawberry or peach topping. To prepare strawberry topping, divide thawed fruit into 5 dessert dishes, reserving a few berries for garnish. Spoon rice cream filling over fruit. Cut ladyfingers in halves crosswise and tuck around edge of dish. Garnish with reserved berries. To prepare peach topping, drain sliced peaches. Spoon a few slices into bottom of 5 dessert dishes. Spoon rice cream filling over peaches; garnish with additional peach slices. Sprinkle with toasted almonds or macaroon crumbs. *Serves 5.*

HONEY RICE

> 2/3 cup honey
> 1/4 cup corn syrup (dark)
> 4 cups cooked rice (about 1½ cups uncooked)
> ½ cup raisins
> 1½ teaspoons lemon rind

1½ tablespoons butter or margarine
1½ tablespoons lemon juice
¼ cup sherry
⅓ cup nuts, toasted, chopped

Heat the honey and corn syrup in a heavy pan and add the cooked rice, raisins, lemon rind, and butter. Cook about 5 minutes. Pour mixture into a well-buttered shallow baking dish. Cover. Bake in a moderate oven (350°F.) until golden brown, about 40 minutes. Remove from oven and stir in lemon juice and sherry. Serve in dessert dishes and top with chopped nuts. *Serves 8.*

SUGGESTION: Rice may be cooked in orange juice and extra orange juice may be substituted for sherry.

RICE PUDDING U.S.A.

5 cups milk
1 cup uncooked rice
½ teaspoon salt
¼ cup heavy cream
¼ cup butter or margarine
½ cup orange marmalade

Heat milk in 3-quart saucepan. When milk reaches boiling point, add rice and salt gradually and stir until it comes to a full boil. Cover saucepan with tight lid and simmer about 50 minutes. Remove rice from heat and add cream and butter. Fold in orange marmalade. Pour into serving dishes. *Makes 10 ½-cup servings.* Serve warm with Marmalade Sauce.

MARMALADE SAUCE

1 cup orange marmalade
⅓ cup sherry
½ cup nuts, chopped fine

Melt marmalade with sherry over low heat. Remove from heat and fold in nuts. Serve warm over rice pudding.

PEACHY RICE PUDDING

1⅓ cups water
1⅓ cups packaged enriched pre-cooked rice
2 tablespoons frozen concentrate for imitation orange juice
2 packages (10 ounces each) frozen peaches in quick thaw pouch
1 envelope whipped topping mix
2 tablespoons confectioners' sugar

Bring water to boil. Stir in rice. Cover and remove from heat. Let stand 5 minutes. Stir in concentrate; chill. Before serving, thaw peaches as directed on package and drain. Then prepare whipped topping mix as directed on package, adding sugar before whipping. Fold peaches and prepared whipped topping into rice mixture. Makes about 6 cups. *Serves 10–11.*

SUGGESTION: Use 2 cups sweetened sliced peaches in place of frozen. *Also:* use 1¼ cups heavy cream in place of whipped topping mix. Just whip the heavy cream with sugar just until soft peaks will form.

APPLE RICE BETTY

1⅓ cups water
½ teaspoon salt
1⅓ cups packaged enriched pre-cooked rice
1 tablespoon lemon juice
1 can (20 ounces) sliced apples
1½ cups firmly packed brown sugar
½ teaspoon cinnamon
½ teaspoon nutmeg
1 cup sour cream
¼ cup unsifted confectioners' sugar

Bring water and salt to a boil. Stir in rice. Cover, remove from heat, and let stand 5 minutes. *Next:* stir lemon juice into sliced apples. Combine brown sugar, cinnamon, and nutmeg. Sprinkle 3 to 4 tablespoons sugar mixture into a shallow 1-quart casserole. Then alternate 2 layers of rice with 2 layers of apples, starting with rice and sprinkling each layer with 5 tablespoons brown sugar mixture. Bake at 350°F. for 30 minutes. *Meanwhile:* combine sour cream and confectioners' sugar. Spread over top of hot apple rice mixture. Return casserole to 350°F. oven for 3 minutes. Serve warm. Makes about 4 cups. *Serves 6.*

SUGGESTION: If desired, sour cream topping may be omitted and dessert may be served with cream.

CALIFORNIA RAISIN RICE

1 cup sliced celery
3 tablespoons butter or margarine, melted
2½ cups water
2 teaspoons grated orange peel
½ cup apple juice
1½ teaspoons salt
2 tablespoons honey
1½ cups uncooked rice
½ cup raisins

Cook celery in butter until tender. Add water, orange peel, apple juice, salt, and honey; heat to boiling. Add rice and raisins. Stir. Cover, reduce heat, and simmer for 25 minutes, or until rice is tender and liquid is absorbed. *Serves 8.*

LEMON RICE PUFFS

1 teaspoon grated lemon rind
¼ cup butter
½ cup sugar
3 egg yolks, well beaten
3 tablespoons lemon juice
¾ cup enriched pre-cooked rice
1½ cups milk
3 egg whites, stiffly beaten

Cream lemon rind with butter until well blended. Gradually add sugar, creaming until light and fluffy. Add egg yolks and beat well. Then mix in lemon juice, rice, and milk. (Mixture will look curdled.) Fold in egg whites. Pour pudding into greased custard cups. Place in shallow pan. Pour hot water around cups to depth of one-half inch. Bake at 350°F. about 25 minutes for porcelain cups or 30 to 35 minutes for glass cups. (Pudding will have a cake-like layer on top with soft custard below.) Serve warm or cold with prepared whipped topping or whipped cream, if desired. *Serves 6–8.*

SUGGESTION: This dessert may also be baked in a greased 1½-quart baking dish. Pour mixture into dish, cover, set in a pan of hot water, and bake at 350°F. for 45 minutes.

INDIAN RICE PUDDING

1 cup plus 1 tablespoon milk
1 cup enriched pre-cooked rice
1 tablespoon molasses
1 tablespoon brown sugar
dash of salt
dash of cinnamon
dash of ginger
vanilla ice cream

Bring milk to a boil. Stir in rice. Cover, remove from heat and let stand 10 minutes. Stir in remaining ingredients except ice cream. Serve hot, topped with a scoop of vanilla ice cream or a dollop of prepared whipped topping or whipped cream. *Serves 4.*

RICE CHEESECAKE

1½ cups enriched pre-cooked rice
1⅓ cups water
1 tablespoon butter or margarine
⅓ teaspoon salt
1½ cups graham-cracker crumbs (about 18 crackers)
½ cup brown sugar
½ teaspoon cinnamon
½ cup melted butter or margarine
2 cups creamed cottage cheese
½ cup milk

1 package instant lemon pudding mix
½ cup sour cream or cherry preserves

Combine rice, water, butter or margarine, and salt; cook as directed on package. Cool to room temperature. Mix graham-cracker crumbs with brown sugar, cinnamon and butter or margarine. With the back of a spoon, press mixture into bottom and ½-inch-up sides of a buttered 9-inch-square cake pan or spring-form mold. *Chill.* Press cottage cheese through a coarse sieve or whip until fairly smooth. Combine with milk and pudding mix and beat about 1 minute. Fold in rice and pour into cooled crumb crust. Chill 1 hour. Before serving, top with sour cream and/or peaches or other fruit. *Serves 6–8.*

OLD WORLD PINEAPPLE CREAM

1 cup cooked parboiled rice
1½ cups milk
2 tablespoons flour
⅓ cup sugar
¼ teaspoon salt
2 well-beaten eggs
1 tablespoon butter or margarine
¾ cup crushed pineapple, drained

Heat rice with 1 cup milk in double boiler for 10 minutes. Combine dry ingredients and add remaining half cup milk. Pour slowly into rice mixture, stirring constantly. Cook until slightly thickened. Add half cup hot rice to eggs and stir into double boiler. Cook, stirring, until thickened. Remove from heat; add butter or margarine and pineapple. Pour into serving dishes. Serve warm or cold. *Serves 4.*

COCOA RICE PUDDING

2 cups enriched pre-cooked rice
2 cups water
½ teaspoon salt
1 teaspoon butter or margarine
2 cups milk

½ cup sugar
1 tablespoon cornstarch
¼ cup cocoa
½ teaspoon salt
½ teaspoon vanilla
½ cup chopped nuts

Combine rice, water, salt, and butter in a large saucepan. Bring to a boil, cover, and lower heat. Cook until all liquid is absorbed; then add milk. Combine sugar, cornstarch, cocoa, and salt. Stir into rice-and-milk mixture. Continue cooking until mixture thickens, stirring constantly. Remove from heat; add vanilla and nuts. Serve warm or at room temperature. *Serves 6–8.*

RICE-FRUIT CRISP

4 cups pared and thinly sliced apples (about 4)
1½ cups enriched pre-cooked rice
2 cups canned pineapple tidbits, drained
1½ cups water

Topping:

1 cup flour
½ cup softened butter or margarine
¾ cup brown sugar
½ teaspoon cinnamon

Arrange half of apple slices in buttered 1½-quart casserole. Mix rice with pineapple and spread over apples. Top with remaining apple slices. Add water. Mix ingredients for topping until crumbly and sprinkle over top. Cover and bake in 350°F. oven for 30 minutes. Uncover and bake 15 minutes longer to brown topping. Serve warm with cream. *Serves 6.*

RICE AND FRUIT FLUFF

⅓ cup evaporated milk
⅓ cup sugar
2 teaspoons lemon juice
¾ cup chopped fruit (peaches, figs, strawberries, etc.)

2 cups cold cooked parboiled rice

Chill evaporated milk and whip. Add sugar and lemon juice. Fold in chopped fruit and rice and spoon into dessert dishes. Top with bits of fruit. *Serves 4.*

BAKED RICE PUDDING

1 cup enriched pre-cooked rice
1½ cups milk
2 eggs, beaten
⅓ cup sugar
1 teaspoon vanilla
¼ cup raisins
nutmeg *or* cinnamon

Cook rice according to package directions. Add milk. Boil gently 5 minutes, stirring occasionally. Combine eggs, sugar, and vanilla. Slowly stir in rice. Add raisins. Pour into 1½-quart greased casserole. Sprinkle top with nutmeg or cinnamon. Place in pan containing one-half inch water. Bake 35–40 minutes in 350°F. oven or until knife inserted near edge comes out clean. *Serves 4–5.*

SUGGESTION: Omit raisins, if that is your preference.

RICH RICE CREAM

1 tablespoon plain gelatin
¼ cup cold water
1 cup cooked parboiled rice
¼ cup milk
¼ teaspoon salt
¼ cup sugar
½ teaspoon vanilla
⅛ teaspoon almond extract
⅔ cup chilled evaporated milk

Soak gelatin in cold water. Heat rice with ¼ cup milk in double boiler for 10 minutes. Add softened gelatin, salt, sugar, and flavorings. Chill until partially thickened. Fold in stiffly beaten evaporated milk. Turn into molds rinsed with cold water and chill until firm. Unmold and serve with favorite fruit or sauce. *Serves 4.*

MAPLE-WALNUT RICE

½ cup brown sugar
2 eggs, well beaten
½ teaspoon maple flavoring
⅛ teaspoon salt
1¼ cups milk
½ cup top milk *or* light cream
¼ cup chopped walnuts
1½ cups cooked parboiled rice

Beat sugar with eggs. Blend in maple flavoring, salt, milk, and cream. Pour over walnuts and cooked rice in buttered 1-quart baking dish. Place in pan of water and bake in 325°F. oven for approximately one hour until a knife inserted in the center comes out clean. *Serves 4.*

SUGGESTION: If your family prefers pecans to walnuts, by all means use pecans—or, if you like, omit the nuts entirely.

MOCHA RICE PUDDING

⅓ cup parboiled rice
1½ cups strong coffee
1 tablespoon butter *or* margarine
2 eggs, well beaten
1 cup milk
⅓ cup dark corn syrup
⅓ cup sugar
½ teaspoon vanilla
⅛ teaspoon salt
cinnamon

Place uncooked rice in coffee in double boiler. Cook approximately 35 minutes or until rice is tender. Add butter or margarine and combine thoroughly with remaining ingredients. Pour into buttered 1-quart baking dish. Sprinkle with cinnamon and set in pan of warm water. Bake in 350°F. oven for about 50 minutes or until knife inserted in center comes out clean. Serve warm or cold, with whipped or light cream. *Serves 4.*

RICE PRUNE WHIP

¼ cup parboiled rice
⅓ cup chopped raw prunes (pits removed)
⅛ teaspoon salt
1¾ cups water
1 tablespoon lemon juice
6 marshmallows (regular size, quartered)
1 egg white
2 tablespoons sugar
½ cup heavy cream, whipped

Combine rice, prunes, salt, and water in saucepan. Bring to a boil. Cover and lower heat. Cook, stirring occasionally, about 25 minutes or until mixture is consistency of preserves. Remove from heat, add lemon juice and marshmallows; fold until partially melted. Chill. Beat egg white until stiff; beat in sugar. Fold into cooled rice mixture. Fold in whipped cream. Turn into serving bowl or individual dishes and chill. *Serves 4–5.*

LEMON RICE PUDDING

1 cup enriched pre-cooked rice
1⅔ cups cold water
¼ teaspoon salt
½ teaspoon butter or margarine
1⅓ cups milk
⅓ cup sugar
1¼ teaspoons cornstarch
2 egg yolks, beaten
1 teaspoon grated lemon rind

Bring rice, cold water, salt, and butter to a boil in a saucepan and stir. Boil rapidly until most of the liquid is absorbed, 7 to 10 minutes. Mix milk, sugar, and cornstarch; add to rice. Cook, stirring, 3 minutes. Remove from heat. Slowly stir in beaten egg yolks and lemon rind. Heat to boiling. Chill the pudding or serve it warm. *Serves 4.*

CHOCOLATE RICE PUDDING

1 square unsweetened chocolate
2 cups milk
1½ cups cooked parboiled rice
2 eggs
½ cup sugar
¼ teaspoon salt

Melt chocolate in double boiler. Stir in milk. Add rice and continue heating. Beat eggs thoroughly, add sugar and salt. Blend egg mixture gradually into rice and milk. Pour into buttered casserole, bake in 325°F. oven for one hour or until set. Chill, serve with whipped cream. *Serves 6.*

BROWNIE RICE PUDDING

2 eggs, separated
½ cup sugar
¼ teaspoon salt
1 teaspoon vanilla
1 square chocolate, melted
1½ cups milk
½ cup chopped pecans or walnuts
2 cups cooked parboiled rice

Beat egg whites until they stand in soft peaks; beat in yolks. Blend in slowly the sugar, salt, vanilla, and melted chocolate (slightly cooled). Add milk and blend. Mix nuts and cooked rice in buttered 1½-quart baking dish. Pour chocolate mixture over. Place in pan of water and bake in 350°F. oven for approximately 50 minutes or until a knife inserted in center comes out clean. *Serves 6.*

CREAMY RICE PUDDING
(Double Boiler)

Mix ½ cup uncooked rice, 2½ cups milk, ¼ cup sugar, and ½ teaspoon salt in the top part of a double boiler. Cook, covered, over boiling water 1 hour, until liquid is absorbed and rice is tender. Stir often. Blend in 1 teaspoon vanilla. Serve Creamy Rice Pudding directly from the cooking pan, if you like, or spoon into dessert dishes and chill before serving. *Serves 6.*

PEACH-BRITTLE TOPPING: This topping is to be used on cooled or chilled Creamy Rice Pudding. Whip ½ pint heavy cream. Fold into whipped cream 1 cup finely crushed peanut brittle candy, 1 can (1 pound, 13 ounces) sliced peaches, drained (reserve 8 slices), ¼ teaspoon salt, and 1 tablespoon lemon juice. Spread topping over cooled or chilled pudding.

VARIATIONS:
Date Rice Pudding: Prepare recipe for Creamy Rice Pudding. When cooked, stir in ½ cup chopped dates and ½ cup chopped nutmeats. Serve with a vanilla or lemon hard sauce.
Orange Rice Pudding: Omit from the ingredients of Creamy Rice Pudding ¼ cup sugar. Cook. Fold into cooked pudding 2 table-spoons butter or margarine, ½ cup orange marmalade, and 3 tablespoons cream. Pour into serving dishes. Add orange topping: Melt ¾ cup orange marmalade with ¼ cup cream sherry; fold in ⅓ cup chopped nuts. Serve marmalade sauce over hot or cold pudding.

RICE MINT WHIRL

1 package (3 ounces) lime gelatin
water
4 tablespoons lemon juice
1 package (1 pound) melon balls (drain
    and reserve liquid)
1 teaspoon mint sauce
2½ tablespoons sugar
1½ cups cooked rice
1 cup grapes, halved and seeded

1 package (2⅛ ounces) whipped topping,
prepared

Combine reserved liquid from melon balls, lemon juice, and
enough water to make 2 cups. Heat to boiling. Pour over gelatin
and dissolve. Add mint sauce and sugar. Chill until partially set.
Stir in melon balls, grapes, and cooked rice. Fold in prepared
whipped topping. Spoon into individual molds. Chill until set.
Serves 8.

VARIATIONS: Substitute a low-calorie fruit gelatin for the lime
gelatin. Omit the mint sauce and use a sugar substitute in place
of the sugar. Use a low-calorie whipped topping, following package directions for preparation.

BAKED RICE CUSTARD

Combine 3 beaten eggs, ½ cup sugar, and ¼ teaspoon salt. Gradually add 2 cups scalded milk, stirring. Add 1 cup cooked rice,
¼ cup raisins, and 2 teaspoons vanilla. Pour into greased 1½-
quart casserole; set in pan of hot water. Bake at 350°F. for ½
hour; stir. Sprinkle with ¼ teaspoon nutmeg; dot with 1 tablespoon butter or margarine. Bake 30–40 minutes longer or until
set. *Serves 6.*

FRENCH RICE CAKE
(Gateau de Riz)

1 cup sugar
3 tablespoons water
2 cups milk
1 cup water
½ cup sugar
½ teaspoon salt
1⅓ cups enriched pre-cooked rice
3 eggs, well beaten
1½ teaspoons vanilla
whipped cream

Combine 1 cup sugar and 3 tablespoons water in a small saucepan.

Simmer and stir over very low heat until sugar dissolves and syrup turns golden brown—about 25 minutes. Brush a thin even coating over the inside of a fluted 1½-quart mold. Set aside. *Next:* combine milk, 1 cup water, ½ cup sugar, and salt in a saucepan. Cover and bring to a boil. Stir in rice. Cover, remove from heat, and let stand 10 minutes (not all of the liquid will be absorbed). *Next:* combine eggs and vanilla. Gradually add some of the hot rice mixture, stirring rapidly. Then add egg mixture to rice. Pour into prepared mold. Bake at 400°F. for 40–45 minutes, or until center of cake is firm. Remove from oven, invert onto a serving plate, and remove mold at once. Serve warm with whipped cream. *Serves 6.*

EGGNOG RICE PIE

3 cups cooked rice
1 quart eggnog, bottled or canned
1 tablespoon unflavored gelatin
2 tablespoons water
3 tablespoons cream sherry
1 chocolate cooky crumb crust
1 package (2 ounces) whipped topping mix
½ cup milk
⅓ cup crushed peppermint candy

Cook rice in eggnog until creamy but not too thick, about 20–25 minutes. Soften gelatin in water and stir into hot rice until gelatin is dissolved. Add sherry. Cool. Turn into 10-inch crumb crust. Chill. Combine topping mix and milk; whip until it stands in stiff peaks. Fold in peppermint candy. Swirl on top of pie before serving. *Makes one 10-inch pie.*

RICE FLOUR BROWNIES

2 squares unsweetened chocolate (2 ounces)
⅓ cup shortening or margarine
1 cup sugar
2 eggs
⅔ cup rice flour, sifted twice before measuring
½ teaspoon baking powder
½ teaspoon salt

Melt chocolate and shortening in a double boiler over hot water. Remove pan from hot water and beat in sugar and eggs. Sift together rice flour, baking powder, and salt. Stir into chocolate mixture; spread into a greased 8-inch square pan. Allow mixture to stand ½ hour before baking. Bake in 350°F. oven for 30 to 35 minutes. A slight imprint is left when the top is touched. Cool slightly; cut into squares. *Makes 16 two-inch squares.*

RICE FLOUR SPONGE CAKE

> 2 eggs, separated
> ⅓ cup sugar
> ¼ cup rice flour, sifted twice before measuring
> 1 teaspoon lemon juice
> grated rind of ¼ lemon
> dash of salt

Sift together rice flour, sugar, and salt. Beat egg yolks until thick and lemon colored. Add lemon juice and rind to egg yolks. Beat egg whites until stiff but not dry. Fold egg yolk mixture and flour mixture alternately in small amounts into beaten egg whites with rubber spatula. Pour into a small loaf pan that has been lined with wax paper. Bake in a 350°F. oven 25–30 minutes. *Serves 4.*

APPLE-FLAVORED RICE TREAT

> 3 cups cooked rice
> 2 eggs
> 2 apples
> ½ teaspoon cinnamon
> ½ cup sour cream
> 1 orange
> ½ cup seedless raisins
> 2 tablespoons butter
> 2 tablespoons sugar

Grate the peel of the orange and mix with rice. Put melted butter, sour cream, thinly sliced apples, sugar and cinnamon in rice and mix well. Beat egg whites stiff and put yolks into it. Mix these slightly and fold eggs into the above mixture. Butter a deep pan or Pyrex dish and bake in moderate oven 30 minutes. Serve hot or cold. *Serves 4.*

FROZEN STRAWBERRY RICE PIE

½ pint heavy cream, whipped
1 8-ounce package cream cheese, room temperature
½ cup sugar
1½ cups frozen strawberries, drained
1½ tablespoons unflavored gelatin
4 tablespoons juice from berries, heated
1 cup cooked rice
1 9-inch baked pie shell

Whip cream and set aside. In a mixing bowl, whip cream cheese with sugar until light and fluffy. Add strawberries. Dissolve gelatin in heated juice from berries. Combine with cream cheese mixture. Add cooked rice and mix well. Fold in whipped cream. Turn into baked 9-inch pie shell. Chill and serve. *Serves 4–6.*

STRAWBERRY SMOOTHIE

3 cups cooked rice
3 cups milk
½ cup sugar
1 teaspoon vanilla
3 eggs, separated
1 cup strawberry preserves

Combine rice and milk. Cook 15 minutes or until slightly thickened. Add ¼ cup sugar and vanilla. Beat egg yolks; spoon some of the rice mixture into the eggs. Blend all into rice mixture. Cook about 1 minute. Remove from heat and chill. *Next:* Beat egg whites until frothy. Add remaining sugar gradually and continue beating until whites are stiff. Fold in ¾ cup strawberry preserves. Spoon rice custard into serving dishes. Top each custard with meringue whip and remaining strawberry preserves. *Serves 8.*

MOCHA RICE PUDDING

2 cups cooked rice
2 cups milk
1/2 teaspoon salt
2 teaspoons instant coffee
1 cup marshmallow cream
chocolate syrup

Combine rice, milk, salt, and coffee in a saucepan and simmer until thick and creamy. Remove from heat and cool. Fold in 3/4 cup marshmallow cream. Spoon into dessert dishes and top with remaining marshmallow cream and chocolate syrup. *Serves 6.*

APPLE RICE BETTY

1 cup enriched pre-cooked rice
1 1/3 cups apple juice
1/8 teaspoon salt
2/3 cup firmly packed brown sugar
1/2 cup raisins
1 1/3 cups diced apples
1 tablespoon butter
1 cup heavy cream

Combine all ingredients except butter and cream in a saucepan. Bring to a boil, cover, and simmer 5 to 10 minutes, or until most of the liquid is absorbed. Remove from heat and blend in butter. Chill. Just before serving, whip cream and fold into rice mixture. Garnish with additional whipped cream, if desired. *Serves 6–8.*

SUGGESTION: To make Glorified Apple Rice, prepare as for Apple Rice Betty, adding 1/4 teaspoon cinnamon to the rice mixture before cooking. Stir in 2 tablespoons coarsely chopped nuts with the butter. *Serves 6–8.*

RED AND WHITE PARFAITS

1 can (1 pound) whole cranberry sauce
1½ cups water
1⅓ cups enriched pre-cooked rice
⅛ teaspoon salt
⅓ cup granulated sugar
¼ teaspoon cinnamon
1 cup diced apples
1 tablespoon butter
1 cup heavy cream
¼ cup unsifted confectioners' sugar
2 tablespoons chopped nuts

Combine all ingredients except butter, cream, confectioners' sugar, and nuts. Bring to a boil, cover, and simmer about 10 minutes or until the rice is tender. Remove from heat, stir in butter. Chill. *Just before serving* whip cream with confectioners' sugar. Fold nuts into rice mixture. Layer rice mixture and cream alternately in parfait or other tall slender glasses (or fold whipped cream into rice mixture and spoon into serving dishes). Garnish with additional nuts and whipped cream, if desired. *Serves 6–8.*

BROILED BUTTERSCOTCH RICE PUDDING

½ cup uncooked rice
1 cup water
¼ teaspoon salt
1 teaspoon maple extract
1 package (3¼ ounces) butterscotch pudding mix
2 cups milk
1 tablespoon butter or margarine

Topping:

⅓ cup maple syrup
2 tablespoons melted butter or margarine
1 cup shredded coconut

Combine rice, water, salt, and maple extract. Heat to boiling over high heat. Stir once. Cover, reduce heat, and simmer for 15 minutes. Blend pudding mix with milk and butter; cook over medium heat, stirring constantly, about 5 minutes. Fold in cooked rice. Spoon into oven-proof serving dishes and chill. When ready to serve, spread with mixture of topping ingredients and broil slowly until golden, 2–3 minutes. Watch carefully so as not to burn. *Serves 6.*

CREAMY RICE PUDDING

2 cups milk
½ cup uncooked rice
½ teaspoon salt
1 small piece of vanilla bean
2 egg yolks, beaten
¼ cup sugar
¼ cup light cream

Combine milk, rice, salt, and vanilla bean in a top of a double boiler. Cook, covered, over boiling water about 45 minutes, stirring occasionally. (Rice should be tender and the milk almost absorbed.) Combine egg yolks, sugar, and cream and stir into rice. Remove top of double boiler from water and cook rice mixture over low heat, stirring constantly until it just reaches the boiling point. Remove from heat. Serve warm or cold with fruit, cream, toasted slivered almonds, coconut, or preserves. *Serves 4.*

SUGGESTION: ¾ teaspoon vanilla extract may be added with egg mixture instead of vanilla bean.

OLD-FASHIONED RICE PUDDING
(Baked Method)

4 eggs, beaten
¼ teaspoon salt
⅓ cup sugar
2 teaspoons vanilla
1½ teaspoons grated lemon peel
3 cups milk
1½ cups cooked rice

Combine eggs, salt, sugar, vanilla, and lemon peel in a buttered 2-quart casserole. Combine milk and rice. Stir into egg mixture. Set casserole in a pan of hot water filled to within 1 inch of top of casserole. Bake uncovered at 300°F. for 1½ to 2 hours. After first 30 minutes, insert spoon at edge of pudding and stir from bottom. Near end of baking time, insert silver knife; if it comes out clean, pudding is done. Serve hot or cold. *Serves 6 to 8.*

VARIATIONS:

Raisin Rice Pudding: Prepare recipe for Old-Fashioned Rice Pudding, adding ½ cup seedless raisins to mixture before cooking. Bake. Spread pudding with 2 cups whipped cream and sprinkle with a mixture of 2 teaspoons sugar and 1 teaspoon cinnamon. Brown quickly under broiler.

Pink Cloud Rice Pudding: Prepare and bake Old-Fashioned Rice Pudding. Cool. Whip ½ pint heavy cream; fold in cherry pie filling (1 lb. can) and 2 or 3 drops each almond extract and red food color. Cut pudding into squares and top with cherry mixture.

Meringue Surprise Pudding: Prepare Old-Fashioned Rice Pudding using the egg yolks only. Bake. Arrange 4 milk chocolate bars (7/8 ounces each) on pudding. Spread with meringue prepared with the egg whites, 6 tablespoons sugar, ¼ teaspoon cream of tartar, and 1 teaspoon vanilla. Bake at 350°F. for 12–15 minutes.

BUTTERSCOTCH RICE PUDDING

1 package (3¾ ounces) butterscotch pudding and
                                       pie filling mix
1½ cups milk
2 eggs, separated
2 cups cooked rice
1 teaspoon vanilla
2 teaspoons brown sugar

Combine pudding mix, milk, and egg yolks. Cook over medium heat, stirring constantly until thickened. Add rice and vanilla. Cool. Beat egg whites with brown sugar until whites stand in stiff peaks. Fold into pudding. Spoon into serving dishes. Chill. *Serves 6.*

VARIATIONS:

Vanilla or your favorite flavored pudding and pie filling may be substituted for butterscotch.

Broiled Maple Rice Pudding: Prepare recipe for Butterscotch Rice Pudding. Pour mixture into baking dish. Spoon *following mixture* on top of pudding: blend together ⅓ cup maple syrup, 2 tablespoons melted butter or margarine, and 1 cup shredded coconut. Broil slowly until golden, 2 or 3 minutes, watching to prevent burning.

Fig Parfaits: Prepare recipe for Butterscotch Rice Pudding. Combine 1 cup fig preserves, 2 teaspoons lemon juice, and ½ teaspoon powdered ginger. Bring to a boil; cook 2–3 minutes. Cool. Alternate layers of Rice Pudding with fig mixture in parfait glasses. Top with whipped cream or coconut macaroon crumbs.

Fruit Parfaits: Prepare Rice Pudding recipe using your favorite flavor of pudding and pie filling mix. Chill. Alternate layers of pudding with fresh, canned, or frozen fruit (drained). Top with whipped cream and fruit.

RICE PUDDING
(Top of the Range Method)

3 cups cooked rice
3 cups milk
½ cup sugar
3 tablespoons butter or margarine
1 teaspoon vanilla

Combine rice, milk, sugar, and butter. Cook over medium heat until thickened, about 30 minutes, stirring often. Add vanilla. Pour into serving dish. Serve hot or cold. *Serves 6.*

VARIATIONS:

Strawberry Smoothie: Follow directions above until pudding is slightly thickened; to 3 beaten egg yolks add enough pudding mixture to blend. Stir egg yolks into remaining pudding mixture. Cook 1 minute or until pudding is thickened. Spoon into individual dessert dishes. Chill. *Strawberry Topping:* Beat 3 egg whites until frothy. Add ¾ cup strawberry (or cherry, pineapple, raspberry) preserves; continue beating until whites are stiff. Top chilled Rice Pudding with meringue whip; spoon 1 teaspoon of preserves on top of whip.

Mocha Rice Pudding: To milk in recipe for Rice Pudding, blend 2 teaspoons instant coffee. Prepare according to directions given. Cool. Fold ¾ cup marshmallow cream into pudding. Spoon into dessert dishes. Top each with additional marshmallow cream and chocolate syrup.

Caramel Rice Pudding: Prepare recipe for Rice Pudding. Into a loaf pan pour ½ cup sugar. Cook over very low heat, stirring constantly until sugar melts and turns a golden color. Tilt pan frequently as sugar melts to coat sides thoroughly. Remove from heat. Pour Rice Pudding into loaf pan. Cover and bake at 350°F. for 30 minutes. Cool. Unmold onto serving dish. Serve plain or with whipped cream.

16.

Bread, Cookies, Rolls

RICE DROP DUMPLINGS

1½ cups all-purpose flour
2 teaspoons baking powder
1 teaspoon salt
1 egg, beaten
½ cup milk
1 tablespoon melted butter or margarine
1 cup cooked rice
3 tablespoons minced parsley
4 cups well-seasoned chicken broth

Sift flour, baking powder, and salt together. Beat egg, add milk and melted butter. Combine with flour mixture and stir in rice and parsley. Beat until smooth. Drop from tablespoon into hot chicken stock. Cover; cook 15 minutes. Do NOT lift cover during time dumplings are cooking. *Do not boil.* If spoon is dipped into hot broth, then into batter, dumplings will slide off easily. *Serves 6.*

SOUTHERN RICE CAKES

⅔ cup water
¼ teaspoon salt
1 tablespoon butter
⅔ cup enriched pre-cooked rice

1 egg, well beaten
⅓ cup milk
2 teaspoons grated onion
¼ cup unsifted all-purpose flour
1½ teaspoons baking powder
1 teaspoon sugar
¼ teaspoon salt
⅛ teaspoon pepper

Bring water, salt, and butter to a boil. Stir in rice. Cover, remove from heat, and let stand 5 minutes. Meanwhile, combine egg, milk, and onion; then mix into rice. Combine remaining ingredients, add to rice mixture and mix *only* enough to dampen flour. Drop by tablespoonfuls onto hot well-greased griddle; brown lightly on both sides. Serve hot with currant jelly or maple syrup as a side dish with meat or as a breakfast or brunch entrée. Makes 10 to 12 cakes. *Serves 5–6.*

SUGGESTION: Add ½ cup diced Cheddar cheese with the egg mixture to add a piquant taste.

RICE CORN BREAD

⅔ cup enriched pre-cooked rice
¾ cup water
¾ cup milk
1 cup cornmeal
½ cup sifted all-purpose flour
2 teaspoons baking powder
½ teaspoon salt
3 tablespoons butter
¼ cup sugar
1 egg, beaten

Combine rice, water, and milk; set aside. *Next:* sift together cornmeal, flour, baking powder, and salt. Cream butter and sugar. Add eggs and beat well. Stir in rice mixture. Add sifted dry ingredients and beat slowly with a rotary beater until flour is moistened. Pour into a greased 8-inch square pan. Bake at 400°F. for 30 minutes or until lightly browned. Serve hot with butter. *Serves 9.*

RICE SPOON BREAD

1 cup cooked rice
2 eggs, separated
1 tablespoon butter
1 cup milk
1 cup boiling water
3 tablespoons white cornmeal
¼ cup flour
2 teaspoons baking powder
1 teaspoon salt
1 tablespoon sugar

Add water to cornmeal and stir; add flour, salt, and sugar. Cook in double boiler until thick, then stir in rice and butter. Add the beaten egg yolks, baking powder, and milk. Fold in stiffly beaten egg whites and pour into a greased baking dish. Place in a pan containing an inch of hot water and bake 40 minutes at 350°F. Serve hot with butter. *Serves 8.*

CALAS

1½ cups hot cooked rice (very soft)
½ package yeast, active dry or compressed
½ cup warm, not hot, water (lukewarm for compressed yeast)
3 eggs, beaten
1¼ cups sifted flour
¼ cup sugar
½ teaspoon salt
¼ teaspoon nutmeg

Mash rice and cool to lukewarm. Soften yeast in warm water and stir into lukewarm rice. Mix well. Cover and let rise overnight. The next morning, add eggs, flour, sugar, salt, and nutmeg. Beat until smooth. Let stand in a warm place for 30 minutes. Drop by tablespoons into deep hot fat (360°F.) and fry until golden brown, about 3 minutes. Serve sprinkled with powdered sugar or sugar mixed with cinnamon. Makes 2 dozen.

NOTE: Calas, a hot fried bread made with rice, is one of the oldest recipes I came across during a culinary discovery trip in New

Orleans. Old Creoles of the last century would sell them right on the streets. Sometimes they made them in saucepans filled with hot oil while their customers waited. Or, they covered the Calas in brown paper while still piping hot and carried them through the streets in market baskets on their heads. Children delighted in running out to buy them when they heard the call "Calas" outside. They would carry them home to be eaten—while still hot and delicious—with milk.

RICE FLOUR MUFFINS

        2 cups rice flour
        2 teaspoons baking powder
        ½ teaspoon salt
        ½ teaspoon baking soda
        2 tablespoons sugar
        2 eggs, beaten
        1 cup buttermilk
        ¼ cup water
        4 tablespoons butter or margarine, melted

Mix and sift the dry ingredients. Mix the egg, milk, water, and butter together and stir into the dry ingredients. Bake in greased muffin tins, ¾ full, at 425°F. for 20 minutes. *Makes 12 muffins.*

17.

Specialties

SUKIYAKI

1 pound beef loin steak, cubed
1 tablespoon salad oil
3 small onions
1 small bunch carrots
1 stalk celery
1 pound green beans
1 bunch green onions
2 green peppers
¾ cup Chinese cabbage or cauliflower
1 cup soy sauce
1 tablespoon sugar
6 cups hot cooked rice

Brown meat in salad oil. Cut vegetables slantwise into small pieces. Arrange vegetables over meat in the following order: onions, carrots, celery, green beans, green onions, green pepper, and cabbage *or* cauliflower. Cover tightly and steam until vegetables are half done. Add soy sauce and sugar and continue steaming until vegetables are tender, but not mushy. Serve over the hot rice with the additional soy sauce. *Serves 6.*

INDIA RICE

1 cup uncooked rice

2 cups beef bouillon
2 tablespoons butter or margarine
½ cup white raisins
½ teaspoon salt
¼ cup toasted slivered almonds

Combine rice, bouillon, butter, raisins, and salt in saucepan. Bring to a boil and stir. Cover and simmer for 14 minutes. Remove from heat. Add almonds and mix lightly with a fork. *Serves 4.*

SPICY RICE

1 cup uncooked rice
2 cups chicken broth
½ teaspoon salt
1 teaspoon celery salt
1 teaspoon soy sauce
⅓ cup slivered toasted almonds
   (optional)

Combine rice, chicken broth, salt, celery salt, and soy sauce in a saucepan. Bring to a boil. Stir well; cover and cook over low heat for 14 minutes or until rice is tender and the liquid is absorbed. For a gourmet touch, stir in almonds. *Serves 4.*

RICE AND EGG STUFFING

1 cup celery, chopped
1 cup onion, chopped
¼ cup butter or margarine
3 cups cooked rice, cooked in
   chicken broth
4 hard-boiled eggs, diced
½ teaspoon salt
¼ teaspoon pepper

Sauté in a saucepan, celery and onions in butter until tender. Combine cooked vegetables with rice, boiled eggs, and seasonings. Mix well. Will stuff four 1½-pound boned fish.

HERB RICE

1 cup uncooked rice
2 cups water
2 chicken bouillon cubes
1 tablespoon butter or margarine
1 teaspoon salt
½ teaspoon rosemary
½ teaspoon marjoram
½ teaspoon thyme

Combine all ingredients in a saucepan. Bring to a boil; stir well. Cover and cook over very low heat for 14 minutes or until rice is tender and the liquid absorbed. *Serves 4.*

RICE LYONNAISE

¾ cup sliced onion
2 tablespoons butter or margarine
3 cups cooked rice
¼ cup diced pimiento

Sauté onion in butter until golden brown. Add rice and pimiento. Cook over low heat until rice is thoroughly heated, stirring occasionally. *Serves 5.*

DEVILED RICE

½ cup chopped onion
½ cup chopped green pepper
2 tablespoons butter or margarine
⅓ cup sour cream
⅓ cup currant jelly
¼ cup prepared mustard
2 tablespoons chopped pimiento
1 teaspoon Worcestershire sauce
3 cups hot cooked rice

In a saucepan, sauté onion and green pepper in butter until tender. Add sour cream, currant jelly, mustard, pimiento, and

Worcestershire sauce. Mix well and heat, stirring occasionally. Combine this mixture with hot rice. Spoon into serving dish and, if desired, garnish with parsley and a topping of jelly. *Serves 5.*

CURRIED RICE

3 tablespoons butter or margarine
1 cup onions, chopped fine
1 cup green peppers, chopped
½ cup currants
2 cups rice, uncooked
½ teaspoon curry powder
1 teaspoon salt
½ teaspoon pepper
1 quart chicken broth

Melt butter and add onions, green peppers, and currants; sauté until tender. Stir in rice and seasonings; brown slightly. Add chicken broth and mix well; bring to a boil. Cover with a tight-fitting lid and simmer for 14 minutes. Remove from heat, toss lightly, and serve. *Serves 8.*

SOUTHERN RICE DRESSING

Roux:

1 tablespoon shortening
1 tablespoon flour

Dressing:

2 cups broth, chicken or beef
1 clove garlic
1 cup chopped giblets or ground meat
1 onion, chopped
2 tablespoons parsley, chopped
4 cups cooked rice
salt and pepper to taste

Mix roux and cook over low flame until brown. Now add broth, garlic, and meat. Let cook for 20 minutes. Add onions and parsley; simmer for 10 minutes. Mix with cooked rice and seasonings. Simmer for about 10 minutes. *Serves 6.*

PIZZA-TUNA-RICE SUPPER

1⅓ cups packaged enriched pre-cooked rice
1 can (1 pound) stewed tomatoes
1 cup water
2 tablespoons salad oil
¼ pound cubed American cheese (¾ cup)
1 can (7 ounces) tuna, drained and coarsely flaked
¾ teaspoon salt
¼ teaspoon oregano (optional)
⅛ teaspoon pepper
¼ cup sliced stuffed olives

Combine rice with remaining ingredients except olives in a saucepan or skillet. Stir. Bring to a boil; then reduce heat, cover, and simmer 5 minutes, stirring occasionally. Top with olive slices and garnish with chopped parsley, if desired. *Serves 4–5.*

RICE LOUISIANA

¾ cup sliced onion
2 tablespoons butter or margarine
4 cups cooked rice
¼ cup diced pimiento

Sauté onion in butter until golden brown. Add rice and pimiento. Cook over low heat until rice is thoroughly heated, stirring occasionally. *Serves 6.*

WILD RICE STUFFING

1 package long-grain and wild rice mix
1 tablespoon butter
2 tablespoons chopped onion
2 tablespoons chopped celery
⅛ teaspoon Tabasco sauce
2 cups toasted bread cubes
1 teaspoon salt
1 teaspoon grated orange rind
3 oranges, sectioned

Cook rice according to package directions. Melt butter in skillet. Add onion and celery and sauté, stir in Tabasco sauce. Add cooked rice, bread cubes, seasoning, and rind. Mix thoroughly, then cut orange sections in half, add to rice mixture, toss slightly. *Makes 6 cups.*

NEW ORLEANS RICE STUFFING

2 cups parboiled rice
3 large onions, finely chopped
4 large stalks of celery, finely chopped
1 green pepper, chopped
turkey heart, gizzard, and liver, ground
turkey fat, finely chopped
⅔ cup chopped parsley
1 cup chopped pecans
2 whole eggs, well beaten
salt, pepper, poultry seasoning to taste

Cook rice according to package directions. While the rice is cooking, sauté vegetables, liver, gizzard, and heart together with rendered or chopped turkey fat in skillet. Cook thoroughly. Add seasonings, stir to blend. Turn off heat under skillet; add rice and fold in eggs, mixing thoroughly. Add chopped nuts and chopped parsley. Remove from skillet, stuff turkey, and bake until done. *Makes about 11 cups.*

SUKIYAKI—TOKYO STYLE

2 tablespoons butter
1 pound lean round steak, cut in very thin slices
½ pound fresh mushrooms, thinly sliced (about 3 cups)
1 bunch green onions, cut into strips (about 2 cups)
1 cup celery strips
1 cup sliced yellow onions
1 can (5 ounces) bamboo shoots, drained
2 tablespoons sugar
⅓ cup soy sauce
1 beef bouillon cube
¼ cup hot water

3 cups fresh spinach
2 cups enriched pre-cooked rice

Heat butter in a large skillet. Add meat and brown very quickly on both sides—takes about 1½ minutes. Add remaining ingredients except spinach and rice. Simmer uncovered, stirring occasionally, 3 to 4 minutes, or until vegetables are almost tender but still crisp. Then add spinach, cover, and cook 3 minutes longer. *Meanwhile:* prepare pre-cooked rice according to package directions. Serve Sukiyaki immediately over the rice (vegetables should be crisp). Sprinkle with additional soy sauce, if desired. Makes about 5 cups Sukiyaki plus rice. *Serves 5–6.*

SUGGESTION: For ease in cutting meat, place in freezer until just firm—about 1½ hours—or only partially thaw frozen meat. Then cut with a heavy, sharp knife and let stand to thaw while preparing other ingredients.

CHILI RICE CON CARNE

1 pound ground beef
2 teaspoons salt
⅛ teaspoon pepper
½ cup chopped onion
2 tablespoons butter
1 can (1 pound) kidney beans
1 can (1 pint, 2 fluid ounces) tomato juice (or use a 1-pound can tomatoes and increase water to 1½ cups)
2 teaspoons chili powder
1⅓ cups enriched pre-cooked rice

Sprinkle meat with salt and pepper. In a large skillet, sauté meat and onion in butter until browned. Add undrained beans, tomato juice, water, and chili powder. Cover and bring to a boil. Stir in rice, cover, and simmer 8 to 10 minutes, or until flavors are blended and rice is tender. *Serves 6.*

PERSIAN RICE

Prepare 1⅓ cups enriched pre-cooked rice as per package directions, omitting butter. Then melt 1 tablespoon butter in another saucepan. Drop rice by spoonfuls into butter, making a cone-shaped mound. Pour 2 tablespoons melted butter over rice. Cover; place over medium heat about 10 minutes, or until mound is browned on bottom. Set pan in cold water a few moments, or just until mound can easily be removed from pan. Lift mound of rice from pan carefully and place on serving platter. Serve with steak and other meats. *Serves 4.*

PINEAPPLE RICE WHIP

    1 3-ounce package flavored gelatin
    ¾ cup boiling water
    1 can (8½ ounces) crushed pineapple,
        drained (reserve juice)
    ⅓ cup sugar
    1¾ cups cooked parboiled rice, cooled
    1 cup heavy cream, whipped

Dissolve gelatin in boiling water. Measure juice drained from pineapple. Add enough water to make 1¼ cups in all. Add to dissolved gelatin. Refrigerate until set. When gelatin is set, whip until foamy and light in color. Add sugar, rice, and drained pineapple. Just before serving, fold in whipped cream. *Serves 6.*

SUGGESTION: Use any favorite flavor such as strawberry, raspberry, black raspberry, cherry, lime, etc. Vary the flavor each time you make this pudding.

SOUR CREAM PILAF

    1 can (4 ounces) sliced mushrooms
    2 chicken bouillon cubes
    1⅓ cups enriched pre-cooked rice
    2 tablespoons butter
    ½ bay leaf

½ cup sour cream

Drain mushrooms, measuring liquid and adding water to make 2 cups. Bring liquid to a boil in large saucepan. Add bouillon cubes and crush to dissolve. Meanwhile, sauté mushrooms and rice in butter until golden brown. Add to bouillon with bay leaf. Cover and simmer 5 minutes. Remove from heat, discard bay leaf, and stir in sour cream. Serve with chicken and other entrées. *Serves 4.*

QUICK "WILD" RICE

¼ cup butter or margarine
1⅓ cups enriched pre-cooked rice
1 cup finely chopped celery
¼ cup chopped celery leaves
¼ cup finely chopped onion
1¼ teaspoons salt
dash of pepper
1⅓ cups water

Melt butter in saucepan. Add rice, celery and leaves, onion, and seasonings. Cook and stir over medium heat until onion is transparent and rice is golden brown—about 8 minutes. Stir in water and bring quickly to a boil over high heat. Then cover, remove from heat, and let stand 5 minutes, or until all liquid is absorbed. Fluff with a fork before serving. Serve with broiled, fried, or roasted meats, fish, or poultry. *Serves 4.*

BROWNED RICE

1⅓ cups enriched pre-cooked rice
2 tablespoons butter
½ teaspoon salt
1⅓ cups water

Sauté rice in butter over medium heat until golden brown, stirring frequently. Add salt; then gradually stir in water, Bring quickly to a boil over high heat. Cover. Remove from heat and let stand 5 minutes. *Serves 4.*

SUGGESTION: To make Browned Rice Pilaf, prepare as above, increasing butter to 3 tablespoons, sautéing ½ cup finely chopped onion with the rice, and substituting 1⅓ cups chicken bouillon for the water. If desired, increase salt to taste.

HOPPING JOHN

8 slices bacon, diced
½ cup chopped onion
1 can (1 pound) black-eyed peas or
   lima beans, drained
½ cup water
1⅓ cups enriched pre-cooked rice
1½ cups water
½ teaspoon salt
dash of pepper

Fry bacon in saucepan over medium heat until crisp. Remove all except 2 tablespoons drippings in saucepan. Add onion and sauté just until tender. Add peas and ½ cup water; simmer about 5 minutes. Stir in remaining ingredients. Bring quickly to a boil over high heat. Then cover, remove from heat, and let stand 5 minutes. Fluff with a fork before serving. Serve as an entrée or as a side dish with ham or other meats. *Makes 5 cups or 6–8 side servings. Makes 4–5 entrée servings.*

TIJUANA RICE

½ cup minced onion
½ cup chopped green pepper
3 tablespoons olive oil
2 cups enriched pre-cooked rice
¼ cup tomato sauce
1 teaspoon salt
1 teaspoon chili powder

Sauté onion and green pepper in oil in a heavy 2-quart saucepan until pale golden. Add water, rice, tomato sauce, salt, and chili powder. Heat to boiling. Cover and simmer over low heat for 5 minutes or until liquid is absorbed. *Serves 4.*

RICE INDIENNE

1½ cups chopped onions
¼ cup butter or margarine
1 can (4 ounces) mushroom pieces,
    drained (or 1 cup sliced fresh
    mushrooms)
⅔ cup enriched pre-cooked rice
¼ teaspoon saffron (optional)
2⅔ cups chicken broth or bouillon
salt and pepper

Sauté onions in butter until lightly browned, stirring frequently.
Add mushrooms and sauté about 5 minutes to blend flavors. Stir
in rice and saffron; then add broth. Season to taste with salt and
pepper. Pour into a 2-quart baking dish, cover tightly, and bake
at 350°F. for 20 minutes, or until all liquid is absorbed. Serve
with creamed chicken, curries, and other entrées. Makes about
5½ cups. *Serves 6–8.*

RICE À LA GRECQUE

1 cup chopped onions
2 tablespoons butter or margarine
2½ cups enriched pre-cooked rice
2 cups chicken broth
⅔ cup green peas
⅔ cup golden raisins
¼ teaspoon salt
⅓ cup grated Parmesan cheese

Cook onions in melted butter in medium skillet until soft. Stir in
rice, broth, peas, raisins, and salt. Bring to a vigorous boil. Cook
over moderate heat, uncovered, about 5 minutes. Stir in grated
cheese. Serve hot. *Serves 6.*

HOT GERMAN RICE SALAD

1 package (12 ounces) frankfurters,
    cut in eighths

3 cups cooked rice
1 cup diced celery
½ cup finely chopped onion
1½ tablespoons flour
½ cup mayonnaise
2 teaspoons prepared mustard
salt and pepper to taste
½ cup milk
hard-cooked egg slices and parsley for
    garnish

Combine frankfurters, rice, celery, and onion. Blend flour, mayonnaise, mustard, seasoning, and milk. Stir into rice and frankfurter mixture. Turn into a greased 2-quart casserole. Cover and bake at 350°F. for 30 minutes. Garnish with hard-cooked egg slices and parsley. *Serves 8.*

RICE CHANTILLY

3 cups cooked rice
1¼ teaspoons salt
⅛ teaspoon pepper
dash of cayenne
½ cup cream, whipped
½ cup grated Cheddar cheese

Season rice with 1 teaspoon salt, pepper, and cayenne. Spoon rice into a greased 1½-quart casserole. Add remaining salt and cheese to the whipped cream. Spread over top of rice. Bake at 375°F. for 30 minutes. *Serves 6.*

RICE O'BRIEN

½ cup diced green pepper
2 tablespoons butter or margarine
1 cup uncooked rice
2 cups chicken broth
1 teaspoon salt
½ cup chopped pimiento

Cook green pepper in butter until tender. Add rice, chicken broth, and salt. Heat to boiling and stir once. Cover, reduce heat, and simmer for 14 minutes or until liquid is absorbed. Remove from heat and toss lightly with pimiento. Serve hot. *Serves 4.*

GLORIFIED LEMON RICE

1 cup water
¼ cup lemon juice
¼ cup sugar
¼ teaspoon salt
1 cup enriched pre-cooked rice
2 cups sliced peaches
¼ cup chopped nuts, toasted
1½ cups prepared whipped topping

Combine water, lemon juice, sugar, and salt in saucepan. Bring to a boil. Stir in rice. Cover, remove from heat, and let stand 10 minutes. Then uncover, stir, and cool. *Meanwhile:* sprinkle peaches with enough sugar to sweeten. When rice is cool, drain peaches, measuring ¼ cup syrup. Add measured syrup and nuts to rice. Fold whipped topping into rice mixture. Add peaches. Garnish with additional drained fruit and a maraschino cherry, if desired. *Serves 8.*

RICE AND VEGETABLE DRESSING

1 cup uncooked rice
2 tablespoons butter or margarine
1 cup finely chopped onion
1 tablespoon minced parsley
1 teaspoon minced marjoram
2¼ cups chicken broth
1 package frozen lima beans
1½ teaspoons salt

Set oven at 350°F. Spread rice in a shallow pan and heat in oven until golden brown about 10 minutes. Stir frequently so as not to burn. *Next:* melt butter or margarine in a 3-quart saucepan. Add onion, parsley, marjoram. Sauté until onion is tender. Now add chicken broth, lima beans, and salt into saucepan. Simmer covered for 5 minutes. Add toasted rice. Bring to a boil. Stir. Reduce heat, cover with a tight fitting lid, and simmer about 20 minutes. Excellent when served as a dressing with roast beef or steak. *Serves 6.*

CHOCOLATE-FILLED MARSHMALLOW BARS

6 cups puffed rice cereal
¼ cup butter or margarine
⅓ cup chunk-style peanut butter
32 large marshmallows
1 6-ounce package (1 cup) semi-sweet
   chocolate pieces

Heat puffed rice cereal in shallow pan in preheated moderate oven (350°) about 10 minutes. Pour into large greased bowl. Melt butter, peanut butter, and marshmallows over low heat, stirring occasionally. Pour over rice cereal, stirring until evenly coated. Firmly press half of mixture into greased 7 x 11 pan; sprinkle chocolate pieces over top. Place in preheated oven (350°F.) two to three minutes or until chocolate is softened. Remove from oven; spread chocolate with spatula. Press remaining puffed rice mixture over chocolate. Cool. Cut in bars. *Makes 32 bars.*

PUFFED "POPCORN"

4 cups puffed rice cereal
¼ cup butter or margarine
½ teaspoon salt

Heat puffed rice cereal in shallow pan in preheated moderate oven (350°F.) about 10 minutes. Melt butter in large skillet; add salt and rice cereal. Heat over high heat about 1 minute, stirring constantly. *Makes 4 cups.*

PUFFED CANDY BALLS

6 cups puffed rice cereal

¾ cup light corn syrup
¼ cup light molasses
½ teaspoon salt
1 teaspoon vinegar
2 tablespoons butter or margarine
1 teaspoon vanilla

Heat puffed rice cereal in shallow pan in preheated moderate oven (350°F.) about 10 minutes. Pour into large greased bowl. Combine syrup, molasses, salt, and vinegar in saucepan. Cook over medium heat, stirring occasionally, to hard ball stage (255°F.) or until syrup dropped into cold water forms a hard ball. Remove from heat; stir in butter and vanilla. Pour over puffed rice cereal, stirring until evenly coated. With greased hands, shape to form candy balls. *Makes 12 candy balls.*

NIBBLE BAIT

3 cups puffed wheat cereal
3 cups puffed rice cereal
1 cup Spanish peanuts
1 3½-ounce can French fried onions
1 6½-ounce package (about 3 cups) cheese pretzel sticks
¼ cup butter or margarine, melted
2 tablespoons grated Parmesan cheese
1 tablespoon barbecue seasoning
¼ teaspoon garlic powder

Place puffed wheat and rice cereals, peanuts, onions, and pretzels in large shallow baking pan. Combine remaining ingredients and pour over cereal mixture, tossing until evenly coated. Heat in preheated slow oven (300°F.) about 30 minutes, stirring occasionally. *Makes about 10 cups.*

CHOCOLATE CLUSTERS

5 cups puffed rice cereal
½ cup peanuts
¾ cup sugar

¼ cup light corn syrup
½ cup water
½ teaspoon salt
2 squares (2 ounces) unsweetened chocolate
1 tablespoon butter or margarine
1 teaspoon vanilla

Heat puffed rice cereal in shallow pan in preheated moderate oven (350°F.) about 10 minutes. Pour into large greased bowl; stir in peanuts. Combine sugar, syrup, water, and salt in saucepan; bring to a boil. Add chocolate and continue cooking to soft ball stage (236°F.) or until syrup dropped into cold water forms a soft ball. Remove from heat. Stir in butter and vanilla. Pour over puffed rice cereal mixture, stirring until evenly coated. Drop by tablespoonfuls onto waxed paper. Cool. *Makes 3 dozen.*

CHOCOLATE NUGGETS

6 cups puffed rice cereal
¾ cup light corn syrup
1½ cups semi-sweet chocolate pieces
1 teaspoon vanilla
finely-chopped nutmeats

Heat puffed rice cereal in shallow pan in preheated moderate oven (350°F.) about 10 minutes. Pour into large greased bowl. Bring syrup to boil; quickly add chocolate pieces and vanilla, stirring until chocolate melts. Pour over puffed rice cereal, stirring until evenly coated. With greased hands, shape to form 2-inch balls; roll in chopped nutmeats. Place on waxed paper until set. *Makes 1½ dozen.*

TRIXIES

8 cups puffed rice cereal
1 14-ounce package caramels
¼ cup water
1 6-ounce package (1 cup) semi-sweet
    chocolate pieces, melted
pecan halves

Heat puffed rice cereal in shallow pan in preheated moderate oven (350°F.) about 10 minutes. Pour into large greased bowl. Melt caramels and water over low heat, stirring occasionally. Pour over puffed rice cereal, stirring until evenly coated. With greased hands, shape to form 1½-inch patties. Cool. Spread each patty with melted chocolate. Press pecan half into chocolate. Refrigerate until set. *Make 4 dozen.*

CONFETTI RICE BALLS

Ingredients	12 Balls	48 Balls
puffed rice cereal	6 cups	6 quarts
chopped peanuts	1 cup	1 quart
cut-up gumdrops	1 cup	1 quart
miniature marshmallows	3 cups	11 cups
butter or margarine	¼ cup	1 cup

Heat puffed rice cereal in shallow pans in preheated moderate oven (350°F.) about 10 minutes. Pour into large greased bowl. Add peanuts and gumdrops; stir to combine. Melt marshmallows and butter over low heat, stirring occasionally. Pour over puffed rice cereal mixture, stirring until evenly coated. With greased hands, shape to form balls. (If mixture hardens before shaping is complete, place in a moderate oven to soften for a few minutes.) Wrap balls in plastic wrap and tie with ribbons.

RICE JACK COOKIES

8 cups puffed rice cereal
1½ cups sugar
¾ cup water
1½ teaspoons vinegar
¼ cup molasses
1½ tablespoons butter or margarine
¾ teaspoon salt

Heat puffed rice cereal in shallow pan in preheated moderate oven (350°F.) about 10 minutes. Pour into large greased bowl. Combine sugar, water, and vinegar in saucepan. Bring to boil; cook 5 minutes. Add molasses, butter, and salt; cook to soft crack stage (290°F.) or until syrup dropped into cold water separates into threads that are hard but not brittle. Pour over cereal, stirring until evenly coated. Spread on two greased cookie sheets; cool. Break into pieces. *Makes 5 dozen cookies.*

CARAMEL NUT BARS

> 5 cups puffed rice cereal
> 1 cup coarsely-chopped nutmeats
> ¼ cup butter or margarine
> one 14-ounce package caramels
> 1 cup marshmallow creme
> ½ teaspoon vanilla

Heat puffed rice cereal and nutmeats in shallow pan in preheated moderate oven (350°F.) about 10 minutes. Pour into large greased bowl. Melt butter and caramels over low heat 20 to 30 minutes, stirring occasionally. Remove from heat; beat in marshmallow creme and vanilla. Pour over puffed rice cereal mixture, stirring until evenly coated. Firmly press mixture into greased 9-inch square pan. Cool at room temperature until firm. Cut in bars. *Makes 16 bars.*

CHOCOLATE EASTER EGGS

> 3 cups puffed rice cereal
> 15 large marshmallows
> 2 tablespoons butter or margarine
> 12 large gumdrops
> 2 6-ounce packages (2 cups) semi-sweet
>   chocolate pieces, melted
> pink confectioners' sugar frosting
> yellow confectioners' sugar frosting
> green confectioners' sugar frosting

Heat puffed rice cereal in shallow pan in preheated moderate oven (350°F.) about 10 minutes. Pour into large greased bowl. Melt marshmallows and butter over low heat, stirring occasionally. Pour over cereal, stirring until evenly coated. With greased hands, shape to form eggs around gumdrops. Chill. Melt chocolate pieces over hot, not boiling, water. Spread eggs with melted chocolate. Chill. Decorate with pink and yellow confectioners' sugar frosting rosettes and green confectioners' sugar frosting leaves. *Makes 12 eggs.*

PUMPKIN FACES

6 cups puffed rice cereal
1 cup light corn syrup
¼ cup sugar
½ teaspoon salt
1 teaspoon vinegar
1 tablespoon butter or margarine
1 teaspoon vanilla
few drops yellow food coloring
few drops red food coloring

Heat puffed rice cereal in shallow pan in preheated moderate oven (350°F.) about 10 minutes. Pour into large greased bowl. Combine corn syrup, sugar, salt, and vinegar in saucepan. Cook over medium heat to soft ball stage (236°F.) or until syrup dropped into cold water forms a soft ball. Remove from heat; stir in butter, vanilla, and food coloring. Pour syrup over puffed rice cereal, stirring until evenly coated. Shape to form pumpkins. Decorate with long *green gumdrops* for stems and *black candy drops* for the eyes and mouth. Wrap in plastic wrap and tie with a bow. *Makes 6 pumpkins.*

HAPPY HAUNTED KATS

6 cups puffed rice cereal
32 large marshmallows
¼ cup butter or margarine
½ cup semi-sweet chocolate pieces
½ cup butterscotch pieces
1 teaspoon vanilla
chocolate confectioners' sugar frosting
miniature marshmallows
red cinnamon candies
licorice sticks
spaghetti

Heat puffed rice cereal in shallow baking pan in preheated moderate oven (350°F.) about 10 minutes. Pour into large greased bowl. Melt marshmallows and butter over low heat, stirring occasionally. Stir in chocolate pieces, butterscotch pieces, and vanilla. Pour marshmallow mixture over puffed rice cereal, stirring until evenly coated. With greased hands, shape to form 8 cats. With chocolate confectioners' sugar frosting, attach cut marshmallow pieces and cinnamon candies for eyes and mouth. Use licorice sticks for tail and broken spaghetti pieces for whiskers. *Makes 8.*

CLOWN CONES

> 5 cups puffed rice cereal
> ⅓ cup butter or margarine
> ½ cup peanut butter
> 32 large marshmallows
> 2 pints vanilla ice cream

Heat cereal in shallow pan in preheated moderate oven (350°F.) about 10 minutes. Pour into large greased bowl. Melt butter, peanut butter, and marshmallows over low heat, stirring occasionally. Pour marshmallow mixture over puffed rice cereal, stirring until evenly coated. With greased hands, press mixture onto bottom and sides of 12 greased custard cups. Chill. Using spatula, gently remove cones from cups. Dip 12 large scoops of ice cream; make a face on each scoop, using pieces of raisins for eyes and mouth and red cinnamon candy for nose. Use chocolate sprinkles for hair. Place in cones and keep in freezer until ready to serve. *Makes 12.*

SUGGESTION: The clown faces can be prepared ahead of time and kept on a cookie sheet in your freezer.

PUFFED SUCKERS

> 6 cups puffed rice cereal
> 32 large marshmallows
> ¼ cup butter or margarine
> 1 6-ounce package (1 cup) semi-

sweet chocolate pieces
½ teaspoon vanilla
12 candy sticks

Heat puffed rice cereal in shallow pan in preheated moderate oven (350°F.) about 10 minutes. Pour into large greased bowl. Melt marshmallows and butter over low heat, stirring occasionally. Add chocolate pieces and vanilla, stirring until melted. Pour marshmallow mixture over puffed rice cereal, stirring until evenly coated. With greased hands, shape to form 12 balls. Insert candy stick in each ball. Cool. *Makes 12.*

JOLLY SNACK MIX

4 cups puffed rice cereal
4 cups puffed wheat cereal
4 cups thin pretzel sticks
¾ cup butter or margarine, melted
1 1⅜-ounce package onion soup mix

Place rice and wheat cereals and pretzels in shallow baking pan. Combine butter and onion soup mix. Pour over cereal mixture, tossing until evenly coated. Heat in preheated very slow oven (250°F.) about 40 minutes. Stirring occasionally. *Makes about 3 quarts.*

PETER COTTONTAIL

6 cups puffed rice cereal
32 large marshmallows
¼ cup butter or margarine
½ teaspoon vanilla
few drops red food coloring
coconut
gumdrops
raisins
pink construction paper
pipe cleaners

Heat puffed rice cereal in shallow pan in preheated moderate oven (350°F.) about 10 minutes. Pour into large greased bowl. Melt marshmallows and butter over low heat, stirring occasionally. Add vanilla and food coloring, stirring until smooth. Pour over cereal, stirring until evenly coated. With greased hands, shape one medium-sized ball for head, one small ball for tail and remaining mixture for body. Assemble bunny with *thick confectioners' sugar frosting.* Use coconut for topknot, gumdrops (cut in half crosswise) for buttons and nose, and raisins for eyes. From construction paper, cut ears and feet. Make two slits in head and insert ears; set bunny on the paper feet. Insert pipe cleaners for whiskers. *Makes 1 large bunny.*

CRUNCHY FREEZE

½ cup regular margarine or butter
2½ cups oven-toasted rice cereal
¾ cup brown sugar, firmly packed
1¼ cups (3½-ounce can) flaked coconut
1 cup broken pecans
½ gallon brick vanilla ice cream, slightly softened

Measure margarine in 13 x 9 x 2 baking pan. Place in slow oven (300°F.) about 10 minutes or until just melted. Add rice cereal, sugar, coconut, and pecans; mix well. Return to oven for about 30 minutes or until evenly browned, stirring occasionally. Cool. Remove half of mixture from baking pan. Spread remaining mixture evenly in pan. Place slices of ice cream on top of rice cereal mixture and smooth tops until even. Sprinkle remaining rice cereal mixture over ice cream. Freeze about 2 hours or until hardened. Scoop the Crunchy Freeze into dessert dishes. Serve immediately. *Serves 12.*

CRUNCHY FUDGE SANDWICHES

1 6-ounce package (1 cup) butterscotch morsels
½ cup peanut butter
4 cups oven-toasted rice cereal
1 6-ounce package (1 cup) semi-sweet chocolate morsels
½ cup sifted confectioners' sugar
2 tablespoons regular margarine or butter, softened

1 tablespoon water

Melt butterscotch morsels and peanut butter in heavy saucepan over very low heat, stirring constantly until melted and well blended. Remove from heat. Add rice cereal to butterscotch mixture, stirring until well coated. Press half of rice cereal mixture into buttered 8 x 8 x 2 pan. Chill cereal mixture in pan in refrigerator while preparing fudge mixture. Set remaining cereal mixture aside. Combine chocolate morsels, sugar, margarine, and water; melt over hot *but not boiling* water, stirring frequently, until mixture is well blended. Spread over chilled cereal mixture. Spread remaining cereal mixture evenly over top; press gently. Chill. Remove from refrigerator about 10 minutes before cutting into squares. Makes about 25 Crunchy Fudge Sandwiches, 1½ x 1½ inches each.

SUGGESTION: Substitute one 6-ounce package (1 cup) chocolate mint morsels for semi-sweet chocolate morsels.

PEANUTTY-CRUNCH PIE

⅓ cup peanut butter
⅓ cup corn syrup
2 cups oven-toasted rice cereal
1 quart vanilla ice cream, slightly softened

Measure peanut butter and corn syrup into large bowl; mix until thoroughly combined. Add rice cereal; stir until well coated. Press cereal mixture evenly and firmly in bottom and around sides of buttered 9-inch pie pan. Chill untill firm. Spread ice cream evenly in pie shell. Freeze until firm. Cut into wedges to serve. Top with golden peach slices or other fresh fruit. *Serves 8.*

ICE CREAM SANDWICHES

½ cup corn syrup
½ cup peanut butter
4 cups oven-toasted rice cereal
1 pint brick ice cream

Measure corn syrup and peanut butter into mixing bowl; mix well. Add rice cereal, stirring until well coated. Press cereal mixture evenly and firmly in bottom of buttered 13 x 9 x 2 pan. Place in freezer or coldest part of refrigerator until firm. Cut into 12 3-inch squares; sandwich a slice of ice cream between each two squares. Cut each sandwich into two bars. Serve immediately or wrap individually in aluminum foil and store in freezer until needed. *Makes 12 Ice Cream Sandwiches, 3 x 1½ each.*

CRAZY DAISIES

3 cups presweetened expanded rice cereal
⅓ cup regular margarine or butter
¼ cup peanut butter, chunk style
6 10-ounce packages (about 40) regular marshmallows
½ cup milk chocolate morsels, melted

Measure rice cereal into large buttered bowl; set aside. Melt margarine, peanut butter, and marshmallows in saucepan over low heat, stirring constantly until smooth. Pour over rice cereal; stir until evenly coated. Using buttered hands, shape cereal mixture into 2-inch patties. Frost center of each patty with melted chocolate morsels. Refrigerate until chocolate is firm. *Makes 25 Crazy Daisies, about 2 inches in diameter for each.*

MINTED RICE AND PINEAPPLE

2 cups miniature marshmallows
1 cup sugar
2 cups milk or cream
3 cups cooked rice
1 tablespoon butter
¼ teaspoon salt
1 teaspoon mint flavor

Sauce:
1 13½-ounce can pineapple chunks, including juice
3 tablespoons sugar
2 tablespoons cornstarch
1 drop yellow food coloring
½ cup chopped pecans

In double boiler, melt marshmallows and sugar in cream. Stir in rice, butter, and salt. Cool. Add mint flavoring. Pour into buttered casserole and garnish with pineapple sauce and sprinkle with chopped pecans. *To make sauce:* combine pineapple with juice, sugar, and cornstarch in saucepan. Cook over low heat until thickened and transparent. Cool. Pour over rice. *Serves 12.*

PRETTY PARFAIT

Into parfait glasses or tall dessert dishes, spoon in alternate layers of cooled cooked rice and canned pie filling—cherry, blueberry, peach, or apricot. Top with whipped cream.

HAWAIIAN RICE DESSERT

1 8¼-ounce can crushed pineapple, drained
2 tablespoons lemon juice
⅓ cup sugar
⅛ teaspoon salt
1 cup heavy cream, whipped
3 cups cooked rice, chilled
½ cup shredded coconut

Combine pineapple, lemon juice, sugar, and salt. Fold mixture into whipped cream. Fold in rice and shredded coconut. Chill before serving. *Makes 6 one-half cup servings.*

PINK PARTY PARFAIT

4 cups cold cooked rice
½ pint whipped cream
a drop or 2 of red food color
¼ cup sugar
½ teaspoon almond flavoring
1 10-ounce package frozen strawberries, thawed

At serving time, whip cream and food coloring, sugar and flavoring. Fold in rice. Alternate layers of rice and strawberries in parfait glasses. *Serves 6.*

RICE COCKTAILS

Apple Juice: Substitute 2 cups apple juice for water and add ½ cup chopped celery and ¼ teaspoon thyme before cooking rice. Cook 20 minutes. Excellent with pork.

Orange Juice: Substitute 2 cups orange juice for water and cook rice for 20 minutes. Chill. Stir in ¾ cup toasted coconut. Serve topped with sweetened orange slices.

Tomato Juice: Substitute 1 cup of tomato juice for 1 cup water and cook rice 15 minutes. Add ⅓ cup grated Parmesan cheese and 1 tablespoon minced chives to the cooked rice.

Bouillon: Substitute beef or chicken bouillon for water. If you like, add ¼ teaspoon saffron or 1 tablespoon curry powder before cooking the rice.

Milk: For 6 servings, combine ¾ cup uncooked rice, 1 quart milk, ½ cup sugar, 3 tablespoons butter or margarine, 1½ teaspoons vanilla, and ½ teaspoon salt in a saucepan. Bring to a boil. Stir well. Cover with a tight lid; reduce heat. Simmer over low heat for 1 to 1½ hours until rice is desired thickness.

RICE AND COCONUT SNOWBALLS

2 tablespoons cornstarch
1 cup sugar
¼ teaspoon salt
2 cups milk
2 cups cooked rice
½ cup chopped pecans
3 eggs, separated
1 teaspoon brandy extract
½ cup finely shredded coconut

Combine cornstarch, ⅔ cup sugar, and salt. Stir in milk. Cook until thickened, stirring occasionally. Remove from heat. Fold in rice and nuts. Beat egg yolks slightly. Add some of the hot mixture to eggs; mix thoroughly. Stir into remaining mixture. Add flavoring. Pour into 6 well-buttered 5-ounce custard cups.

Set cups in shallow pan. Pour hot water around them one-inch deep. Bake at 350°F. about 30 minutes or until set. Cool slightly. Unmold and place on greased baking sheet. Beat egg whites until stiff but not dry. Gradually beat in remaining sugar and continue beating until whites stand in stiff peaks. Spread on top and sides of custards. Sprinkle lightly with coconut. Return to oven and bake 5 minutes or until flecked with brown. *Serves 6.*

SUGGESTIONS: *In Winter*—substitute finely chopped dates for pecans and ½ teaspoon vanilla for brandy extract. *In Spring*—substitute finely chopped fresh pineapple for nuts and ½ teaspoon vanilla for brandy extract. *In Summer*—substitute finely chopped fresh peaches for nuts and almond flavoring for brandy extract. Add 1 tablespoon lemon juice to fresh peaches to prevent discoloring.

RICE 'N' CHERRIES IN THE SNOW

3 cups cooked rice
3 cups milk
½ cup sugar
1 tablespoon butter or margarine
1 tablespoon unflavored gelatin
⅓ cup milk
1 teaspoon almond extract
1 cup heavy cream, whipped

Sauce:

1 can (1 pound) tart pitted cherries
⅔ cup sugar
2 tablespoons arrowroot
red food coloring

Combine rice, milk, ½ cup sugar, and butter. Cook over low heat until thickened, about 25 minutes. Soften gelatin in ⅓ cup milk. Dissolve over hot water. Stir into rice mixture with flavoring. Cool. Fold whipped cream into rice mixture. Turn into 10 individual ½-cup molds or a 1-quart mold. Serve with sauce. *Next:* Drain juice from cherries. Reserve cherries. Combine ⅔ cup sugar and arrowroot and stir into juice. Add enough food coloring to obtain preferred color. Cook over low heat, stirring, until thickened. Add cherries. Cool. *Serves 10.*

SUGGESTION: For a bit more glamor, pour a little Kirsch over dessert and flame.

RICE SURPRISES

Tomato Rice:
Combine 1½ cups uncooked rice, 3 cups chicken broth, 1 tablespoon butter or margarine. Cook according to package directions. Chill. Toss with 2 fresh chopped tomatoes, 1½ cups diced celery, ¼ cup chopped onion, ¼ teaspoon garlic powder, 1 teaspoon salt, and a dash of pepper. Serve on lettuce leaf with your favorite salad dressing. *Serves 6.*

Pineapple Rice:

Combine 3 cups hot cooked rice with one No. 2 can crushed pineapple (drained), ⅓ cup brown sugar, ⅓ cup melted butter or margarine, ⅓ cup diced green pepper, 1 teaspoon soy sauce, ½ teaspoon prepared mustard. *Serves 6–8.*

Confetti Rice:

Toss lightly together 3 cups hot cooked rice with ¼ cup melted butter or margarine, ¼ cup finely chopped onion, ½ cup chopped pimiento, ¼ cup ground fresh green pepper, and one 6-ounce can tuna fish. *Serves 6–8.*

CRANBERRY RICE RELISH

¾ cup cooked rice, marinated in
  ⅓ cup Sauterne
2 cups fresh cranberries, chopped fine
1 orange, quartered and ground fine
½ cup brandy-flavored mincemeat
½ cup sugar
½ cup broken nut meats, pecans

Marinate rice in sauterne for about 3 hours. Chop or grind cranberries and orange. Add sugar, mincemeat, and nuts. Let stand

and chill while rice marinates. Combine cranberry mixture with marinated rice. *Makes 2½ cups of relish.*

RICE INDIENNE

1 cup uncooked rice
2 cups bouillon
2 tablespoons butter or margarine
½ cup white raisins
½ teaspoon salt
¼ cup toasted slivered almonds

Combine rice, bouillon, butter, raisins, and salt in saucepan. Bring to a boil and stir. Cover and simmer for 14 minutes. Add almonds and mix lightly with a fork. *Serves 4–6.*

GOOD AND EASY

1 package yellow saffron rice mix
1 pound hot dogs
½ cup barbecue sauce

Cook rice according to package directions. Heat hot dogs in barbecue sauce over low heat for 10 minutes. Top rice with hot dogs and pour remaining sauce over all. *Serves 4–6.*

HOLIDAY GREEN RICE

1⅓ cups water
pinch of poultry seasoning
½ teaspoon salt
2 tablespoons butter
1 chicken bouillon cube
½ tablespoon chopped onion
1⅓ cups enriched pre-cooked rice
¼ cup chopped parsley
¼ cup coarsely chopped pistachio nuts *or* almonds

Combine water, seasonings, butter, bouillon cube, and onion in a saucepan. Bring to a boil. Stir in rice. Cover, remove from heat, and let stand 5 minutes. Add parsley and nuts and fluff with a fork before serving. Serve with roast turkey, chicken, and other entrées. Makes about 3 cups. *Serves 4.*

HOLIDAY RED RICE

1⅓ cups enriched pre-cooked rice
1 can (1 pound) whole cranberry sauce
1½ cups water
⅛ teaspoon salt
⅓ cup sugar
¼ teaspoon cinnamon
1 cup sliced apples
1 tablespoon butter

Combine all ingredients except apples and butter in a saucepan. Bring to a boil, cover, and simmer 10 minutes, or until rice is tender. Remove from heat; stir in apples and butter. Cover and let stand at least 10 minutes. Fluff lightly with a fork just before serving. Serve with roast turkey, chicken, and other entrées. Makes about 4 cups. *Serves 5–6.*

QUICK CHEESE SAUCE

1⅔ cups (14½-ounce can) evaporated milk
2 teaspoons dry mustard (optional)
½ teaspoon salt
2 cups (8 ounces each) grated process American or
Cheddar cheese

Combine milk, mustard, and salt in a saucepan. Cook over medium heat to just below boiling—about 2 minutes. Add the cheese; then stir over medium heat until cheese melts—about 1 minute longer. *Makes about 2½ cups sauce.*

PARTY FONDUE

1. Bring 1¼ cups chicken broth to a boil. Add ½ cup par-

boiled rice. Cover tightly; cook over low heat until all liquid is absorbed, about 25 minutes. Cool.

2. Beat 2 eggs lightly. Combine with cooked rice, ¾ cup crumbled crackers, 1 tablespoon minced onion, 1 tablespoon parsley flakes, 3 tablespoons melted butter or margarine.

3. Mix well. Chill until mixture holds together. Form into 1-inch balls. Place on baking pan; bake in 450°F. oven 15 minutes or until brown (*makes 40 balls*).

4. While rice balls bake, make fondue. Peel 1 clove garlic and rub over the bottom of a chafing dish. Mix 4 cups (1 pound) grated Swiss cheese with 1½ tablespoons flour.

5. Heat 1½ cups milk (or white wine, if you prefer) in chafing dish until almost to boiling point. Add floured cheese slowly, stirring constantly as cheese melts.

6. Season cheese mixture with 1 teaspoon salt, ⅛ teaspoon white pepper, dash nutmeg. When mixture comes to a boil, serve at once; keep bubbling in chafing dish.

7. Each diner spears a rice ball with a fork, "dunks" in the fondue, twirls to capture dribbles, cools the ball a moment, eats the ball—and repeats.

8. *To make a meal:* for a party, serve cooked ham cubes to dip in fondue as well, crisp vegetable relishes and olives, and mixed fruit with minted sour cream for dessert. *Serves 6.*

TUTTI FRUTTI RICE

1. Combine 2 cups cooked parboiled rice, 1 cup water, ½ cup canned apricot nectar in a 3-quart saucepan. Bring to a boil; cover and lower heat. Simmer until most of liquid is absorbed, about 15 minutes.

2. Remove from heat. Add ½ cup apricot nectar and ¼ pound of marshmallows. (If miniature marshmallows are used, leave whole; if regular size, cut into quarters.) Fold in marshmallows until they are half melted.

3. Chill mixture until cool and partially set. Then fold in 1¾ cups orange sections (canned mandarin oranges, well drained, may be used) and ⅓ cup well-drained halved maraschino cherries.

4. Add the juice of ½ lemon. Whip ½ pint (1 cup) heavy cream until stiff. Fold into the fruit mixture. Pile in individual serving dishes or a serving bowl. Chill at least 3 hours or until set. *Serves 12.*

RICE COCKTAIL MIX

In a saucepan, melt 1/4 cup butter. Add 1/2 teaspoon each of curry powder, garlic salt, and celery salt. Pour over 4 cups crisp rice cereal squares and toss to coat evenly. Spread the cereal squares on a baking dish and heat at 350°F. for 10 minutes. *Serves 4.*

RICE NOSEGAY PARTY FAVORS

1. To tint rice, add 1/2 to 1 teaspoon of any vegetable coloring to 1 cup cold water. Add 2 cups uncooked rice and soak 5 minutes. Drain.

2. Spread drained, tinted rice on cookie sheet and dry in oven at 250°F. for 15 minutes. If you like, make different colors.

3. Wrap 2 teaspoons of tinted rice in a 5-inch square of Saran Wrap. Twist corners together. Punch three small holes in center of a small paper doily. Thread ends of 3 rice packages through holes. Fasten ends with a rubber band. Tie with colored ribbon.

RICE PIZZABURGER

2 cups cooked rice
2 tablespoons melted butter or margarine
1 egg, beaten
12 cooked sausage links, diced
1 cup tomato sauce
1/2 cup grated onion
1/2 teaspoon salt
1/4 teaspoon oregano
dash of pepper
6 ounces Mozzarella cheese, sliced
2 tablespoons grated Parmesan cheese

Combine rice, butter, and egg. Line bottom of a 12-inch skillet or pizza pan with rice mixture, making a rim around the edge about 1/4 inch high. Bake at 350°F. for 10 minutes. Arrange sausage on crust. Combine tomato sauce and onion. Spoon over sausage. Sprinkle with salt, oregano, and pepper. Cover with Mozzarella cheese. Sprinkle with Parmesan cheese. Bake at 375°F. for 20 minutes. *Serves 6.*

RICE ROMANOFF

1⅓ cups water
½ teaspoon salt
1⅓ cups enriched pre-cooked rice
1 cup (about) dry macaroon crumbs
4 tablespoons Cointreau
4 tablespoons brandy
2 cups heavy cream
3 tablespoons sugar

Bring water and salt to a boil in a saucepan. Add rice, cover, remove from heat, and let stand 5 minutes. Then chill. *Meanwhile,* mix macaroon crumbs, 2 tablespoons Cointreau, and 2 tablespoons brandy; set aside. Combine cream, sugar, and remaining Cointreau and brandy in a bowl; whip. Fold into rice. *Next:* place a third of the rice mixture in large glass serving bowl. Sprinkle with about a third of the macaroon mixture. Continue, making 2 more layers of each. Chill 3 to 4 hours. If desired, serve with a strawberry sauce. *Serves 8–10.*

SUGGESTION: For macaroon crumbs, crush 8 to 12 macaroons. If macaroons are soft, break into pieces, place on baking sheet, and bake at 275°F. for 10 minutes. Cool; then crush.

DEVILED RICE

½ cup chopped onion
½ cup chopped green pepper
2 tablespoons butter or margarine
¼ cup prepared mustard
⅓ cup sour cream
⅓ cup currant jelly
1 teaspoon Worcestershire sauce
2 tablespoons chopped pimiento
3 cups cooked rice

Lightly cook the onion and green pepper in butter or margarine. Add prepared mustard, sour cream, currant jelly, Worcestershire sauce, and chopped pimiento. Mix well and heat, stirring occasionally. Combine with the rice (freshly cooked and hot). Garnish with parsley and serve with a topping of jelly. *Serves 5.*

GLAZED FRANKS WITH PARSLEY RICE

1 cup orange juice
⅓ cup honey
2 tablespoons prepared mustard
¼ teaspoon oregano
2 tablespoons sherry
1 pound frankfurters, cut with diagonal slits
3 cups hot cooked rice
3 tablespoons melted butter
3 tablespoons chopped parsley

Blend orange juice, honey, mustard, and oregano. Heat until syrup is slightly thickened. Add sherry and frankfurters and continue cooking until franks are glazed. Toss rice with butter and parsley. Serve glazed frankfurters over rice. *Serves 6.*

CALICO RICE IN FRANKFURTER CROWN

¼ cup salad oil
2 tablespoons vinegar
2 tablespoons prepared mustard
1½ teaspoons salt
⅛ teaspoon pepper
4½ cups hot cooked rice (1½ cups rice cooked in 3 cups chicken broth)
2 hard-cooked eggs, diced
1¼ cups sliced ripe olives
1 cup diced celery
¾ cup chopped green onions
¼ cup chopped sour pickle
½ cup crumbled crisp bacon
1 teaspoon celery seed
1½ pounds frankfurters

Blend together salad oil, vinegar, mustard, salt, and pepper. Pour over hot rice; mix well. Add hard-cooked eggs, olives, celery, green onions, sour pickle, bacon, and celery seed; toss together. Cut frankfurters in half and stand them on end in a casserole to form a crown. Fill with rice mixture. Cover and bake at 450°F. for 15 minutes. *Serves 8.*

18.

For Parties

Rice in various colors or in one color to match or complement the party or wedding theme may be used as favors. The rice may be placed on small squares of net or tulle, lined with polyethylene, and tied with ribbon.

The use of rice for decoration is not limited to weddings. You have many ways to use tinted and perfumed rice for parties and special occasions. Colored rice may be utilized for decorative and unusual holiday adornments and is easily glued to centerpieces and ornaments. It is attractive when layered or mixed in clear vases or jars for year-round appointments.

Tinted rice can be used for mosaic paintings or caught up in netting for unique corsages. With the use of simple ingredients and a minimum of time, rice can be made a party festivity by the following directions:

Ingredients: Vegetable coloring, as desired (2 teaspoons yellow, 2 teaspoons blue, 3 teaspoons green, or 3 teaspoons red), 3 cups cold water, and 4 cups uncooked rice (1 pound, 12 ounces).

Method: Mix desired coloring with water. Add rice and soak until desired shade is obtained. Drain tinted rice, saving colored water for re-use it needed.

Fragrance: A few drops of your favorite perfume or cologne may be added to the water after the vegetable coloring has been blended into it.

Final Step: Spread drained, tinted rice on a cookie sheet and dry in an oven at 250°F. for 15 minutes. Makes about 32 bags or 2 tablespoons each.

Suggestion: Use regular milled white rice for pastel colors. Parboiled rice is best for deeper colors.

Hawaiian Rice Luau Party

Rice plays an important part in the traditional celebration feast known as a Luau. The Luau is a completely informal feast. The feast may be set on a "tablecloth" of ferns and other leaves spread on the ground. In Hawaii, they use no plates, forks, or other eating utensils. Everything is eaten with the fingers. The native's love for rice was brought to the island by the orientals, so rice is included in the Luau in various dishes. Color, in both food and decorations, is a must for the Luau.

Table Decorations: Tablecloth may be of fish net. A white cloth decorated with leaves (cannon leaves are good) may be used. Fern and flowers may be spread on the table or pinned to the tablecloth sides.

Table Centerpiece: Should be made from fruits and flowers.

Suggestion:

1. "Island Scene Centerpiece." On tray, tiny or large depending on size of table, lay a sea blue paper and on it set an island of green modeling clay covered with sand. In the clay, anchor small palm trees, tiny figures, and perhaps a little shack made by gluing brown rice to a box. Keep everything to scale.

2. "Palms from Pipe Cleaners." For trunks of tiny palm trees, use pipe stem cleaners cut various lengths, dipped in brown dye and dried. Peel back fuzz at one end leaving a bit of the exposed wire. On this wire, impale ends of seven or eight palm fronds cut from green paper. Anchor base of tree in modeling clay and bend to give a palm-like effect.

3. "Outrigger Canoe Nut Cup." Canoe is made from brown paper. Ends are stapled together to form a boat. Outrigger is fine wire wrapped in brown tissue paper.

4. "Indoor Party." If the Luau is to be inside, decorate with fish net. Fish may be made from paper plates, painted to resemble tropical fish with colored paper tissue fins. The post or pillows in the room could be decorated with paper flowers or fresh flowers. Keep the decorations colorful.

POLYNESIAN RICE MINGLE

1 cup brown rice
1 cup white rice
3 tablespoons minced onion
3 tablespoons soy sauce
4 chicken bouillon cubes
4 cups boiling water
½ cup Macadamia nuts (other nutmeats
    may be substituted, such as pecans,
    walnuts, peanuts)
parsley for garnish

Combine rice, onion, and soy sauce in a 2-quart casserole. Dissolve bouillon cubes in boiling water and stir into other ingredients. Cover and bake at 350°F. for 30 minutes. Remove cover and bake for 15 minutes more. Sprinkle with chopped nutmeats and garnish with parsley. *Serves 8.* NOTE: The two-tone effect of combining the two types of rice is most attractive.

PARTY-TIME FRIED RICE WITH ALMONDS

2 tablespoons salad oil
1 small onion, chopped
½ medium green pepper, chopped
2 cups cold cooked rice
½ cup blanched almonds, split lengthwise
2 tablespoons soy sauce
½ teaspoon garlic salt
¼ teaspoon pepper

Cook the onion and green pepper in oil for 5 minutes. Add the rice, almonds, soy sauce, garlic salt, and pepper; mix well and cook 10 minutes or until thoroughly heated. *Serves 4.*

SUGGESTION: Festive with sweet and sour spareribs, chicken, or shrimp. It is easy to serve party buffet style. It can be prepared in advance and reheated at the last minute.

HAWAIIAN KAUKAU (SALAD)
(Ka-oo Ka-oo means food and meat)

2 cups cold cooked rice (in cooking
　　the rice, tint pale yellow)
1½ cups diced cooked veal
1 cup halved seedless grapes or raisins
1 cup minced celery
½ cup broken nutmeats
¾ cup salad dressing
1 tablespoon lemon juice
½ teaspoon salt

Combine rice, veal, grapes, celery, and nutmeats. Blend together salad dressing, lemon juice, and salt. Pour over rice-meat mixture and toss lightly. Chill thoroughly. *Serves 6.*

SUGGESTION: Serve in lettuce cups in individual salad bowls and garnish with parsley and small clusters of seedless grapes. Serve with additional salad dressing.

ALOHA PINEAPPLE RICE PUDDING

4 cups cold cooked rice
1 No. 2 can crushed pineapple, drained
¾ cup maraschino cherries, chopped
　　(use juice for cooking rice)
1 cup (½ pint) heavy cream, whipped
¼ cup sugar
1 teaspoon vanilla extract

Combine the rice, pineapple, and chopped cherries. Flavor the cream with sugar and vanilla and fold into the pineapple-rice mixture. Chill. *Serves 8.*

CHICKEN CURRY IN COCONUT NEST

1 5-pound stewing chicken
1 onion, cut very fine
4 tablespoons chicken fat

2 tablespoons melted butter or margarine
2 tablespoons curry powder
5 tablespoons flour
5 cups boiling chicken stock
2 cups fresh coconut milk (see below)
½ teaspoon finely chopped ginger root
2 teaspoons mango chutney, chopped fine
1 teaspoon Accent
2 teaspoons salt
3 cups cooked rice
4 fresh coconuts, cut in half

Clean chicken, cover with water, and simmer until tender, about 1½ to 2 hours. Then remove from liquid. Remove chicken from bone and cut into bite-sized pieces. Reserve stock. *Next:* Cook onion in 3 tablespoons chicken fat until lightly browned. Remove onion and brown the chicken in remaining fat and butter. Add curry powder and flour. Cook 2 minutes. Add chicken stock and remaining ingredients, except rice and coconuts, stirring constantly, and cook until thickened. Now serve in fresh coconut nests. Place hot rice in center of coconut and spoon chicken curry over the rice. Sprinkle with grated coconut. To make coconut nests, cut fresh young coconuts in half. Cut off about ½ inch of the bottom of each coconut so it will stand. *Serves 8.*

SUGGESTION: To make coconut milk, pour 2 cups boiling milk over 4 cups grated fresh coconut or packaged coconut. Let stand 20 minutes. Strain through a thin cloth (a double thickness if cheese cloth is used). Press to remove all liquid. Coconut milk should be stored in the refrigerator. If coconut milk is to be heated, bring to the scalding point, stirring constantly to avoid curdling. *Makes 2 cups.*

RICE AND PINEAPPLE FESTIVAL

Split 4 medium-sized fresh pineapples in half, cutting carefully through green tops to prevent breaking. Scoop out pineapple pulp, leaving about ½ inch all around shell. Cut pulp into bite-sized chunks.

4 cups chunk pineapple

¼ cup sugar
4 cups cooked rice (cooked in chicken stock)
4 cups cooked chicken, cut into bite-sized pieces
¼ cup crystallized ginger, slivered
3 cups chopped pecans

Into a mixing bowl, pour pineapple and sprinkle with sugar. Let stand about 5 minutes. Toss together with remaining ingredients. Spoon into pineapple shells. Chill. Garnish with maraschino cherries and lime slices. *Serves 8.*

FRUITED RICE FILLED CROWN ROAST OF PORK

1 crown roast of pork, 24 ribs
salt and pepper
3 cups cubed and pared apples
1 cup chopped celery
⅔ cup chopped onion
¼ cup drippings, from roast
4 cups cooked rice (cooked in consommé)
1 cup raisins
1 teaspoon grated lemon peel
1 teaspoon salt
dash each of thyme, rosemary, marjoram,
      and pepper

Have butcher prepare crown roast of pork. Wipe with damp cloth. Season inside and out with salt and pepper. Place roast on rack of roast pan. If desired, rib ends may be covered with pieces of bacon or aluminum foil. Bake at 350°F. for about 2½ hours or until meat at the center registers 185°F. on your meat thermometer. *Next:* sauté apples, celery, and onion in meat drippings until tender but not brown. Add cooked rice, raisins, lemon peel, and seasonings. Mix well. About 45 minutes before roast is done, remove from the oven and fill center of roast with rice dressing. Cover crown with aluminum foil (this is to prevent rice from becoming too dry). Next, return to oven to finish cooking. Allow 3 ribs per serving. *Serves 8.*

TROPICAL DESSERT MOLD

1 3-ounce package lemon gelatin
water
1 No. 2 can crushed pineapple, drained
2 bananas, crushed
1 cup cooked rice (½ cup rice cooked
    in 1 cup water and 1 teaspoon walnut
    extract)
½ cup heavy cream, whipped

Heat pineapple juice and enough water to make 2 cups. Pour over gelatin and stir until dissolved. Chill until mixture begins to congeal. Stir in pineapple, banana, and rice. Fold in whipped cream. Turn into a 1-quart mold and return to refrigerator to congeal. *Serves 8.*

19.
As Leftovers

RICE MEAT LOAF

⅔ cup packaged enriched pre-cooked rice
1 pound ground beef
1 egg, slightly beaten
¼ cup chopped onion
1 tablespoon chopped parsley
2 teaspoons salt
⅛ teaspoon marjoram
dash of pepper
2 cans (8 ounces each) tomato sauce
2 strips bacon

Combine all ingredients, except ¼ cup of the tomato sauce and the bacon, mixing lightly. (Mixture will be soft.) Shape into a loaf in a shallow baking pan. Place bacon strips over top. Cover with heavy duty aluminum foil and bake at 350°F. for 30 minutes. Then remove foil, spoon remaining tomato sauce over top of loaf, and bake 30 minutes longer, uncovered. Serve with additional heated tomato sauce, if desired. Makes one loaf. *Serves 4–6.*

TEXAS HASH

½ cup diced green pepper
½ pound ground beef
2 tablespoons butter or margarine

1 cup uncooked rice
2 cups beef broth
1 teaspoon salt
½ cup chopped pimiento

Cook green peppers and ground beef in butter until peppers are tender; stir once or twice. Add rice, broth, and salt. Heat to boiling; stir once. Cover, reduce heat, and simmer for 14 minutes or until liquid is absorbed. Remove from heat and toss lightly with pimiento. Serve hot. *Serves 6.*

SUGGESTION: Substitute one cup cooked diced chicken for the beef, and chicken broth for the beef broth. Add the chicken, rice, and broth; cook as directed above.

RICE PIZZA

¼ cup chopped onion
1 tablespoon cooking oil
1 can (8 ounces) tomato sauce
1¾ cups water
1½ teaspoons salt
garlic seasoning, oregano or basil, pepper,
    and sugar (to taste)
¾ cup parboiled rice
pepperoni, mushrooms, and/or anchovies
3 to 6 ounces Mozarella cheese, sliced
⅓ to ½ cup grated Parmesan cheese

Sauté onion in oil; remove from heat. Add tomato sauce, water, salt, and other seasonings to taste. Add rice. Bring to a boil. Stir well. Cover and lower heat. Cook 20 to 25 minutes or until rice is tender and sauce is cooked down thick. Stir to prevent sticking; add a bit of water if needed. Turn mixture into a well-oiled pizza pan or 2 pie pans. Spread, making a slight rim. Arrange pepperoni, mushrooms, and/or anchovies over top. Cover with cheese slices. Sprinkle with Parmesan. Slip under broiler to brown. Cut in wedges. Serve on plates. *Serves 5–6.*

SPECIAL RICE HASH

1½ pounds ground beef
1 package (⅝ ounces) onion soup mix
2 tablespoons oil
1 can (3 ounces) mushrooms, stems and pieces
3 tomatoes, coarsely chopped
1 cup uncooked rice
2 cups beef bouillon
1 teaspoon salt
½ cup cooked peas
1 pimiento, diced

Combine ground beef and soup mix. Form into 12 patties. Brown on each side in oil; drain off excess fat. Add mushrooms, tomatoes, rice, bouillon, and salt. Heat to boiling. Cover, reduce heat, and simmer for 20 minutes. Add peas and pimiento and cook until heated through. *Serves 6.*

RICE MEAT LOAF

1 cup cooked parboiled rice
1 pound ground beef
2 eggs, well beaten
⅓ cup minced onion
2 tablespoons minced green pepper
¼ teaspoon pepper
1½ teaspoons salt
1 teaspoon Worcestershire sauce
dash of cayenne
1 cup (8-ounce can) tomato sauce

Thoroughly combine all ingredients, reserving half of tomato sauce. Form mixture into loaf in greased baking pan. Pour remaining tomato sauce over loaf and bake in 350°F. oven about 1 hour. *Serves 4.*

SUGGESTION: Before pouring reserved tomato sauce over meat loaf, add to sauce 1 tablespoon brown sugar and 1 tablespoon vinegar.

TEXAS HASH

3 tablespoons fat
½ cup chopped onion
1½ cups chopped green pepper
1 pound ground beef
½ cup parboiled rice
2 cups cooked tomatoes
1 teaspoon chili powder
1 teaspoon salt
¼ teaspoon pepper

Melt fat in a skillet; add onion, green pepper, and ground beef and brown well. Add remaining ingredients. Cover tightly. Cook over high heat until steaming freely, then turn heat down and simmer for about 30 minutes. *Serves 6.*

COMPANY-STYLE BEEF STEW

2 pounds boneless beef chuck, cut in 1½-inch cubes
2 tablespoons all-purpose flour
2 teaspoons salt
⅛ teaspoon pepper
1 tablespoon butter
1 tablespoon salad oil
2 cups chopped onions
2½ cups water
1 can (1 pound) tomatoes
1 bay leaf
1 clove garlic, sliced
3 medium carrots, cut in 2-inch pieces
2 medium onions, cut in half
¼ pound fresh mushrooms, sliced (about 1½ cups)
¼ cup Burgundy or other dry red wine
2 cups enriched pre-cooked rice

Dust meat with flour, salt, and pepper. Heat butter with oil in a large Dutch oven until quite hot. Add meat; brown thoroughly. Add chopped onions; cook until brown. *Next:* Stir in water, tomatoes, bay leaf, and garlic. Cover and simmer 1 hour or until meat is almost tender. Add carrots and onion halves; cook 30 minutes. Stir in mushrooms and wine; cook 15 minutes or until vegetables are tender. Discard bay leaf. *Meanwhile:* prepare enriched pre-cooked rice as per package directions. Spoon stew over rice. *Serves 5–6.*

LEFTOVER RICE FOR LUNCHEON

Quick Trick: Leftover rice? Serve it to the children for lunchtime dessert. Mound rice in a sauce dish, pour cream over, give them cinnamon sugar or brown sugar to sprinkle on. Makes a good breakfast dish, too.

MEAT LOAF MAGNIFIQUE

2 cups enriched pre-cooked rice
1½ pounds ground beef
1 egg, slightly beaten
½ cup finely chopped onion
½ cup finely cut celery
½ cup cooked tomatoes
½ cup milk
1½ teaspoons salt
⅛ teaspoon pepper

In mixing bowl, combine all ingredients in order listed, mixing well. Pack lightly in ungreased 9 x 5 x 3 loaf pan. Bake in moderate oven (375°F.) about 1 hour. After removing from oven, let stand in pan about 5 minutes before turning out onto heated platter. Slice and serve. *Serves 8.*

20.

Glossary of Rice Definitions

The rice industry, like all industries, has terms that are personal to it alone. In order to understand about rice, you should have a knowledge of its terms. Following is a list of the more commonly used words of the rice trade.

ROUGH RICE—Also known as Paddy Rice. This is rice with the hulls on, as it comes from the farm. It is rice without any portion of the stalk. The rice arrives by truck to the mill with debris, such as weed seeds, pebbles, granules of dirt, etc., which are removed before the milling process begins.

BROWN RICE—Edible rice with only the hull removed, yet still containing the bran layers and most of the germ. Its light brown color is caused by the presence of the rice germ and 7 bran layers. Because of this color and a relatively long cooking period, this highly nutritious rice has always remained a specialty food, and in some cities it is available only in health food stores.

MILLED RICE—May be either polished or unpolished. It is rice from which the hulls, germ, outer bran layers, and most of the inner bran layers have been removed. In trade circles, polished milled rice is commonly termed simply "milled rice," and unpolished milled rice is commonly termed simply "unpolished rice."

COATED RICE—Rice that has been coated with an edible substance, usually glucose and talc.

UNCOATED RICE—Rice that has no other substance applied to it as a coating.

PARBOILED RICE—Rice that has been subjected to a steam or hot-water treatment prior to milling. The purpose of the treatment is to diffuse vitamins from the bran layers into the starchy kernel of the grains. Because of this process, the rice retains more natural nutrients, but requires a longer cooking period (25 minutes) than regular rice (20 minutes). Since this process eliminates the surface starch common to regular rice, it insures a separateness of grain that is especially desirable for kitchens preparing rice in large quantities.

RICE HULLS—The outer husk of the rice grain. A few years ago, the hulls were of no value except as boiler fuel for the rice mills. Modern technology, though, has discovered many industrial uses, for example, as polish for semi-precious gems, as abrasive in mechanic's soap, and as filler in ceramic ware.

RICE BRAN—The pericarp or outer layers and germ of the rice grain. Rich in nutrients.

RICE POLISH—The next layer removed from the final stages of milling is composed of new white bran, protein-rich aleurone layers, and starchy endosperm. It is easily digestible in valuable nutrients, the polish is included in many baby foods because of high fat content and highly concentrated carbohydrate.

HEAD RICE—Whole kernels of milled rice.

SECOND HEAD RICE—Broken kernels of milled rice that are at least one-half as long as a whole kernel. A non-gluten flour that is used in dry mixes and bakery products.

SCREENINGS—Broken kernels of milled rice that are about one-fourth to one-half the length of a whole kernel.

BREWERS RICE—Broken kernels of milled rice that will pass readily through a sieve. It is composed of the smallest pieces of broken rice. It gets its name from the fact that it is used as an adjunct in beer-making. It is regarded a concentrated source of carbohydrates.

How to Become a Gourmet Rice Cook

Problems do occur, even with the best of ingredients and cooks. Here is a chart that will help you identify the cause of the problem and what to do:

Problem	Cause	Solution
Sticky rice	Washing before cooking	Don't wash.
	Inaccurate measuring	Measure rice and liquid.
	Over-cooking	Time accurately.
	Leaving in cooking utensil too long	Remove from utensil within 10 minutes after cooking.
	Utensil too deep	Turn into shallow container (s) .
All liquid not completely absorbed	Cooking time too short	Time accurately.
	Excess liquid for amount of rice	Measure rice and liquid.
	Lifting or removing lid during cooking	Keep lid on tightly to prevent steam from escaping.
Mushy rice	Cooking time too long	Time accurately.
	Excess liquid	Measure rice and liquid.
	Leaving in utensil with lid on too long	Remove lid at end of cooking time and test for doneness. Immediately turn rice into shallow pan (s) and fluff with a fork or slotted spoon.
Hard rice grains (or center of grain hard)	Not enough liquid	Measure rice and liquid.
	Utensil not properly covered	Use foil if lid does not fit tightly.
	Utensil overloaded	Use larger utensil.
	Uneven temperature	Adjust temperature as specified in directions.
	Cooking time inaccurate	Time accurately.

Rice packed	Utensil overloaded	Use larger utensil.
	Heat unevenly distributed	Be sure utensil is no larger than heat unit.
	Left in container too long	Immediately turn rice into shallow pan (s) and fluff with fork to allow steam to escape.
Rice sticks to utensil	Heat too high	Control heat.
	Hot spots on utensil	Check pan for hot spots.
	Not enough liquid	Measure rice and liquid.

Index

263